The Worst Day of My Life

May 18th, 2024

Unease gripped me as I turned onto Abbot Kinney Blvd. I pulled into my spot in the alley, jumped out, and entered through the back gate. I expected her things to be gone, but everything was still on the picnic table. The back door and side gate stood open. *Maybe she changed her mind. Maybe she's planning something special.*

I stepped into the house, greeted by an ominous orange hue filtering through the closed blinds. The front closet doors were open—she'd been there. I moved to the bedroom but didn't see her, though something black lay on the bed. I checked the office, then the bathroom, pulling back the shower curtain.

Then it hit me. *What was on the bed?*

It was my shotgun.

Melanie was lying on the floor, her legs folded underneath her. She looked so innocent, a trickle of blood from her nose, a small pool forming beneath her.

The sliding glass mirror was shattered with buckshot. I left our room in shock.

"No, you didn't. No, you didn't," I lamented, hurling my necklace to the floor and then punching into the drywall.

"This is not happening. This isn't real."

I called 9-1-1 at 6:53 p.m.

"My girlfriend shot herself in the chest with my shotgun. She's gone."

Dispatch attempted to settle me down.

"Does she have a pulse?"

I went back inside and pressed my fingers to her neck. She was warm but lifeless. Then, I saw a perfect circle in the center of her chest, the size of a

1

barrel. I staggered back and stumbled outside, pacing in circles between the front and backyard.

"This is not happening today. We were breaking up; she was picking up her stuff. I need to wake up."

I had been grieving the relationship all morning, but this broke my heart.

"My life is over. Everything I was doing was for us. I'm ruined. How could she do this to me?"

"Stay calm, sir; the police are on the way," the operator said.

Long, painful "Ohhs" poured from my soul.

I looked up at the police helicopter circling over my house.

"Are you wearing a white t-shirt, sir?"

"Yes, that's me."

The police cruisers arrived next.

"She's in the bedroom," I told the approaching officers.

"I need you to turn around and put your hands behind your head, sir," the lead officer ordered.

I immediately dropped to my knees and placed my hands on my head.

"Stand up, sir. We're not cuffing you. Hands behind your head, please," he said as they patted me down.

Two officers went inside to investigate while the rest watched me in silence.

"Are there any other guns in the house?"

"Not in the house, no," I responded.

"Was the shotgun loaded, sir?"

"I didn't have any guns before COVID. It had been sitting up there since then."

"Did she mention that she was thinking about killing herself?"

"She said she was having suicidal thoughts, but it felt manipulative. She was breaking up with me."

"She didn't say how she was thinking about doing it?"

"No."

"Did she live here?"

"Sometimes, yeah. She had a bunch of her things here but also had an Airbnb in Topanga and stayed with her sister in Malibu. She never fully moved in. We were breaking up. She was grabbing the last of her things."

"Did she have a key?"

"She did, but she gave it back yesterday."

"How did she get into the house?"

"I was at work. She asked me to leave a key so she could do a final sweep. I left it on the picnic table for her. You can check my phone."

I handed it over.

Melanie: "Hi! Can you leave a key somewhere this evening so I can come by and grab the coffee machine and any last things, please?"

Beau: "I'll put everything on the picnic table in the backyard."

Melanie: "There are some other things I'd like to grab. If you could leave a key, that would be great... there's some other stuff I'm forgetting, I think... I'd like to do a sweep if that's okay with you. I'll be quick."

Beau: "Already swept the medicine cabinet and closet... everything's on the picnic table, but I'll leave a key under the ashtray so you can double-check. Maybe check the front closet by the door."

3

Melanie: "Thank you."

Beau: "If there's anything you don't want to take, please just throw it away."

Melanie: "Appreciate you."

"This can't be real."

"I'm sorry, sir, but it is," the lead officer said.

I headbutted the fence post of the back gate in a moment of rage, checking the officers for a reaction, but they remained still, simply watching over me like guards.

My mind was on a loop, processing a gauntlet of thoughts.

Why did I leave her the key? This is a bad dream.

My breath tightened in my chest. I pressed my fists into the dirt, trying to wake myself up.

"I'm not okay right now, guys. Can we go for a walk?" I asked the officers.

"You need to stay here, sir," the lead officer replied, confining me to my front yard.

"I need to call her mom."

"That's not a good idea, sir. She might be driving."

"Can I call somebody to come be with me?"

"Go ahead, sir."

The officers weren't comforting. I understood they were doing their job, but I needed someone.

I called Justin. After several tries, he finally answered.

"What's up, bro? I'm at dinner in Asheville."

"Mel just killed herself with my shotgun."

"No, she didn't."

"Yeah, she's gone."

"Oh my god. I'd be there if I were home," he said. "I'm so sorry."

"Okay. No worries. I gotta go."

I called my friend Roger, my first friend in LA and my dad's fraternity brother at Stanford.

"What's up, kid?"

"My girlfriend killed herself with my shotgun."

His tone shifted. "Did you call the police?"

"Yeah, they're here now."

"I'm on my way."

"I need to call her mom," I reiterated.

"That's not a good idea, sir," the lead officer replied.

I called her anyway and reached her voicemail. I called again, but still nothing.

Then, I heard a familiar voice. "Is my boy Beau here?"

It was my friend, Troy—finally, someone I could hold on to.

"I'm so sorry, bro. Justin just called me. It's not your fault. It's not your fault, man," Troy said as I wept in his arms.

"I keep trying to undo it, but I can't."

Troy continued to comfort me, but the thoughts in my head drowned out his words.

"I need to wake up.

This isn't real.

I need to call her mom."

This time, she answered.

"Hello," Liz said, unaware of what was coming.

"Hi, Liz. It's Beau. I have horrible news… Mel shot herself in the chest with my shotgun. She's gone, Liz," I choked on my words.

"What? Not my sweet, beautiful Melanie," she replied, her voice breaking.

"She's gone, Liz. She's gone. I'm so sorry," I said, joining her in tears.

The line went silent.

"Okay… okay, where are you? I'm in San Diego, but I'm going to call Becky and have her come to you. Text me your address."

"Okay," I whimpered.

I texted Liz my address, and then my phone rang.

"Beau, it's John. Text me your address. Katie and I are going to drop off the kids; then we're on our way."

I started to get cold and asked the officers if I could grab a sweatshirt.

"Where are they? I can get one for you," one of the officers offered.

"In the bedroom closet," I said.

He brought back my Aspen sweatshirt.

"That was her favorite sweatshirt," I cried as the tears poured.

"I've got another one in the car," Troy mentioned.

Shortly after, Roger showed up and gave me a big hug. He suggested I speak with the crisis counselors from the Mayor's office who had just arrived.

"How are you feeling?" one asked as they introduced themselves.

"It's really cold," I replied.

"He's in shock. We need to warm him up," Roger said.

Roger, a former lifeguard and police officer trained in trauma response, guided me to the couch in the garage. He wrapped me in blankets and rubbed my arms, working to restore my circulation.

"Is there anybody you need to call for work?" he asked.

"Yeah, I left The Victorian. I should probably tell them I'm not coming back. I also have an event at Baja tonight."

Roger handled those calls while I poured my heart out to the crisis counselors.

"We were breaking up. I had been grieving the relationship all morning. She was coming to get the last of her things. We were just in Italy. How did this happen? It happened so fast. I didn't see this coming."

"There's no way you could have, bro," Troy said softly.

"There's nothing you could have done, Beau," Roger added.

"This isn't on you," Troy reiterated.

Shortly after, her sisters Becky and Katie and her brother-in-law John arrived. Their embraces comforted me, but the relief was fleeting. A tsunami of sadness and guilt swallowed it whole. We cried in each other's arms until the officers pulled them aside for their statements.

My mind spiraled on what I could have done differently, desperately trying to undo the impossible. *Why didn't I call her? Why did I leave the key?*

"I decided to stay sober today because I figured she was going to show up at my house tomorrow, and I wanted to have my wits about me so we could talk things through.

If I had gone the other direction and decided to have a bunch of drinks today, I would have come home to this at two o'clock in the morning and seen that with a bunch of cocktails in me.

I'd be lying there next to her right now."

"Don't say that. No, you wouldn't have. This isn't your fault," Roger said.

"I told her I was going to sell the Chris Stapleton tickets when she said she wanted no attachments. It was only fair." I said.

One of the counselors reassured me. "That was fair."

The other approached gently. "The medical examiner is going to take her body out now. They asked if you would like to see her one last time before they do."

"I can't see her like that again."

Becky offered me a guest room at her house in Newport, but Troy's place was familiar and just down the road.

The officers told us they were all done inside and allowed us back into the house.

"You don't know when you're coming back, so pack like you're leaving town for a month," Roger advised.

I asked Roger and Troy to give me a moment alone. Closing the bedroom door behind me, I kneeled at the corner of the bed.

"I'm so sorry. I'm sorry I wasn't here for you today," I confessed, my heart aching.

Buried beneath the shock, I felt a light tingling sensation in my body.

"I love you so much, and I forgive you. Please go to the light when you're ready. Please go to the light when you're ready."

I finished packing the last of my things, and on my way out, I grabbed Mel's scarf from the nightstand.

Melanie Taylor ended her life with my shotgun on May 18, 2024, in Venice Beach, California.

Beau & Mel Thanksgiving 2023

One Year With My Soulmate

Dedicated to the Angel with Butterfly Wings

Melanie Taylor

October 29, 1991 – May 18, 2024

What Are the Chances of Finding Your Soulmate?

1997

I attended Phillips Academy in Andover, Massachusetts, for a postgraduate year, repeating my senior year to attract a college football scholarship after an MCL injury at Gunn High School in Palo Alto, California.

During my first trimester at Phillips, I took an English literature class with Mrs. Edwards and my defensive coordinator, Coach Lou. One assignment asked us to write a poem. I wrote mine as a letter to my soulmate.

Dear Soulmate

I know you're out there, watching time slip by,
A heartbeat away, beneath the same sky.
A bond unseen, still pulling me near,
In time, love will make our purpose clear.

But first, I must walk the map of my soul,
Gather each fragment, and make myself whole.
Only by plumbing the depths of my own
Can I offer a heart that's truly grown.

I'll face down my shadows, embrace every hue,
Until I stand whole, ready for you.
And when the stars whisper the moment is right,
Our worlds will collide in a radiant light.

So wait for me, love, as I journey within,
Learn, unearth, and shed what has been.
For you are the fire that burns this boy blue,
And someday, my path will lead me to you.

What are the chances of actually finding your soulmate?

Former NASA scientist Randall Munroe explored this question mathematically.

"Let's suppose you make eye contact with an average of a few dozen new strangers daily. If 10 percent of them are close to your age, that's locking

eyes with around 50,000 potential soulmates in a lifetime. Among 500,000,000 potential soulmate matches in your age range, that sets the odds of finding that one true love at 1 in 10,000 lifetimes."

Chris Barnard, an actuary at *Allianz*, pointed out that Munroe considered himself *"pretty introverted."* The odds were better for more outgoing people, especially those in front-facing jobs. Someone who meets hundreds of new people daily might lock eyes with 500,000 potential soulmates in a lifetime, bringing the odds down to *"1 in 1,000 lifetimes."* Still rare, but the chances have improved tenfold.

Eye Contact

2015 - 2018

I spent sixteen years as a nightlife promoter in the Los Angeles beach communities, a career that fell into my lap and one I embraced for the flexibility it gave me to explore other ventures. The lifestyle brought a constant stream of new people into my orbit. Of all the women who walked through the doors of the thousands of events I organized, it was Melanie Taylor who always had my eye.

Our paths first crossed in 2015 at The Buffalo Club in Santa Monica. I was heading to the front door to greet a client when she walked in—dark hair, striking, wearing a black leather jacket. Her curls bounced slightly as she moved. Then I locked on her brown eyes, beautiful, magnetic, and charged with energy.

I doubled back and found her at the bar, still holding me with that confident gaze.

Who is that?

Too nervous to approach her directly, I turned to the manager.

"Brayner, send that young lady a drink on me, whatever she wants," I said, smiling at her before disappearing into the crowd.

I wanted to make an impression. Years later, I learned that she already knew who I was. When she moved to Santa Monica, her older sister Sarah told her, "You have to meet Trey and Beau. They throw the best parties on the Westside."

The Buffalo Club had become Mel's go-to spot on Friday nights, and I was the promoter she relied on for her weekend outings.

For her twenty-fifth birthday on Halloween, I set her up with a free table and complimentary bottle service at 41 Ocean. Mel packed the house. Dressed as a kitty cat, she was the center of attention, effortlessly lighting up the room.

Our connection grew through playful flirtation. One night at The Buffalo Club, she greeted me with a kiss on the lips. A couple of weeks later, I moved to kiss her in the private courtyard, but she pulled away.

"What are you doing?" She glared.

"It's going to happen sooner or later."

She squinted, unconvinced, then turned and walked away. A drunken swing and a miss. At the time, I didn't think twice about it.

We ended up at each other's places for after-parties. At hers, I met Sarah and her dog, Lady. At mine, Becky joined us as we put on tie-dye onesies and danced late into the night.

Our first two years were a blur. Money came easily, and life was a party. But I wanted more with Mel. She was a dedicated yogi, dancer, and fitness enthusiast, so I invited her to a private boxing session with my trainer. When she said yes, I was fired up.

I stayed away from the booze that Friday night at work. By ten the next morning, I was at the gym, warming up and waiting. I texted her: *You still coming?*

I kept glancing at the door between rounds, half-expecting to see her walk in. No text. No explanation. Her no-show hit me like a right cross.

The disappointment cut deeper than I wanted to admit. I questioned whether I'd misread every signal between us. Maybe that magnetic energy I felt was just one-sided after all.

Weeks later, our eyes met at a brunch event in the bathroom line. The sting of being stood up hit me all over again. I turned away and walked out.

Months passed. Then, out of nowhere, she texted. She was moving into a new place and needed help picking up a coffee table. Despite everything, I still wanted to see her.

I picked her up, Lady in tow, in a borrowed truck, and we moved the coffee table to her new apartment in Santa Monica. After rearranging her living room, we caught up on the couch.

"So, what do you have up your sleeve these days?" Mel asked.

"What do you mean?"

"You're always working on something. What have you been up to?"

"I'm putting together a music festival in Bali."

"That sounds fun."

"Have you ever been?"

"I haven't."

"You should come."

"Maybe. Are you seeing anybody?"

"I'm so buried right now. I don't have a lot of free time."

Lady rested her head on my lap, gazing up at me sweetly.

"Wow, she really likes you," Mel said.

I knew Lady was her world. Her approval felt like a good sign.

Mel's eyes were unwavering. She always studied me with quiet reserve and curiosity. I felt the pull to kiss her like she was giving me the green light. Then I remembered my failed attempt at Buffalo Club, and her words: "What are you doing?" Fear of rejection held me back, so I opted for a goodbye hug.

As I walked back to my car, I replayed the moment in my head, feeling that I had missed my opportunity. I was upset at myself for not taking the risk, but my biggest promotion ever was pulling me under, and the thought faded into entrepreneurial chaos.

She never made the trip to Bali.

The festival happened, but it nearly broke me. We were way over budget, and when I arrived ten days before the event, a volcano warning greeted me. Mount Agung, dormant since 1963, was on the verge of erupting. Tourism plummeted, and I returned home buried in debt.

Mel had disappeared from the party scene.

I rebuilt my finances, focusing on new venue partnerships, while the festival debt slowly shrank.

In April 2018, Mel wanted to "catch up."

We met for dinner at The Penthouse in the Huntley Hotel.

"How was the festival?" she asked.

"Magical. One of the coolest festivals I've ever been to."

"That's amazing."

"It was also a nightmare. We lost a fortune, and I'm trying to figure out how to bring it back."

"How are you going to do that?"

"For starters, I gave up alcohol. I'm eighty days sober."

"That's got to be hard in your business. I'm proud of you. I'm not drinking either."

Instead, we clinked espresso shots.

"What's new with you? Are you seeing anybody?" I asked.

"I am, but it's not serious. What about you?"

"I am, yeah."

"Is it serious?" she asked.

"It's still early. She's an OC girl."

"Where's she from? Do I know her?"

"Costa Mesa. She's into dirt bikes and is kind of a river rat. Loves taking trips to Laughlin."

Mel laughed. "I'm more of an ocean kind of gal. I grew up sailing with my family."

"Are your parents still married?"

"Yeah, still madly in love."

"How did they meet?"

"My dad was aggressively pursuing my mom for a date, and her boyfriend at the time said, 'Well, if you want to see what that's about, go ahead.' My mom took him up on that offer and never looked back."

I couldn't shake the thought: *That could be us.*

At the valet, we shared a long hug. Our eyes met in an intense, lingering moment when we pulled apart.

I wanted to kiss her, but the timing wasn't right.

The next day, I could not escape the feeling Melanie constantly stirred in me. When I was with my girlfriend later that week, all I could think about was Mel's eyes. The guilt was immediate, but so was the clarity. I started pulling away, and soon, we broke up.

I had been sober for a hundred days, but I broke my streak at my best friend's bachelor party in New Orleans and again at his wedding.

The following Tuesday, Melanie and I went to yoga.

"That was rough," I said.

"Yeah, you were breathing really heavily."

"I have a confession to make. I broke my hundred-day sober streak at my best friend's bachelor party, and I'm still hungover from his wedding this past weekend."

"You can always start a new streak."

My nervous system was shattered from the weekend, and I felt myself retreating.

"Let's hang again soon," I hugged her before leaving.

A few days later, she invited me to walk Lady at the beach.

I eagerly agreed but never heard back.

Not long after, photos of her with her new boyfriend surfaced on Instagram.

Even though our paths seemed to be diverging, I wanted her to know how I felt before letting go.

I sent her a poem.

Beautiful Someday

Majestic souls
Exploring roles
Long to share

Adventures rare
Nature's gift
Due to shift

Bestow a kiss
Endless bliss
Anatomically intertwined
Unlocking time

She responded, "*That's beautiful.*"

"*You look happy. Maybe we'll get our chance in another life.*"

I moved on. It felt like a final goodbye.

A House in Mourning

May 19th - May 22nd, 2024

Mel's mom invited me to stay with her family in Newport. After a sleepless night at Troy's, I was still too rattled to drive. Katie and John picked me up in Venice. Mel's niece and nephew sat with their mom in the backseat. I did my best to hold back my tears for their sake.

Her parents, Liz and Jim, and her brother, Jimmy, greeted me with tearful embraces. As more family members arrived, we struggled to make sense of the unthinkable.

"We were breaking up," I said. "She was going back to her ex."

"I didn't know she was going back to him," Liz confirmed.

"I knew we were in trouble when she brought him up in Italy," I added.

"He gave her an ultimatum... that if she got on the plane with you, things were over between them," John said.

"She told me he found her grandmother's ring, and that's why they met up," I explained.

"Grandmother's ring?" Katie asked.

Nobody seemed to register what I was talking about.

"When I asked her if she told him about Italy, she said no. She lied to me," I continued.

"She said you walked ahead of her the entire time on your hike," Liz confirmed.

"Because she told me she missed his friendship and asked me if I would be okay with them being friends," I explained.

"She didn't tell me that," Liz acknowledged.

"She stopped breathing a couple of months ago," I said, telling them Mel had abandoned her evening ritual of essential oils, sage, and breathwork.

"I noticed that too," Katie said softly. "I didn't even think about it, but she did stop breathing."

"She told me she was on 80 milligrams of Adderall a day three years ago. She realized she had to get away from her ex and off the Adderall, which she did. That's when she found breathwork."

"That's a lot," Jim said. "I use it occasionally for paperwork, but 80 milligrams is a lot."

"She used to say Jim and I fought all the time," Liz said, turning to Katie. "Did we?"

"No, I don't remember that."

"Her ex did something to her. I know he did." Liz's voice hardened with certainty.

"When I told him, he showed no emotion," John said.

"She had a thirteen-minute phone call with him before going to Beau's," Becky added.

"What did she say on the call? If you were going to…" Katie started.

"'If you were going to shoot yourself, would you shoot yourself in the head or the chest?'" John finished. "He said, 'I wouldn't shoot myself at all.'"

The words settled heavily in the room.

"Every time she came over last week, she twisted the knife in a little deeper. She said I manipulated her into the relationship."

"She probably got that from him, Beau," Liz said. "He was manipulative. She was confused."

"The next day, she apologized by text," I continued. "Said it wouldn't happen again and blamed her new meds. Said they were making her crazy. When I asked what she was on, she said Concerta."

"What's that?" Liz asked.

"Some kind of generic Ritalin."

"Her therapist sent me her notes," Becky said. "Melanie asked for something lighter… she didn't like how the Adderall was making her feel."

"When did she start taking Adderall again?" I asked.

"February," Becky confirmed.

"I asked her multiple times if she was back on it, and she said no." *Another lie.*

"You know, the night before was his fiftieth birthday," Liz added tensely.

"She used to talk about wanting to do Molly with me," I said. "They used to do it together."

"What's Molly?" Liz asked.

"It's Ecstasy, Mom," Becky explained.

"What? I didn't know she did that."

"I wouldn't be surprised if they did some at his birthday party," I said.

"When we talked to him, he said, 'No illicit drugs were used that night.' Who says that?" Katie noted.

"He did something to her. I know he did," Liz said.

"He also said she kept getting up in the middle of the night, pulling her hair out in front of the mirror, saying, 'I'm psychotic, I'm psychotic,'" Katie added.

"When she left his house to go to Beau's, he said, 'she was all jacked up,'" John added.

"She told me she wasn't in love with him anymore," I said.

"He told us the same thing… she told him she didn't love him anymore," John confirmed.

Becky had arranged for a priest to say a prayer. When he arrived, he stood quietly at the edge of the room, taking in our grief.

Jim stepped forward.

"Life always felt so effortless," he began, his voice steady but heavy. "Like we kept getting pop flies and easy ground balls. College graduates, daughters getting married, new homes... everything fell into place.

We were long overdue for something like this. But I don't know how we're supposed to get through it.

We've been blessed for so long, and now this... It doesn't make any sense. But whatever comes next, we'll figure it out together."

His voice softened as he turned to me.

"We're all shaken up over this... Beau, maybe more so than the rest of us."

"We're all shaken up, Jim," Liz said firmly but gently.

She was right. Aside from Saturday, this was the most challenging day of my life. The collective pain was almost unbearable.

When the priest finished his prayer, I excused myself to Mel's room to email her breathwork teacher, David, so that he could inform her community.

Hoping to find peace, I turned to the practice Melanie had introduced me to. I lay in her bed with her scarf draped across my eyes and began pranayama: one inhale to the belly, another to the chest, then a swift exhale. After about twenty minutes, the energy began to move—vibrating through me until it lulled me to sleep.

I awoke suddenly in the middle of the night, after my first real sleep since losing her. My left hand lifted two inches off my right. *That's strange. I didn't do that. It has to be Mel.*

In Crested Butte, I had taught her a signal: three hand squeezes for "*I love you*," one for each word. I raised my hand and squeezed three times, waiting for her to squeeze back twice, asking, *"How much?"* I then put all my energy into one last big squeeze when nothing happened, signaling, *"This much!"*

Suddenly, all my chakras lit up with an intense tingling warmth, like goosebumps. She was there. I felt her presence.

I spent the rest of the night tossing and turning, replaying the moment. Was it real, or was my mind grasping for something to hold onto? At dawn, I thought again about my hand defying gravity. *I didn't do that. And those vibrations in my chakras...*

The sadness and guilt lingered as I lay there, shattered and exhausted, having barely eaten in two days.

I wanted to call my family, but the thought of breaking my dad's heart tore at me. He had just had his second cardiac ablation surgery. I called his best friend first.

"He can handle it," his friend said gently. "He'd want to be there for you. Call him."

"Hi, pal," Dad answered warmly.

"Dad... I've got terrible news," I said, my throat tightening. "We lost Mel."

"What?"

"She committed suicide, Dad."

"Oh no. Oh, Beau... I'm so sorry. Where are you?"

"I'm staying with her family in Newport." I paused. "Dad... it's worse. She did it with my shotgun. I found her at the foot of our bed."

A tense silence followed.

"Oh Jesus," he whispered. "Oh, Beau... that's just awful. I'm going to figure out how to get down there."

"I need to call Mom."

"Okay, I love you, son," he said, choking back emotion. "Remember who you are and stay strong. I love you."

"I love you too, Dad."

I dialed my mom.

"Hi, Mom... I've got terrible news. We lost Mel."

"What!?"

"She killed herself, Mom. She did it with my shotgun."

"Oh honey... oh honey," she cried. "Where are you? You need to come to me. Can you come to me?"

"I'm at her parents' house in Newport. Dad's coming down... Maybe you can come with him and stay at Sue's."

"Okay, honey. I'm so sorry. I love you."

"I love you too, Mom."

The heartbreak in their voices made those two phone calls the hardest I had ever made. I was relieved they were over and grateful my parents were coming.

Before heading back out to check on the family, I decided to breathe again. It was the only thing that helped me manage the pain.

My hand rising in the middle of the night replayed in my mind. I was eager to share my experience and told Liz.

"Last night, I woke up from a dead sleep, and my left hand rose two inches off my right hand completely involuntarily. Mel was with me."

"Wow," Liz replied, but I could see in her eyes that she thought I might be losing it. I wondered if she was right.

CNN droned in the background as family came and went. Throughout the day, flowers and food arrived from friends. I picked at some fruit, forcing down what little I could.

25

I shared videos and photos from our year together. "She was always so excited for our next adventure."

Watching a video of her dancing in my living room, Liz revealed a painful chapter from Mel's past.

"She got screwed over in dance," Liz said. "Becky had been captain and cut this one girl. Then, when that girl's younger sister became captain, she cut Melanie to get revenge. It was such bullshit. Melanie was the best dancer of all my girls. And then, on top of everything, we found out the dance teacher was using cocaine. We ended up in this huge lawsuit. It was a lot for her."

Liz's wheels continued to turn. "She just got her teeth cleaned on Wednesday. Why would she get her teeth cleaned?" Then, "Was her breathwork thing a cult?"

"Not at all," I said firmly. "When Melanie was breathing, she was at her best. Through breathwork, she discovered that her depression at fifteen was caused by the sexual abuse she experienced at four years old."

"I didn't know what to do when she told me. We didn't have Google back then," Liz said softly. "I didn't tell Jim."

"That's why she didn't want to go to the yacht club events. She didn't want to see that boy's family. She was upset that you didn't understand."

"Well, she shot herself with your shotgun," Liz said sharply.

"I know." The guilt ravaged me. "I shouldn't have left her the key. I didn't think she knew where it was."

I needed to be alone. I retreated to Mel's room to breathe, then spent the rest of the day working on her eulogy. An email notification from Chris Stapleton popped up on my phone. It contained a link to his new song with Dua Lipa at the ACM Awards.

"I think I'm in love with you. I didn't know it at the time." The lyrics crushed me. It felt like Melanie was speaking through the music.

Tears fell as the guilt churned, thinking about how excited she'd been for his show at the Hollywood Bowl. I wondered if telling her I was going to sell the tickets had made her lose hope in us.

There was a knock at the door.

"Come in," I said, drying my eyes.

Becky was returning my house key. She had taken it to Venice with her fiancé, Ray, to get Mel's keys and pick up her car. I noticed she was slightly tipsy from drinks at the Brig.

"You should wear this," she said, revealing Mel's sun and moon necklace.

As she clasped it around my neck, the lights began to flicker.

"That's Mel," I said with certainty.

Becky looked at me like I was crazy. *Did she not notice the lights?*

"Call me if you need anything. I love you, Beau," she said softly.

"I love you too," I replied, hugging her.

I stared at the ceiling in bed until the sun came up, wondering if I was delirious.

The next morning, work was crippling. Tasks that had once been second nature now seemed impossible. *This must be how Mel felt on her bad days.* The weight of everything pulled me under, and soon, I found myself battling suicidal thoughts of my own.

I opened up about our breakup on a walk with Mel's longtime trainer.

"She was constantly asking if I thought she was fat or pretty. I was always like, *are you kidding me?* She was the most beautiful woman I had ever seen. She never had to work for that validation with me, but her ex used to put her down a lot."

"She knew he wasn't good for her," he confirmed. "She did the same thing with me. I told her how much better and healthier she looked when she finally got off the Adderall."

Back at the house, when I brought up Mel's struggles with Adderall, Jim cut me off.

"Let's not talk about the Adderall anymore," he said sharply. It struck a nerve, much like the subject of her sexual abuse did with her mom.

We shifted to music, playing some of Mel's favorites.

"I was looking forward to going to the Chris Stapleton show with you guys in June," Jim said.

"I still have the tickets. We should all go."

"That would be special. Let's do it," he said. "I'm going to see if I can reach out to his team. It would be amazing if we could get some lyrics to him and have him create a tribute for her."

"My dad actually knows one of his songwriters," I added.

"I'll start putting some lyrics together," he said. "You know, I used to have all these nicknames for her. She was '99' because she got 99 out of 100 on all her schoolwork. I also called her 'Melani,' like a Hawaiian version of Melanie, which is what I named my boat. And she and Sarah were the 'bookends' because they looked so much alike."

Liz walked through the front door and announced:

"Becky found utility rope in the back of her car, Beau. She was going to do it that day anyway, so you're off the hook with the shotgun."

Relief and sorrow tangled, spilling into more tears.

"We have a bunch of food, Beau. The neighbors keep bringing it over. You need to try and eat something," Liz urged.

I nibbled on some quiche, but my appetite was gone.

Mel's uncles, Joe and Manny, arrived, setting off the dogs.

"What's up with these dogs?" Manny said, crouching down to calm them.

"It's because you're Mexican," Jimmy joked.

"You remember, Lady? Man, was she mean," Manny said. "She used to growl and show her teeth every time I came over."

The shotgun came up again. I couldn't escape it.

"Are you a hunter?" Joe asked.

"Yeah, but it was for home protection," I replied.

"Was it loaded?"

"How am I supposed to load it if I'm in a situation where I need it?" I explained.

"I understand that," Liz said quietly.

"I didn't think she knew where it was," I repeated as tears flowed.

Manny pulled me into a hug. "Beau, I know we don't know each other, but I can already tell I love you, brother. You're part of the family now."

"Her ex did this to her. He knew he was losing her. He manipulated her. I know he did," Liz said, her voice trembling with anger.

"I want to fuck him up," I whispered to Liz, rage tightening in my chest.

I needed to clear the dark energy. I stepped into Mel's room, hoping to steady myself with breathwork. Thirty minutes was all it took to shift my mood.

When I returned, Manny was waiting on the patio with his Bible.

"Can I read you a passage from Luke?" he asked.

"*Love for Enemies*

But to you who are listening, I say: Love your enemies, do good to those who hate you, bless those who curse you, pray for those who mistreat you... Be merciful, just as your Father is merciful."

Mercy wasn't going to bring Melanie back. I sat on the couch, still searching for answers, as if scrolling through my phone could alter the outcome. I read her text out loud.

"I'm trying to see if I can get some support from my family. Thank you for everything." Looking up at Liz, I said quietly, "I thought you guys knew. I thought she was getting help from you."

"She never said anything to me," Liz said.

"I would have called you, but you know how she was. She would have been so upset."

"Oh, she would have been pissed if you called us," Liz agreed.

"She was always so secretive."

"She was a very secretive girl," Liz echoed softly.

"Can I see the texts?" Becky asked.

I handed her my phone.

"Can I screenshot the conversation?" she asked next.

"Sure," I said.

A moment later, she frowned. "Why does it stop here?"

The text message history ended on May 13th.

"She broke up with me on the 9th, so I deleted her number and our conversation history to stop myself from reaching out."

Becky looked at me, confused.

"When she came over on the 10th, she was sweet, and after her next text, I re-added her number," I continued.

Ray nodded with understanding.

Becky discovered an edited message with two blue heart emojis in our chat history. I had no idea you could view the original. It devastated me as she read it aloud.

"Hi. I just want to let you know I'm going to stay at my grandma's in Agoura for a while, and she is going to help me. I will schedule NAD sessions there if I can. I just wanted to let you know, in case you don't hear from me, that I'm okay and I'll be with her. I started taking a different stimulant this week because I've been so depressed and hoped it would help, but it actually just made me feel crazy. I am so sorry, and thank you for everything. I need to get over this hump. I will reach out when I'm feeling more stable because it's not your job to take any blame. All you've been is amazing. I'm so sorry."

"I can't believe I missed that," I said.

"I looked in the closet," Becky added. "The shotgun wasn't that hidden."

"She ripped it down from the hooks. It was up high. She would've had to jump to get it down. Did you see the hook on the ground?"

Becky shook her head. "The hooks were still up there when I looked."

"That was for my rifle during COVID," I clarified.

"How many guns did you have?" Becky asked, her eyes narrowing.

"Two handguns, a rifle, and a shotgun."

"Were they all loaded?" she pressed, looking at me like I was crazy.

"Crime in LA has been out of control since COVID."

"How did she know you had them?"

"A couple of months ago, on Easter morning, a homeless man tried to break in to my house.

'Someone's trying to break in,' Mel said.

I banged on the door and yelled, 'Get the fuck out of here!' Then I told her, 'The rule of thumb is, you use the handgun to get to the shotgun.'

I showed her the handguns under my nightstand and desk. When she asked about the shotgun, I told her not to worry about it because it was too big for her. She used to go into my closet for my hoodies and could have seen it then, but I didn't think she knew where it was.

She wanted to learn how to use the handguns. We were supposed to go to Oak Tree Gun Club."

"When was this?" Becky asked.

"The Sunday after Nicole's bachelorette party... when she was at Britt's in San Diego."

"April 28th?" she replied.

"She was late getting back that day, so we went for a bike ride instead."

Becky's voice softened. "Did you know she was having suicidal thoughts?"

"No," I lied.

I felt guilty instantly. But Becky was a lawyer, and this felt like an interrogation. I understood the family needed answers, but it only amplified the guilt I was already drowning in.

"It's not your fault, Beau. She was going to find a way to do it that day. Do you want to see the utility rope we found in her car?" Ray asked.

He showed it to me, which wasn't comforting at all. I was desperate for a mental break from the thoughts crashing in my head. A brief reprieve came during the Celtics-Pacers overtime game; her uncles and dad provided some comedic relief. But the guilt of lying to Becky only made it worse. I called her in tears.

"I did know Mel was having suicidal thoughts," I admitted, my voice breaking. "She was breaking up with me. They seemed manipulative."

Becky joined me in tears. "Did she ever say anything bad about me?"

"She just said you two were competitive over boys. But I know she loved you, Becky. She told me she loved you."

The next day, my dad picked me up. I watched as he and Jim bonded over Stanford stories. The moment was bittersweet. I had imagined this scene since learning Jim went to Stanford, but Mel's absence made it unbearable.

"I thought you were going to propose to her in Italy," Jim said.

"I never would have done that without asking for your permission."

Liz handed me a framed photo of Melanie, and Becky gave me a bouquet to take with me.

We said our goodbyes, and I made plans to return for the viewing and service.

The love from Mel's family was there, but so was the judgment. Still, I was hardest on myself. I was beyond broken and ready to grieve with my own family.

A Quick Catch Up

November, 2021 - October 2022

Three and a half years had passed since we last spoke or saw each other. During that time, I went through three relationships, but none gave me the feeling Mel did. When she liked a photo I had posted on my company's Instagram in November 2021, I was surprised she still followed me. I took it as a sign to reach out.

After months of messaging, Mel agreed to meet. Since she was living with her parents in Newport Beach, I suggested meeting halfway in Palos Verdes. I scoured Instagram looking for signs of her relationship. *Was she finally single? Was this the opportunity that I had been waiting for?*

I arrived early at Terranea Resort, unsure of where the restaurant was located. After ten minutes of searching the massive cliffside property, I finally found it. I told Mel I would meet her in the parking lot. Back at my car, I took a final look in the rearview mirror, feeling nerves creep in.

The lot was huge, so I set out to find her. My heart quickened when I spotted her. Her smile drew me in for a hug, and I could sense her nerves, too. Then she took off her glasses. Our eyes met, and the tension faded.

The four-hour brunch at Mar'sel was on the outdoor patio overlooking the Pacific. I asked about her relationship, curious if it was the same "it's not serious" guy from our dinner at the Penthouse.

"We met at my niece's seventh birthday party," she said. "His daughter was friends with her."

"How old is he?"

"He was forty-four when we met. He's eighteen years older than me."

"I couldn't do the stepdad thing."

"Yeah, that was always in the back of my mind, but he was a really good dad. His daughter was the result of a one-night stand."

"That must've been hard on him."

"She's really sweet, though," she added.

"Why did you break up?"

"He's an actor. When COVID hit, things got really hard. We moved in together so I could help him with bills, and then things got chaotic. When Lady died, I couldn't do it anymore."

"It sounds like you made the right decision."

"We tried couples therapy with his life coach, but it felt like they were ganging up on me. He was so manipulative, treating me like a child, and I was the one paying for everything." She shook her head. "It's hard because I really wanted it to work out."

"It doesn't sound like you're over him."

"No, it's over. But I'm still grieving the relationship."

As she spoke, white foam gathered in the corners of her mouth. I wondered if she was taking medication but kept it to myself, not wanting to make her uncomfortable. After years of idealized memories, I was also concerned for what she might be going through. A familiar tension built within me— disappointment that she might not be ready for something new.

"What's up with you?" she asked.

"I finally recovered from the festival, then COVID shut down my business and put me back in debt. My girlfriend at the time thought I was nuts for questioning the vaccine, and we broke up over it."

"What do you think the vaccines are going to do?"

"I don't know. Heart problems. Cancer. Maybe make it harder for people to have kids. Probably take years off people's lives."

"I didn't want to get it," she admitted. "But I wanted to see my sister's kids, and she wouldn't let me until I did."

"My whole family took it except me."

We walked off brunch along the cliffs, down to where the water met the rocks.

"Do you think I'll be able to have kids?" she asked.

I hadn't expected the question and tried to soften my stance.

"The human body has a remarkable way of healing itself. You're young and healthy. I'm sure you'll be fine. Just stay away from the boosters."

"Thank God I didn't get any boosters."

"Did you ever get COVID?" I asked.

"No, did you?"

"I did. At Lollapalooza last summer."

"You did? Was it bad?"

"I was down bad for two weeks, struggling to breathe, until I got my hands on some ivermectin. The day after I took it, my lungs finally opened up. The last place I wanted to end up was on a ventilator in the hospital."

COVID had changed everything, and this conversation felt like more than just small talk. We were feeling each other out, testing where our worldviews aligned and where they didn't.

I walked her to the car, and she gave me a ride to mine on the other side of the lot. My heart raced, and I debated whether to go for a kiss, but the only thing that was there was the electricity she stirred in me. Melanie was in her head, still tangled in the breakup. The heaviness of our conversation likely didn't help either. I opted for a warm hug as she dropped me off.

On the drive home, I called Justin, buzzing with energy over my connection that day.

"There's something about this girl that I can't shake."

But in the following months, when she became distant, I respected her space.

In the summer of 2022, Mel reached out while I was dating someone else. She mentioned travel plans for a trip to Colorado and asked if I knew anyone there, since I went to college in Boulder. Maybe she wanted someone to show her around, but I still had feelings for her, and I wasn't about to offer up one of my friends as her tour guide—not when there was a chance it could turn into something more. Deep down, I was still holding on to hope for us.

By October, she suggested we catch up again, but I was happy with a new girlfriend. My previous attempts to get closer to Melanie had consistently failed, and I wasn't going to jeopardize another relationship over lingering feelings. I responded briefly, wondering if we were meant to circle each other indefinitely without ever getting a chance to collide.

Remember Who You Are

May 23rd - May 29th, 2024

That morning felt different. Although I was still miserable, waking up with my parents at Aunt Sue's was refreshing. I had no memory of the three of us under the same roof, but there we were, having breakfast together for the first time in more than forty years.

My parents divorced when I was a baby. They had been high school sweethearts in this house—my mom's childhood home. We walked Mom's dog, Baylee, as they reminisced. Our stroll led us to Chapman University, where a prominent sign greeted us at the entrance.

"I can liken life before you to that of a ship with its prow pointed toward the great ocean as it leaves the harbor for the distant shore. Storms may come and they will, for no ship ever sailed the seas but had to face the storm. If it is strong from keel to top, from bow to stern, well maintained and intelligently directed, it rides the storm and goes on its way. So you will meet obstacles, storms. If you are strong in faith, clear headed, honest, trusting for divine guidance and with a character built on the solid rock, you will meet all troubles in life victoriously."

-Charles E Chapman

The sign struck a chord. I snapped a photo and sent it to Mel's family with the message: *"There is no victorious ending to this storm, but together we can do our best to get through it."*

As we continued our walk, the idea of *getting through it* brought me back to my earlier conversation with Mel's dad about putting some lyrics together for her. A personalized tribute from Chris Stapleton seemed impossible, but asking for a song dedication might give us a shot.

"Didn't you tell me you knew one of Chris Stapleton's songwriters?" I asked my dad.

"Yeah, he's my buddy."

"I'm planning to take her family to his show at the Hollywood Bowl on June 26th. There's this new song, 'I Think I'm in Love with You.' Do you think you could ask him to see if Chris would dedicate it to Mel during the show?"

"I'll see what I can do, pal."

As we passed Orange High School, where my parents first met, they talked about their teenage years, old friends, and those they'd lost. My thoughts were scrambled, making it difficult to fully appreciate the moment.

After considerable walking, I checked on my dad, fresh off his heart procedure.

"How are you feeling, Pop?"

"Pretty good. Finally able to catch a full breath."

That was a relief.

When we got back, I joined him outside for a game of cribbage. It was mentally exhausting, and by the end, a wave of sadness left me completely drained.

"I need to go breathe again," I said.

I retreated to my bedroom, pressed a ten-second kiss to Mel's photo, imagining the last one she gave me on May 10th, and then settled into bed, covering my eyes with her scarf to breathe.

Revitalized, I found my parents deep in their own game of cribbage. It was heartwarming to see them together. Memories of teaching Mel how to play surfaced. She found it challenging, and without an early start, she lacked the energy to finish. I understood her exhaustion now.

I didn't have the mental capacity for more cards, but my sister Brittany was coaching the girls' 4x400-meter relay team at her alma mater, Monte Vista, in the California State Track Meet. My dad was eager to watch.

As they prepared for the boys' 4x400, my mom brought up my race in the California state semifinals my senior year.

"Remember when you filmed the wrong guy?" she asked my dad.

"How could I forget? I butchered that one pretty good, didn't I? Filmed the only other white kid in the race."

"He was Asian," I corrected.

They all laughed.

"Well, it was a good season, I thought. I looked up after the kid handed off the baton, and Brian was already halfway around the track. I couldn't believe it. I missed the whole race. Got some great footage of that Asian kid, though."

Another round of laughter.

"How many guys did you pass on your leg?" my mom asked.

"I got the baton in seventh and passed it off in third."

"What was your split?" my dad asked.

"48.3."

"I couldn't believe I missed it. Best race of your life. What was your time?"

"3:18.5."

I was curious to see how our times compared. The 3:18.5 in 1997 would have earned us seventh place in 2024, exactly where we finished.

I remembered how hard I had pushed myself during track and the pain that always followed. Reliving those memories with my parents was a welcome distraction, and their banter subtly rebuilt my confidence. I thought about what my dad told me when I called with the bad news: "Remember who you are."

My parents and I drove back to Venice Sunday morning to retrieve my car. As we pulled off the 90 freeway, my thoughts turned to Mel. She hadn't been herself the last couple of times I saw her. My Melanie, the one with that familiar look in her eyes, was gone.

"I need to buy some sage in case there are any evil spirits still with her," I said.

"Okay. Where do we do that?" my dad asked.

I directed him to Rainbow Acres, where I picked up some white sage. I asked my parents to wait outside while I cleansed the house. Mel's voice from our first breathwork session echoed in my mind: "Make sure to set an intention. Speak it like you mean it."

I lit the bundle, waving it like a wand as I walked through every room.

"Only love and light is welcome here. Evil spirits, you must go. The spirit and soul of Melanie Taylor, you are welcome to stay as long as you need. You are free to go whenever you're ready to go."

I repeated my intention throughout the house, then walked the exterior, speaking the same words.

"You did a great job with the sage," my dad said. He was genuinely supportive, though I wasn't sure he fully understood. I didn't think my mom did either.

When my parents left, I sat at my desk, staring at the empty closet where her clothes used to hang. My office had been Mel's room and workspace. I could still see her sitting cross-legged on the floor in front of the mirror, getting ready for date night.

When the tears finally subsided, a deep peace enveloped me. I wasn't sure where it came from, only that it felt like Mel had taken my pain away. As the weight lifted, I turned to my work, grounding myself in the small tasks of the weekend.

I might be able to come back here.

False Start

February 2nd - June 15th, 2023

The timing never seemed to be on our side. In February 2023, I was in Huntington Beach and asked if Mel was up for a last-minute meetup. I never heard back.

A month later, she texted me to say she had an Airbnb minutes from my place in Venice. I was out of town.

Three weeks passed before she reached out again. It was her last day in Marina del Rey. I hadn't known it was a multi-week stay.

She genuinely wanted to see me, so we made plans for dinner in Malibu on April 6. When I saw her, I was captivated all over again. Her eyes were sharp and full of life, so different from the last time I saw her in Palos Verdes over a year ago.

"I'm sorry I've been so distant," she said. "I was in a dark place."

"I could tell you weren't over your ex the last time we saw each other."

"It wasn't that," she said. "I was on 80 milligrams of Adderall a day when we broke up. It was making me crazy. You know how they say dogs take on the energy of their owners? Lady died of liver failure. I think she was processing the Adderall for me."

"Wow. I had no idea. If I'd known you were on Adderall like that, I probably wouldn't have pursued you the way I did."

"Honestly, I probably would have died if I didn't get off it."

"80 milligrams a day? That's insane. How did you stop?"

"Breathwork," she said. "It saved my life. I've been clean for a year now. No Adderall, no alcohol, no coffee. I'm actually training to become a breathwork therapist."

"I'm proud of you. It shows. You look amazing. Your skin, your eyes… you're glowing."

"Really?" She beamed.

As I listened, I realized how different she was. She was open and vulnerable, something I had never seen from her before.

"So, what's up with you?" she asked.

"Business is booming again. I'm out of debt from COVID and the festival. My events at The Victorian have been taking off, and I'm stacking my crypto bags."

"That's amazing. Any projects I should be looking at?"

I rattled off a few names.

"Merrill still hasn't invested," she said. "They're waiting on regulatory clarity."

"You're still at Merrill?"

She nodded. "Yeah, but I'm working remotely so I can focus on my mental health."

"Are you thinking about leaving?"

"I'd like to, but it's a good situation for now. What else is new? Are you seeing anyone?"

"Yeah, I have a girlfriend," I admitted.

I saw her heart drop in her eyes. Mine fluttered. I had never seen that kind of interest from her before.

Disappointment threaded through her voice. "Why are you here then?"

"Because every time I look in your eyes, I feel the same magic I did the first time I saw you at The Buffalo Club."

She held my gaze, waiting for me to flinch. Time froze as our eyes locked in a moment of truth.

"What about your girlfriend? Is it serious?"

"We're going to Bali next week, but I don't see a future with her."

"Then why are you going?"

"She wanted a label, so I gave it a shot. But it's never felt right."

"Are you using protection?"

"She was on the pill."

"Be careful. You don't want a baby with someone you're not in love with."

I was stunned by how much she cared. I should have canceled the trip, but the flights were booked, and I didn't think it was the right thing to do at the time.

After dinner, she asked about my plans. She was house-sitting for her sister nearby, and as much as I didn't want the night to end, I knew this was a test. Instead of giving in to temptation, I told her I had things to do before my trip.

In the parking lot, I pulled her into a long hug, then drove back to Venice, my head spinning the entire way home.

What if Mel met someone else while I was gone?

I had a three-week trip to Bali planned—ten days with my girlfriend.

The next day, I made a mistake. I texted Mel: "*You should come to Bali.*"

I was trying to figure out how to have her come for the first part of the trip while still honoring the back end with my girlfriend, whom I knew I would break up with when I got home.

Mel's response was immediate: "*What about your girlfriend?*"

The question hung there. I had nothing. No clever response, no way to justify what I had just suggested.

Bali was rough. Mel was in my head the entire trip, and my girlfriend could tell something was off. When I got back, we didn't speak for a week. Eventually, I told her the truth: I didn't see a future for us. It was hard; she was a good person, and I had grown attached to her dog. But sometimes, happiness demands hard choices.

I finally had the green light, and I believed Melanie was interested. I reached out, but there was no response.

Maybe she wasn't single.

I waited a few days and tried again, unsuccessfully.

Had I ruined my chance by inviting her to Bali?

After a week of silence, I made one last attempt. *Three strikes and you're out*, I thought, deleting her number to stop myself from trying again. Then, a text from a *949* number changed everything.

"Are you still with your girlfriend?"

"We broke up."

She invited me to visit her in Ojai. My heart raced at the thought. The excitement and longing had been building since I first saw her. A week later, on May 16, I arrived for our first actual date.

"I thought you had a truck?" she remarked.

"Nope, been driving this Prius since 2008," I said with a smile, thinking back to when I borrowed a truck to help her move the coffee table.

"Let's take my car," she suggested. We climbed into her Audi SUV and went to a park on the main street.

We spread a blanket on the grass but didn't stay long. Fleas jumped on me, and bite welts started to form as we walked down the street to get sushi.

"How come you're staying all the way out here?" I asked.

"Ojai has great energy. Plus, my teacher David lives here, and it's not too far from my sister and the kids in Malibu," she said.

"Are you just bouncing around between Airbnbs? Doesn't that get expensive?"

"I stay with Katie in Malibu and Sarah in San Diego a lot, but when I need my space, I get an Airbnb. It's kind of nice. I'm also spending a lot of money on healing, which helps me save. You should come to a retreat with me sometime. There's a big New Year's Eve event in New Mexico where we do a fire walk."

"What do you mean, a fire walk? You walk on fire?"

"They're hot coals. But yeah, we walk across them."

"That sounds pretty sweet."

"It fills up fast. You should look into it."

"New Year's Eve is tough for me with work, but I'll try."

"How was Bali?" she asked.

"It was good. There are a lot of people in Bali who practice breathwork. My friend Joe was out there teaching at a retreat."

"What kind of breathwork does he teach?"

"I'm not sure."

"David specializes in pranayama. It's an ancient breathing technique that helps activate your intuition."

"Any cool realizations on your journey?" I asked.

"When I was fifteen, I had just started high school and began taking a real interest in boys for the first time. As those feelings surfaced, so did the sexual abuse trauma I'd suppressed."

She collected her thoughts.

"My parents didn't understand why I was struggling in school, and my doctor prescribed me Adderall.

Breathwork helped me realize that my inability to focus was tied to depression, which was linked to the sexual abuse I experienced when I was four."

Her eyes held steady as she continued. "I've worked hard to release the abuse and addiction energies... my next step is to heal the relationship with my parents... and then I want to teach breathwork to help girls who are struggling with similar issues."

"I had no idea you went through all that."

Here was Melanie, revealing her deepest pain while demonstrating remarkable strength in transforming it. I felt my heart open even more for her, not just out of attraction but in deep admiration for her resilience and her desire to help others heal.

"Would you be open to breathing with me sometime?" she asked.

"I would love to."

I felt a connection building and opened up about similar struggles my sister Morgan was going through.

"It's probably energetic," she said gently. "She needs to release that trauma from her body. I would love to help her, but it has to be her choice."

As we returned to her Airbnb, a rush of nerves swept over me. This time, there was no way I was leaving without a kiss. I got out of the car to say goodbye. Unsure if she would invite me in, I made my move. Brushing my fingers through her hair, I leaned in and planted one on her. She responded eagerly, and we pressed against her car, lost in the moment.

After a couple of minutes of accelerating desire, I regained my composure. She gave me that same smile and look she had the first night we met, then disappeared behind the gate.

I drove back to Venice exhilarated. Something about Melanie had sparked my creative energy. It was her passion—the way she spoke about breathwork, transformation, and intuition. It was as if she had unlocked a part of me I had forgotten. On the drive home, I called my friend Brian to pitch an app idea I had been mulling over. Unlike my previous attempts to get it started, the words flowed effortlessly this time.

Brian gave a simple response. "I'll start working on it tomorrow."

That night, EventReply.com was born.

When I arrived home, a sweet text from Melanie was waiting:

"Thanks for a wonderful evening and the hot kiss. I had such a great time with you. You should come back up and breathe soon!"

Without hesitation, I replied. *"Let's do it next week."*

But Mel had an even better idea. A few days later, she spontaneously invited me to Malibu. She was staying at her sister's house and wanted to show me her favorite beach.

After lunch on the Malibu Pier, she took me to Lechuza, a hidden gem north of Pepperdine. I brought a deck of cards and a cribbage board. We spread a blanket on the sand, and I began teaching her how to play.

Mel's eyes grew distant as the waves rolled in.

"Lady loved this beach," she said softly. "We'd spend hours together here. I miss watching her run along the water."

"Have you thought about getting a new dog?"

"I have, but it wouldn't be fair to the dog until I have a more permanent place, you know?"

Our game was interrupted by a disheveled homeless man spinning a broomstick.

"Where did she go?" he demanded aggressively. "Don't ignore me. Which way did she go?"

"I don't know who you're talking about, man," I said calmly.

"Don't lie to me. Did she go that way?" His tone sharpened.

I locked eyes with him, adrenaline surging. *This guy's nuts, but I can take him.* If he got any closer, it would get physical. *He might have another weapon.* I had to be ready. I envisioned slamming him into the sand, wrenching the broomstick away, and choking him out with it.

Sensing the tension, Mel cut in with the perfect suggestion.

"I think she went that way," she said, pointing down the beach.

"Yeah, I think she went that way," he muttered, shuffling off.

"I thought I was gonna have to take that broomstick from him and shove it up his ass," I joked.

Mel burst out laughing.

"Were you scared?" I asked.

"Not with you." She smiled.

I dropped her off at her sister's house. Just before the gate, she gestured to the security camera.

"Not ready for this to be caught on camera," she smiled.

I leaned in and gave her a long, lingering kiss before leaving.

We'd barely made it through two dates, but something was different this time. The walls she'd kept up for so long had come down. Three days later, I made the journey back to Ojai. I picked her up in the Prius this time, and we drove to her favorite hiking spot.

"The Prius doesn't suit you; you should get a truck."

The Prius felt small for me at 6'3" and 220 pounds, but I shrugged it off. I rarely drove far from the Westside of Los Angeles.

"My driving expense is $130 a month, and I'm trying to buy a house."

That sparked her curiosity. "Where?"

"I'd like to get out of the city," I confessed.

"Me too… I feel like something terrible is going to happen in LA next year," she shared with clear resolve.

As we parked for the hike, she made a request: "You know I'm old-fashioned; it would be nice if you opened the door for me when I get out of the car."

I had waited almost a decade for this. "I can get behind that," I assured her. She deserved a gentleman after her last relationship, and I wanted to fill that role.

Her yoga class had been intense the last time we went to the gym, so I anticipated a challenging hike. However, I was pleasantly surprised when she set a leisurely pace, pausing to admire flowers. She even wore a pouch around her waist to collect trash until we found a proper bin. Her dedication to environmental stewardship was impressive. "We need to be mindful of our exchange with Mother Earth," she emphasized.

After our hike, we had dinner at an Indian restaurant, where we continued our conversation about leaving the city.

"I would love to move to Colorado," Mel said, reminiscing about her enjoyable time there in the summer of 2022.

"Colorado is amazing, but the altitude can be tough, and the dry air bothers my sinuses," I replied, sharing my concerns.

I recounted a memorable visit to Flathead Lake, Montana, when I was 16, describing its beauty.

"My dad's junior college football coach retired in a three-story log home with a big grass field that led down to a dock on the water. Something like that would be a dream for me."

"With some babies?" Mel asked, her tone serious yet inviting, drawing me in.

"And a couple of big dogs," I replied, expanding the vision.

Intrigued, Mel admitted she had never been to Montana.

"We should go sometime," I suggested.

"I'd also like to visit Colorado again."

"We'll catch a Buffs game in the fall," I said, imagining the adventure.

After dinner, we returned to her Airbnb. She spread a blanket on the floor of the small studio, lit sage and candles, and sprayed her cleansing mist. Then she asked me to set an intention, but I needed more clarity, so I asked her to explain.

"An intention is what you want to get out of the session," she said gently, noticing my hesitation. "Take your time."

"Do I tell you what it is?"

"That's up to you."

I set the intention of discovering a new purpose, keeping it to myself. She directed me to lie down and placed eye pillows over my eyes. Guiding my breath, she instructed deep inhalations: first into my belly, then into my chest, followed by a swift exhale, repeating the pattern continuously. She started the music.

At first, as I began breathing, tension filled my chest. It felt like there was a block, and I struggled with the rhythm. She encouraged me the entire time, her presence steady and reassuring.

Midway through the session, intense emotions surfaced. Tears welled up under the eye pillows and streamed down my cheeks.

"What's coming up for you?" she asked.

"I feel like a failure," I said. "Like I lack appreciation for my achievements and always fall short of my goals."

"You're not a failure. Let it go."

Tension released with the tears, and eventually, I settled into a rhythm. Breathing grew easier as energy began to flow.

"Are you feeling any vibrations?"

"I am, yeah."

She had me switch to a single inhale through the mouth, then a single inhale through the nose. With each change, the vibrations became more palpable.

"Okay, now we're going to start bringing you back," she said.

She instructed me to rotate my wrists and ankles and stretch my arms, legs, and back. Then, she added, "Remove the eye pillows when you're ready… no rush."

I took off the eye pillows, which were soaked with my tears.

"Sorry, I got them a little wet."

"That's okay. How do you feel?"

"I feel pretty good."

"Do you want to talk about what was coming up for you?"

"I feel like I've accomplished everything I've set out to do in my life, but for one reason or another, I always come up short.

I lacked discipline in my football career and struggled with injuries because of it.

I didn't have enough money to shoot my film the way I wanted and had to cut forty pages because it wasn't in the budget. The New York and LA Times criticized me for underwriting the script.

When I put on the music festival in Bali, the Mount Agung volcano crippled tourism on the island.

Every time I've gone big on something I thought I could be proud of, it's fallen short of my expectations."

"But you still did all of that. You should be proud of yourself; you're not a failure!"

I lost myself in her empathetic gaze, warmed by her compassion.

"I want you to feel something," she said, placing my hand on her chest. "Can you feel that?"

"What is that?" I asked, feeling her chest purring like a kitten. It was magical.

"That's my heart chakra vibrating."

The attraction intensified as I sank deeper into her eyes. Unable to resist, I pounced like a tiger, moving in for a kiss, which she met with anticipation. The heat of the moment enveloped us in a whirlwind of escalating desire. As I began to kiss her waistline, Melanie froze, unsure how to move forward, until she suddenly sat up, leaving a lingering tension in the air.

"Are you okay?" I asked.

"Yeah, I just felt this weird, energetic shift. I'm really tired now. I need to go to bed."

I hugged her goodbye. Anxiety crept in on the way home. The energetic shift was massive; I wondered if I had somehow ruined my chance with her. On the drive home, I replayed the evening, trying to pinpoint what went wrong but couldn't. Maybe it was the Indian food, or perhaps it had to do with her earlier mention of past sexual abuse. *Had something surfaced during our intimacy?* I never figured it out.

Something shifted after the breathwork date. In June, we finally got our boxing date in with my trainer, planning to grab a bite afterward, but the easy connection we'd found retreated behind her walls again.

When the session was over, Mel was quick to end our plans. "I think I'm going to head back to my sister's in Malibu."

"Okay," I replied, trying to mask my disappointment.

"Are you mad?" she asked. "I'm sorry, but that was intense, and I'm exhausted."

"It's all good."

I was now 0-2 on boxing dates with her. A couple of days later, I reached out again, hoping to make new plans. She didn't respond. I stared at my phone, knowing exactly where this was going. By then, I had learned that chasing Melanie didn't work. I deleted her number to stop myself from pushing her further away, hoping she would come back around.

My 44th birthday passed without any wishes from her. The number had always felt meaningful to me; my college football jersey was assigned by chance when I showed up on campus. Not hearing from her was disappointing.

My friend Vanessa came to my birthday party at The Victorian. "Are you dating anyone?" she asked.

"I'm dating a Newport Beach gal," I said, the words feeling uncertain even as they left my mouth.

Vanessa, who was from Newport, asked, "Who? Do I know her?"

"Do you know Melanie Taylor?"

"No way, I grew up sleeping over at their house. Becky and I were really close when we were younger. They're a great family."

I had only heard great things about them. It only made it harder to accept that she was slipping away again.

Rest In Paradise

May 28th - June 1st, 2024

I still wasn't ready to spend the night at my house. It felt cold and empty, and I feared the dark loneliness waiting for me when the sun went down. Justin insisted I stay with him in Westchester so I could take care of things in LA.

When I arrived, I told him everything, every dark and tangled detail, including Mel's sexual abuse.

"When we first heard about it, we were pissed at her for doing that to you. But I feel for her, man. My first girlfriend in LA was abused by her uncle, and her mom never did anything about it.

She said it was a cultural thing. Her family was Mexican, and they kept it quiet. She had to live with it and hated her mom for it."

"Mel's mom said she didn't know what to do… blamed not having Google back then. I don't get it. Unless she didn't believe her or something."

"How old was she?"

"Four."

"Yeah, that's fucked up."

My mind spun on Mel's abuse. I knew it was at the root of her issues, and I never felt like I got the full truth. I retired to the guest room to breathe on it. Not long after, I received a text message from Kia, one of Mel's closest breathwork friends, asking if I was available for a call.

She always told me he understood her in a way that few others did. We shared the same crushing guilt over not being there on Saturday. In hindsight, the signs were obvious. We had both missed them.

"We had dinner Thursday night. She told me she was having suicidal thoughts," he admitted. "I'm right there with you, brother. I want you to know that she spoke highly of you, Beau. Thank you for treating her right."

"She valued your friendship, Kia. I was looking forward to meeting you and Lauren. I'm sorry that dinner never happened," I said, fighting back tears.

Before heading back to Orange County, I cleaned up my home—carrying the shattered sliding glass mirror doors to the garage, sweeping up the broken glass, and scrubbing the floor clean of the blood that remained. I remade my bed with the sheets Becky had washed. Somehow, none of the white bedding had any blood on it, and the room was exactly as Melanie had picked it out—ready for me to come back to after her service.

Mel had encouraged me to grow my hair out, and I wanted to make sure I looked clean-cut for her memorial weekend. I'd been on a spaghetti diet for two days, and my stomach was a mess from reintroducing food. I excused myself from the barber's chair. When I returned and shared the news, it hit him hard. I promised myself I wouldn't do that to anyone else, and bottled it up until the day of Mel's viewing.

Sarah posted the service details on Instagram, tagging me.

"It was time to rip the bandaid off," she texted.

I followed her lead, sharing photos and videos of our special moments with the caption:

"Life isn't fair. Love is beautiful. Nothing else matters. Rest in paradise, my beautiful butterfly."

Condolences poured in, but no amount of love could change what was coming next.

I stopped for roses on my way to Mel's parents' house, where I was staying.

Liz drove us to the cemetery.

I had never been to a viewing before. It was for immediate family.

A slideshow of Mel's life played above her casket, snapshots of a little girl I never knew.

Each frame was another reminder of a life I failed to protect.

I drowned in sadness, paralyzed with guilt.

When they opened the casket, I waited. Her family mourned first. Then I approached slowly, kneeling beside her. I placed my hand on hers, folded across her abdomen. They didn't feel human.

"I'm so sorry, Melanie. I'm so sorry I wasn't there on Saturday," I whispered.

I hoped for something, a sign, a shift in energy, like when my chakras responded a few nights earlier. But there was nothing—just a cold goodbye.

I offered to help prepare for the celebration of life. Normally, this would be where I shine, but I felt dead inside as I sat at Becky's house, scanning additional photos from Mel's childhood to add to the slideshow. Ray's family sorted through pictures, handing me piles. The planning seemed to distract everyone from the weight of it all. A couple of hours later, Jimmy picked me up and brought me back to her parents' house.

I continued to busy myself, refining Mel's eulogy before bed when half of it suddenly disappeared from my phone. Panic set in until I discovered I could recover the text by shaking my device.

But I hadn't deleted it. Was that Mel? Did she not like something I wrote? Was she tired of hearing it?

I remembered when my hand rose in the middle of the night. The final part of the "*I love you*" gesture was supposed to be a firm squeeze and a shake to signal, I love you, "*This much!*"

That was exactly how her eulogy reappeared when I forcefully shook my phone. Maybe that was her way of finishing her part from the other night, telling me how much she loved me.

I raised my hand and squeezed three times.

"I love you."

The next day, Mel's service and celebration of life took place. I rode with her parents and Jimmy to the church in Newport Beach.

When the hearse arrived, I stepped forward as a pallbearer, hand on her casket as we wheeled her down the aisle. The church was packed, the air heavy with quiet grief. Only standing room was left at the back. I fought to hold it together, but my eyes brimmed with tears.

This was never how I had imagined walking down the aisle with her.

I settled into the front row next to Liz and Jim, shifting over to make room for Jimmy beside his mom.

Sarah and Becky read passages before Mel's dad spoke. He was composed and held back most of his emotions as he talked about his love for his wife and family, expressing our shared thoughts. This was not the church speech he envisioned giving for his youngest daughter.

The support was overwhelming. My dad, stepmom, all three of my sisters, Aunt Sue, two of my mom's best friends from high school, my college scholarship donors, Troy, Justin, and four other close friends from LA had all made the trip.

Among them was an unfamiliar face, but I knew immediately who he was.

"Beau," he said.

"Kia," I replied, placing my hand on his heart.

"I knew that was you."

The moment was moving, but my mind was elsewhere. The weight of delivering Mel's eulogy pressed on me. I kept thinking back to a question she had asked me in our kitchen less than three weeks ago.

"What would you say in my eulogy?"

Now, it had become my reality. It still didn't feel real.

Becky organized a beautiful celebration. The slideshow was perfect, and the acoustic musician added to the atmosphere. The only thing that didn't feel right was the location. I understood the convenience on short notice, but Melanie had deep-rooted pain tied to the yacht club.

When the eulogies began, Jim went first, followed by Sarah, then John and Katie. The emotion built with each speech as Becky announced there was a final speaker.

I had never given a eulogy before. I thanked Mel's family for their love and support, then began the letter I had written. My whole body trembled, not from nerves but under the paralyzing weight of my grief.

"My Dearest Mel,

I was hoping to save this story for our wedding day… 10 years ago, you walked into Buffalo Club in your classic black leather jacket, and our eyes locked. I was hooked by your beautiful brown eyes… a magnetic gaze and electrifying smile that froze me. It was a feeling I had felt few times where I truly knew that you were going to be an important part of my life. I was so nervous to talk to you that I walked over to the manager at the end of the bar and asked him to send you a drink. Buffalo Club became your stomping ground on Fridays, and it always brightened my night when you showed up.

In the early years, we went on a couple of dates even though you refused to acknowledge them as such. This past year, we joked about how you 'friend zoned' me so hard back then… and you had no idea how I got out of it.

It started with a poem I wrote for you called *Beautiful Someday,* where I truly believed that even though you were in a new relationship… we would have a chance to build something special one day. I moved on and dated other women, but they weren't you. Four years later, you opened the door when a little heart landed on an Instagram post. I reached out to you, and we had a wonderful brunch and a beautiful walk at Terranea in Palos Verdes. It was clear to me that you were not yet ready… but that electrifying gaze and the feeling it gave me never wavered… of all the women that I met in the thousands of events that I've thrown. It was always you that I felt an overpowering connection with. 10 months after Terranea we finally got our chance. And it was a magical year, Mel.

I'm so proud of you for all of the hard work that you were doing. You were disciplined, determined, and courageous, and as the months passed, our love grew stronger. You loved to hike and spend time in nature. You were grateful for the trees and used to put your hand on them to say hello, which I always thought was so special. You wore a litter pouch on your hikes and were adamant about picking up other people's trash. You cared deeply for Mother Earth. You loved dogs, and you missed your sweet Lady every day. I cherish the passion that you had for your family. You were drawn to the innocence of your nieces and nephew. I had so much fun with you at the baseball game and school play. I loved how excited you would get to show me new videos of Sarah's daughters.

You loved a good Airbnb and were always excited about our next adventure. I'm grateful we were able to fulfill your travel dream in Italy. I can still feel the embrace of your hand and the waves of our sound bath in Moltrasio.

You loved your music and introduced me to some amazing new acts. We saw Portugal. the Man, Hozier, Ray Lamontagne, and Nathaniel Rateliff, whose last name I could never get right... I can still hear the frustration in your voice... 'it's not Ratliff, it's Rateliff.'

You constantly expressed that you were grateful for me and that you were really happy about what we were building. You challenged me to be a better man in so many aspects of my life. You always said I was so independent and that you wished I needed you more. I always needed you... you were my motivation... you wanted out of the city, and I was going to give that to you... I woke up excited to attack each day with that in mind... I've never needed a person more than I need you right now, Mel. The pain is deeper than anything I have ever felt... but you showed me a way through when you introduced me to breathwork. It was your passion... it was your dream. And I will use it to move on and connect with you for the rest of my life.

You would have been an incredible mother. You were my beautiful butterfly. You had amazing, colorful wings... I so wanted to see you fly the way I knew that you could. Upon my arrival at the gates of heaven... I will ask Saint Peter where I can find the Angel with the butterfly wings... We will reunite for another round of deck life in the next chapter, my love. Rest in paradise, my beautiful butterfly!"

By the time I finished, I was a puddle of tears, snot streaming down my face. Mel's sister, Sarah, hugged me.

"That was beautiful, thank you."

I rejoined my family. My twin sisters, Brittany and Morgan, wrapped their arms around me.

"I loved the Nathaniel Rateliff part," Morgan said with a smile.

"Now it makes sense, Beau," my scholarship donor said, pulling me into a hug. "Can we get you a beer?"

I accepted his offer and did my best to visit with family and friends.

"Thank you for honoring her," Kia said, embracing me.

"That was the emotion we all needed," Justin said, offering his hug.

My dad was proud of the eulogy I gave. He wanted to capture the moment with pictures, as the ceremony had brought together so many important people from my life. However, photos were the last thing I wanted to take, and the images revealed how crushed I was.

As things wound down, I walked my family out, said our goodbyes, and made plans to meet them Saturday at my place. I stayed behind, having a couple more beers with Mel's family, hoping it might ease the pain.

The celebration gradually died down, and conversations became quieter. I found myself wandering through the room, watching the slideshow, and studying the mementos of her life. As people began cleaning up, I spotted Mel's sound bowls on display. I placed them in front of her niece and goddaughter.

"Mel would want you to have these," I said. "It would mean a lot to her if you learned how to play them."

She began playing the bowls with her brother as we listened to music. I put on "Keep The Wolves Away" by Uncle Lucius, remembering how I used to sing the chorus to Mel: "*I fought like hell to keep the wolves away.*" Tears flowed when "Something in the Orange" by Zach Bryan played, reminding me of our first dance in my living room.

A drunk family friend tried to comfort me.

"Don't cry," she said. "Let's play a happier song."

I wasn't in a happy place. The beers weren't helping, and I didn't want a hangover. Three were enough. I decided to walk back to Mel's parents' house. The neighborhood was the American dream, but I was still living in a nightmare.

As I approached, I heard blood-curdling moans from upstairs. It was Jim. He'd kept his composure for the past two days, and I wondered if this was his way of grieving. But it didn't sound like emotional pain. It was physical.

I went to Mel's bedroom to breathe. When I came back, he was still writhing in agony.

"I need to go to the hospital. Something's wrong with my kidneys," he bellowed.

"Okay, we'll go," Liz said.

She came downstairs, and I asked, "Is he alright?"

"He's being a big baby," she replied.

In the morning, Jim admitted he felt much better.

"What was going on?" I asked.

"I thought it was my kidneys, but it must have been a nerve in my back," he said. "I'm feeling a lot better now."

I was relieved, but I wondered if the universe or Mel was making him feel the weight of his loss differently.

I was ready to head back to Venice. I said goodbye to Jim before Liz, Jimmy, and I went to see John, Katie, and the kids for breakfast burritos. They were staying at a friend's place nearby.

While we waited for the burritos, the kids watched *Crazy Rich Asians*. I had never seen it, but it took me back to my first session with Mel's breathwork teacher, David. I told him I had lost faith in Hollywood and abandoned my dream of writing screenplays. He mentioned that one of his clients had once come to him with an idea for a book but nearly gave up, convinced no one would care—then went on to write *Crazy Rich Asians* after David encouraged him to keep going. The coincidence struck me, but grief was still pulling me under.

Deck Life

July 5th - July 13th, 2023

Magic Hour painted Lake Arrowhead as I snapped a photo from the deck of our rental. "*Something to look forward to,*" I texted Mel, hoping to spark some excitement.

She had reached out wanting to "*catch up,*" opening with a belated birthday wish before apologizing for being distant while focusing on breathwork. Between mentions of her upcoming trips to Joshua Tree and Maui, I suggested a mountain getaway, knowing how much she wanted to escape LA. I was surprised and thrilled when she agreed.

The two-story home sat high up the mountain, its spacious deck overlooking the lake. I had chosen a place with multiple bedrooms, conscious of our undefined status. As night settled in, I anticipated uninterrupted time together.

By morning, I had worked out while waiting for her "*on my way*" text and then went grocery shopping. Midway through, she called about a flat tire. Past experiences had me bracing for a cancellation and calculating the cost of a shortened stay. When she texted that AAA had fixed it, I channeled my relief into making guacamole, swapping bell peppers for chips knowing she was health conscious.

She arrived at four, wrapping me in a warm embrace before I showed her to the downstairs master.

"I swear there's this dark energy that doesn't want me to see you," she said.

"I thought you were going to flake again."

"When did I flake on you?"

"Remember our first boxing date that never happened?"

"I'm so sorry," she said sincerely. "Will you please forgive me for that?"

"You wouldn't be here if I hadn't already."

"I just thought you were another douchebag promoter with lots of girls. I didn't know you were so sweet."

I laughed it off. It wasn't wedding bells, but we were making progress.

She made a salad in the kitchen while I grilled fish on the deck.

"This is nice," she said at dinner. "I'm having a really nice time with you."

"So am I. Thanks for coming."

After dinner, we moved to the fire pit, tucking into blankets on cushioned rocking chairs. She pulled out a deck of cards with questions on them to spark meaningful conversation. As the sun set, "deck life" began.

"Have you ever had your heart broken?"

"I've never been broken up with," she said proudly, "but I've had my heart broken. My ex used to gaslight me constantly, always making me feel like I didn't know what I was talking about because he had all this life experience on me.

He somehow got me to alienate myself from my family and friends… but I knew it was over when he didn't get me anything for my thirtieth birthday. I gave him some of the best years of my life."

"You've still got a lot of good years left."

"What about you?"

"My college girlfriend broke my heart. She loved me when I was a starting tight end on a top 25 football team, but when we moved to New York and I was starting over, I became deadweight. That fucked me up for years."

"Sounds like you're not over her."

"I am, but I didn't let anyone get close for a long time. Quick, physical relationships were all I was interested in. After the music festival, I got sober for nine months. It shifted my focus from hookups to patience and commitment. I got close to a couple of women, but I feel like all those relationships were preparing me for this."

"How long did it take to get over her?"

"Fully? Almost a decade."

Her jaw dropped. "I hope it doesn't take me that long."

Mel still wasn't entirely over him. I could see it in her eyes.

"Have you ever used illegal drugs?"

"My ex and I used to do Molly in Joshua Tree," she said. "We'd stay up all night and connect. We should do it sometime."

"My Molly days are behind me."

"What about mushrooms?"

"In the right setting, I'd be down."

"They'd be fun here." She knew I had to head back to LA the next day. "Can you get some?"

"I have some chocolate I can bring on Saturday."

I thought back to my own experiences with MDMA.

"You know Molly is the love drug. That's why they call it ecstasy. Had you ever done it before?"

"I hadn't," she said, her gaze scanning for answers. "I never thought about that."

"It sounds like he used MDMA to deepen his connection with you... almost like Stockholm syndrome."

She exhaled sharply.

"Wow, I just felt this huge release." Her voice dropped. "The sexual abuse energy from when I was a little girl... is the same predatory energy in him that I was attracted to."

The realization hit her hard.

"Thank you for talking to me about this. I need to breathe on it."

She went to her room for a breathwork session. The smell of burnt sage drifted upstairs as I got ready for bed. When she returned, she climbed into bed beside me.

"I want to stay in bed with you," she said, "but we aren't getting fresh tonight, okay?"

It was our first night sleeping in the same bed together, and I happily welcomed her cuddle until the next morning.

After breakfast, I encouraged her to join me for a YouTube HIIT class in the living room. Fifteen minutes in, she gave up, which surprised me. She had always been a fitness enthusiast, so I expected this to be her kind of workout, but she said it was too intense. It reminded me of our boxing class, which had also pushed her limits.

Despite her resistance to structured exercise, she was eager to hike. When she stepped out of the car, she started picking up trash. Inspired, I joined in, turning it into a game so she could relax and enjoy the trail.

"Humans are gross," she said. "We're the only species that trashes Mother Earth."

"I don't disagree, but hearing that from the girl who hates on my Prius is funny," I laughed.

"You'd be better suited in a truck, and it's nice to be picked up in a nice car."

As we neared the top, she said, "I'm going to say hi to that mama tree."

She approached a towering oak and placed her hand on its bark. I admired the moment's sweetness.

"Do you think I'm weird?" she asked.

"That's why I like you."

We settled onto a rock with a view of the lake, slipping off our shoes to ground our feet in the dirt. The breeze carried the scent of pine as sunlight filtered through the branches. We sat in silence before sharing a kiss on the mountaintop.

"It's so pretty and peaceful up here," she said. "I can't wait to get out of the city."

"It would be tough to leave LA with my business, but I could see myself in Arrowhead or Ojai."

"I love Ojai."

I continued to brainstorm the idea on my way back to the car. The two-hour commute to and from work on weekends would be tough, and I'd probably need to give up drinking to make it work. As I tried to piece together the possibility, a dragonfly landed on my arm, and I flicked it away, thinking it was a fly. Regret hit me the moment I realized it wasn't.

"Do you like what you do?" Mel asked, her mind seemingly running futuristic scenarios as well.

"I used to, but keeping up with the kids is tough. Promoting is like wrangling cats," I said, drawing a laugh from her.

"I don't know how you do it."

That evening, I drove back to LA for work. When I arrived at The Buffalo Club, she texted a picture of herself on the deck.

"Missing deck life with you."

She missed me. This is going somewhere.

I got back late Saturday night after my day party at The Victorian. She was already in bed and asked me to shower and burn sage to cleanse my energy before joining her. As I slid into bed, we started kissing passionately. I was sensitive to our previous hookup in Ojai and conscientious of her history with sexual abuse. A rush of nerves came over me. I was afraid of hurting her and felt myself retreating through the motions.

"What are you doing?" she asked, pulling away.

"I'm sorry, I just got really nervous all of a sudden."

I wished I had opened up about what I was feeling. Instead, she rolled over, became the little spoon, and we fell asleep.

In the middle of the night, I woke up to us making out intensely. She pulled away.

"Whoa, that was crazy. I don't know what happened there," she said as we emerged from the daze. "We have to be careful. I've got this baby energy circling me."

"What do you mean?"

"I can feel a baby girl circling me, waiting to be born."

That was a wild statement, but as I held her, I could see her as the mother of my child.

Sunday morning we grabbed coffee in Lake Arrowhead Village while waiting to ride the tourist boat. Mel ordered a matcha.

"David thinks it's best for me to stay away from stimulants," she confessed.

"That makes sense."

When her matcha arrived, I asked how it was.

"They can never get it right. Can I have a sip of your foam?"

I laughed as she sucked down the top layer of my cappuccino.

"I miss coffee so much," she said.

The lake was the only way for non-residents to access the water. The boat was packed, and I could tell Mel wasn't enjoying herself. An obnoxious woman and her child crowded her space. Another woman, complaining about the cold, shut the window nearest us.

"Would you mind opening the window back up? It's really stuffy in here," Mel asked.

I tried to make the most of the tour. "Pick out your dream house," I said. "What about that one?"

She wasn't feeling it. She was sensitive to the energy of others and didn't like large gatherings or crowded spaces. She reminded me of my mom in that way, both Scorpios.

Back at the house, away from the crowds, Mel relaxed into our familiar routine.

"Let's do another round of deck life," she suggested, reaching for the cards.

"What's the hardest thing you've ever done?"

"Dance was intense growing up. There was a lot of pressure to be the best and the prettiest. We juggled tight schedules with school, rehearsals, and practices. My mom bused the five of us around in her van, managing pickups and drop-offs," she said, referencing her four siblings.

"Mom sounds like a badass."

"She was. Dad was always busy working, but Mom had it down to science. We were constantly on the move, doing homework and napping in the van while waiting to pick each other up. What about you?"

"The film I made was tough, and the music festival was stressful, but playing college football in the Big Twelve was the hardest. I thought I would be a wide receiver at Colorado. When I asked our offensive coordinator for the playbook, he told me I was playing tight end and needed to put on thirty pounds if I ever wanted to see the field."

"I don't know much about football."

"I was small for my position and got beat up pretty good. I spent a lot of time in the training room recovering from injuries. Football is brutal because, eventually, your body gives up on you. Coming back from injuries again and again is exhausting, physically and emotionally. But I wouldn't trade that experience for anything. It made me who I am."

"What are you looking for in a partner?"

"A best friend to be my rocking buddy," I replied.

Mel looked intrigued.

"I went to North Carolina with my business partner who was going through a breakup. His father told us we needed to find our rocking chair buddy, someone to sit on the porch with and talk to when the physical attraction fades. 'Your mother and I don't have sex anymore,' he told us, 'but we sit on the porch every night and talk, and it's nice. You boys need to find yourselves a rocking chair buddy.'"

"My parents are still passionately in love. I hope I never get to a point with my husband where there's no sex."

"I hope that doesn't happen either," I replied. "But I've talked to a lot of older men, and they say things slow down after kids. Looks fade, stress takes over, and family life becomes the new passion. That's why I want a best friend."

"I hope I don't lose my sex drive after kids. I want to be madly in love with my husband."

"True love takes time to build."

"I thought I had that with my ex. I realize now what I thought was love was actually chaotic codependency, but it's still hard to let go, you know?"

I didn't understand. Chaos was something I avoided in relationships.

That night, we shared some chocolate mushrooms, wrapped in blankets on the couch, and listened to Ray LaMontagne. As the trip deepened, we switched to Pink Floyd. I closed my eyes, our bodies intertwined as reality shifted. A vision of Mel's soul hovered before me—a translucent green goddess floating in the darkness, tethered to the earth by an angelic white cord pulsing with energy. The moment felt perfect.

Mel went downstairs to breathe. I sauntered into bed, still deep in the trip, my mind drifting to a recent conversation with my mother about having children. "I'm not sure I want to bring kids into such a cruel world." Her response echoed in my head:

"But your child might be the one who makes a difference."

A sudden clicking from behind the screen door snapped me out of my thoughts. It was too rhythmic to be the wind. I felt it before I understood it—something was there. The message wasn't spoken, but I heard it anyway:

"Your child is going to change the world."

Overwhelmed, I raised my hand, silently asking it to leave. The clicking stopped. Seconds later, the carbon monoxide alarm pierced the silence.

I went downstairs and found Mel just finishing her breathwork. Unable to silence the alarm, I removed the batteries. I wondered if the entity had triggered it. When I told her about my experience, she shrugged it off.

"It's a full moon. I'm going to sleep under the stars."

She slept on the patio, then climbed into bed with me at sunrise.

We were supposed to check out in the morning, but Mel was still on her spare tire, and we didn't think it was safe for her to drive back to Malibu. I asked if she wanted to stay while we found a place to get it fixed. She agreed, and we extended our trip for two more nights.

On our hike that day, I asked if she'd be okay with me running to the top for a workout. As I passed a broken tree, I spotted a black snake stretched across the trail. I waited to make sure it didn't catch her off guard. She smiled when I pointed it out.

"Snakes are a good omen."

I pushed on to the top and settled onto our rock. When she arrived, I had already kicked off my shoes and dug my feet into the dirt. I leaned in for another kiss, but something was off. Maybe it was the mushrooms from the night before, but Mel seemed distant. I couldn't tell where her head was.

That night, we played another round of deck life.

"What was your toughest day?"

"Last year, I testified in the trial of a college teammate who shot someone in the arm while he was strung out. He had played in the NFL and was using CTE as a defense for temporary insanity. It's complicated, but I ended up as a witness after the prosecution served me and flew me to Colorado to testify about his cocaine use."

"Did you ever see him using it?"

"One time, yeah. When the defense attorney had his chance for cross-examination, he shifted to CTE and asked what happened to another teammate of ours... Drew, his best friend. The prosecution objected, but the judge overruled it and allowed me to answer. I said, 'He shot himself in the heart with a shotgun,' and immediately broke into tears."

"Why did he kill himself?"

"We think he had CTE. Drew also played in the NFL, and my teammate who was on trial believed he shot himself in the chest so his brain could be studied, which my friend had been trying to arrange for him. It was an emotional day."

"That sounds intense. Thank you for sharing that with me."

"What was your hardest day?"

"I don't know if there's one day in particular, but my breakup was really hard. I know I've been out of it the last couple of days. I'm still really grieving that relationship," she said.

"What about the big energetic release a couple of days ago? You said he was toxic and that he had dark energy."

"I know, but he's really not that bad of a guy. He's a good dad. He was the one who encouraged me to get off the Adderall."

I appreciated her honesty and understood that she needed to work through this on her own. At the same time, I felt confused and unsure about where we stood.

The following day, we picked up Mel's car. I didn't need to be back at work until Friday, and Mel had no plans to stay elsewhere. I asked if she wanted to spend an extra night at the Lake Arrowhead Resort, and she agreed.

We spent the day at the resort beach, the only way to swim in the lake besides owning a house on the water.

Mel pulled out her teacher David's book on healing.

"Would you consider seeing David for a breathwork session?" she asked.

I knew she valued his opinion and could tell she was still unsure about me.

"Absolutely," I confirmed.

"His sessions fill up fast. You should jump on it."

She went for a dip in the lake, then said she wanted to go back to the room to do some breathwork.

"Can I borrow your book?" I asked.

I was curious about David and wanted to learn more before booking a session. Mel was enthusiastic about me diving in and was happy to leave it with me.

One passage in the book stood out. It talked about dragonflies symbolizing the arrival of good fortune. I regretted flicking the one that had landed on me during our hike. As I continued reading, another dragonfly landed on my arm. I let it stay this time, and we held eye contact for about thirty seconds before it took off.

When I returned to the room, I told Mel about the dragonfly and how I had just read about their meaning in the book she gave me. Her excitement didn't match mine.

Something in her had shifted.

"Is everything okay?"

"I think I'm gonna go," she said.

My joy collapsed into regret.

"I've got a place to stay. You should stay; I'll go."

I stuffed my clothes into my suitcase, trying to leave before my emotions got the best of me. What had been a great week was slipping away, and I didn't understand why. I started down the hall with my bags.

"I don't want you to go," she said.

"I don't want to stay here alone. I got the room for us. I'm not going to feel good about waking up here in the morning by myself. You need a place to stay. You can stay."

I teared up as I started toward the elevator.

"I'm sorry. I don't want you to go. Please stay."

"I'm confused, Mel. I want to stay, but only if you want me to."

"I know. I'm sorry. I don't know why, but I'm scared I'm going to push you away. I don't want to lose you. Please stay."

"Okay."

I couldn't figure her out.

Mel's energy had shifted again. One moment of fuss, and she was a different person.

"I really appreciate you, and thank you for a great trip. Is there anything I can do for you?" she asked.

"A back rub would be nice."

"You got it."

She grabbed some lotion and massaged me to sleep.

In the morning, the dragonfly's promise of good fortune came true. Ripple, a cryptocurrency I had invested in, had a breakthrough in its case with the SEC. As we lay in bed, we watched my portfolio value climb by nearly $20,000.

The gains continued through breakfast but felt secondary to our time together.

I walked her to her car. We kissed goodbye, then went our separate ways.

Learning to Fly

June 2nd - June 5th, 2024

My dad stayed with me the night after Mel's service. The next morning, we had breakfast around the corner from my house, where he shared a curious detail.

"You know, when I spoke with Mel's mom, I said, 'I guess there was another guy,' and she said, 'There was no other guy.'" Dad furrowed his brow. "Which was odd because you had already told me about him. Mel's Aunt overheard us and said, 'No, there was another guy.' I don't understand why she lied to me."

"I think she just didn't want people talking about that at the service," I said.

"Her dad was touched when you said you never would have proposed to her without his blessing."

"It was the truth. Were you ever able to find out about that song request?"

"My buddy wasn't comfortable with it, but he told me to ask his agent, who's also a friend of mine. I guess Chris is with William Morris, who is their biggest competitor, but we're trying."

"Thanks, Pop," I said, knowing it was a long shot.

Back at the house, Dad hugged me goodbye. "Don't forget who you are. You're going to get through this."

I settled into my room for a breathwork session, saging the space and starting David's 28-minute meditation. When it ended, I turned off Spotify and asked the question I had pondered since losing her.

"Mel, are you here?"

Before the words finished leaving my mouth, my chakras lit up like I had hit the jackpot on a slot machine, sending a euphoric shot of electricity through my body. Goosebumps multiplied by a thousand. *Holy shit. She's here.*

The questions poured out:

"Are you okay? Are you stuck here?" The sensation returned.

"Are you by yourself?" Nothing.

"Is someone with you?" Another surge.

"Is Lady with you?" Energy pulsed again, relief washing over me that they were reunited.

I could ask yes-or-no questions. Excitement built.

"Do you want to see Katie and John?" She buzzed me.

"Do you want to see your mom and dad?" No response.

"Do you want to see Sarah?" Nothing.

"Do you want to see David?" Silence.

"Do you want to see Kia?" A loving pulse.

But as I kept asking, the energy faded. I realized I was rushing, making it harder to understand her responses. I let her rest, grounding myself before returning to the living room.

A strange digital moment followed. While searching: *"Can the dead communicate through vibrations?"* My phone suddenly had a mind of its own, scrolling down four pages and buzzing. The blue copy-and-paste dots appeared, highlighting an article:

"If a loved one dies in your home, how long does their soul or spirit stay in the house with you? When do they know that they can continue to go to the other side?"

Is she stuck here? The thought hit me hard, images of trapped souls flashing through my mind.

I searched for mediums who help lost souls transition and found a psychic in Australia. The moment I opened her site, vibrations charged through my body again.

I had more questions. After another breathwork session, I remained in meditation.

"Are you stuck here?" Nothing. *Good.*

"Are you waiting for something?" A buzz.

"Do you want me to finish what you started with *Butterfly Breathwork*?" She lit me up.

"Do you want your story told?" A strong surge of energy.

"Is it hard for you to communicate like this?" Another large pulse.

"Do you want me to find a medium so you can communicate with us?" An intense charge flowed through me.

"Okay, I'll find someone."

I hesitated before asking my next question. "Did you love me, Mel?"

Nothing. No buzz. No answer.

It saddened me, but I understood it was hard for her to communicate like this. Maybe my feelings weren't what she needed to focus her energy on. Perhaps the only answer I needed was that she wanted me to find a medium.

That night, I called Katie, convinced Mel's spirit was still in my room. She and John planned to come over so I could teach them how to connect with her.

The next day, she messaged me, *"Beau, my mom is coming as well."*

Earlier, when I asked if Mel wanted to see her parents, she hadn't responded. I asked again, assuming nothing would happen since I wasn't in meditation. But to my surprise, she lit me up.

When Katie, John, and Liz arrived, Liz wanted to retrace Mel's steps.

"She came in through the front gate," I said, leading her through it.

I pulled up my ADT camera footage, showing Mel's final walk across the grass.

"She went around the side, got the key from under the ashtray on the picnic table, and entered through the back door, which was open when I got home.

All her things were on my bedside table. I think she sat here," I said, sitting on the bed.

"My handgun was normally mounted here, on the magnet under this drawer." I patted the underside of the bedside table.

"When she didn't find it..." I walked Liz to the closet by the front door. "I think she rummaged through here. Both sliding doors were open."

Back in the bedroom, I pointed to the closet where the shotgun had been.

"Then she found the shotgun. It was mounted on two red hooks up here." I pointed to the holes in the wall.

"She would have had to jump to pull it down. One of the hooks was on the floor."

Liz's voice broke. "Why did she do this to us, Beau?"

"I don't know, Liz," I said softly.

I set up a breathwork session for them in my room, providing stones from my backyard, lighting candles, and saging the space. Katie had tried breathing with Melanie, but Liz was unfamiliar, so I walked them through the two-step breathing technique before leaving them with David's twenty-eight-minute meditation.

When they finished, I asked, "Can you guys feel yourselves vibrating?"

They all confirmed they were.

"Okay, whoever feels like they're vibrating the most, start asking yes-or-no questions," I instructed. "Give her time to answer, and if you feel something but aren't sure, ask, 'Is that a yes?'" I left the room and closed the door behind me.

Immediately, I heard an outpouring of emotion. I knew they felt what I had, so I gave them their space with her.

When they emerged, all three were in tears. John was the first to speak. "That was incredible. I've never experienced anything like that," he said.

"Were you able to communicate with her?" I asked.

"Yeah," he replied. "I asked if she was scared, and she said yes."

"I asked if she was okay, and she said yes," I added. "I wonder what she's scared of."

"Katie, did you feel anything?" I asked.

"I could feel it in my hips whenever it was a yes for me," Katie said. "She knows I have bad hips."

"This sounds like something you might be into, Beau," Liz remarked.

"I don't know about that. I've never experienced anything like this either."

"Can you send me that meditation?" John asked.

"Yeah," I said.

Liz wiped her tears. "Why would she do this to us?"

"She wanted to tell her story but never felt like she had your blessing. I need your blessing to tell it, Liz."

"You have my blessing," she said, and we both broke down.

"She told me it's difficult for her to communicate like this, and she wants us to find a medium," I added. "I'm going to reach out to some people in the breathwork community for recommendations."

I figured Mel's breathwork teacher, David, might know someone. I booked a session with him in Ojai and braved two hours of LA traffic to see him. It was my third visit, but the first time, I felt like I needed it.

David admitted, "I told her that if she was going back to her ex to see if anything was still there, she needed to be honest with you and do it the right way." I agreed with his advice.

When the topic of sexual abuse came up, he said, "You know, my sister gave her a colonic at one of our retreats in New Mexico. People tend to pour their hearts out during those. I'm pretty sure she said Melanie told her all her siblings were abused."

"She told me it was a fifteen-year-old boy, but that doesn't make sense if it happened to all of them. She was always vague about it. I wanted to respect her feelings, figuring she'd open up when ready, but it never made sense."

"Yeah, I'll double-check, but I'm pretty sure that's what she told me."

I shifted the conversation to her Adderall use. "I found out she started taking Adderall again in February."

"I noticed a shift in her mood in November," David said.

That lined up closely with when she started drinking coffee again.

"I had to talk her into attending our last retreat in March," David continued. "She admitted to Bear then that she was back on it."

"She kept saying she felt like a fraud; now I understand why. She stopped her breathwork practice, too. I'd love to talk with Bear. I know they were close," I said.

He then guided me through a meditation, taking me back to that night. I recalled the long, painful "Ohhs" that poured from the depths of my soul.

"Go ahead and let them go," David encouraged.

"Ohh! Ohh! Ohh!" I cried as tears streamed from beneath my eye pillows. It reminded me of my first breathwork session with Mel; only these emotions were deeper.

David said he would contact some people and get back to me about a medium.

On the way home, I stopped at Mel's nephew's baseball game in Malibu. He played with an *M* on his wrist, checking the stands on his way to the batter's box. His face lit up when he saw me. After the game, we went to Mel's niece's choir concert, where I updated Katie on my Medium search. When it was time to leave, I said my goodbyes and drove back to Venice.

Back on my couch, I replayed the videos I had recorded that day, sharing them like Mel was sitting beside me. I began to question my sanity. *Am I really talking to a ghost?* Exhaustion pulled me to bed, but sleep offered no relief.

I dreamt I was searching for her, desperately calling her name, but she was nowhere to be found. As panic set in, an electric shock jolted me awake. It felt like something tried to enter my body but was blocked, like being hit with defibrillator paddles.

Later that morning, I had a phone call with David's psychic referral, Chris.

"I'm sensing tremendous guilt and anger," he said. "I want you to know that she was in a state of despair when she woke up that morning. Her serotonin was completely gone."

The anger must have been suppressed because all I felt was guilt and sadness. I shared with him my newfound ability to ask yes-or-no questions.

"She was this beautiful butterfly, ready to take flight, training with David to be a breathwork therapist.

I told her she should call her business *Butterfly Breathwork*, envisioning butterfly eye pillows. It was a great branding opportunity," I explained.

"It sounds like that was your idea, Beau," Chris said. "The yes-or-no questions were likely you, communicating with your spirit."

"I think she might be stuck here. I'm pretty sure she wants us to find a medium so she can communicate directly."

"Spirits don't get stuck. That's not how it works. It's not like what you see in Hollywood."

"I still think she wants us to do a reading."

"I won't do a reading for at least a year after someone passes because I believe it takes that long for loved ones to be ready for what the spirit might have to say."

This was David's referral, which is why she didn't want to talk to him. Chris wasn't going to do a reading for us.

"Your home has been violated, Beau. If you can get out of town, I'd recommend going for at least seven days. Ideally, though, twenty-two days would be best to reset your soul."

There was only one place that felt like home—where I believed I might actually be able to heal from this.

"I've been thinking about going to Bali."

"If you can afford the time off, you should go."

"Okay, I think I'm going to do that," I responded. "Thank you for your time, Chris."

"Be kind to yourself, Beau. You should find yourself a soft-spoken female therapist. I'm also getting the color blue for you. You should think about wearing a lot of blue. If you need to talk, please feel free to reach out."

Shortly after, Kia texted to say his medium friend had already sensed she was meant to help someone. He suggested we set up our communication during the new moon when the veil between Earth and the spirit realm is believed to be thinnest. He sent me the number of his psychic friend, Brandie, and told me she was expecting me to reach out.

I texted her:

"Hi Brandie, Kia referred me to you. I would love to talk to you about my girlfriend, Melanie."

While I waited for her response, Chris called me back.

"Are you a writer, Beau?" he asked.

"Yeah."

"You should get a journal and write down everything that's about to happen to you. Make sure you take the time to reflect on what you have written before you develop any beliefs," he advised.

"Okay. Thank you," I said.

"Take care of yourself, Beau," he added.

Thirty seconds after I got off the phone with Chris, Brandie texted me back. She understood the urgency, asked for my availability, and reassured me she'd make it work despite the time difference in New York. She loved Kia's idea of the new moon for its refreshed energy and asked for a few pictures of Mel to help with the session.

When I asked if Mel's family could join, Brandie cautioned that multiple people might complicate communication but said she'd check with Mel. Less than a minute later, she confirmed Mel wanted her family there.

Dancing with a Butterfly

July 30th & August 6th, 2023

I knocked, expecting Mel, but the door swung open to a woman with a startled expression. For a second, I wondered if I had the wrong house.

"Is Melanie here?"

"She's upstairs getting ready. Come in."

"Hi, I'm Beau."

"I'm Liz, Melanie's mother."

My heart skipped at the unexpected introduction. Liz didn't miss a beat.

"Can I get you something to drink? Water, soda, or would you like a beer?"

"I'm okay."

"Let's have a beer," she insisted. My nerves welcomed the suggestion.

As we talked, we found an easy connection. I learned her husband Jim had gone to Stanford, like my dad, though their paths never crossed. Liz and I were also Geminis—a fitting coincidence, since Mel and my mom were both Scorpios.

I was already on my second beer when Mel finally appeared at the top of the stairs. The tension on her face was clear. Liz suggested we stay to greet Sarah and Dave, who were due home any minute with their newborn daughter.

"We've got to go, Mom." Mel rushed me out of there, barely acknowledging the flowers before heading for the door.

We ran into Sarah and Dave on the porch on our way out. Five years had passed since I last saw Sarah, but Mel's urgency cut the reunion short.

"I wasn't ready for that. Did you get my text? I asked you to wait in the car."

"I'm sorry, I'm just seeing it now. I wanted to bring the flowers in."

"It's okay. Thank you for the flowers; that was sweet of you."

At Del Mar, the crowds swelled around us as we settled in by the fourth race. Mel still seemed slightly off, her earlier tension lingering beneath the surface. I tried to lighten the mood, letting her pick the first few horses, hoping it would pull her out of it.

"Why did you come back from Maui so soon?" I asked. "I thought you were staying for a month."

"I was worried about being away from my remote work address for that long. I also didn't love it, to be honest. My setup wasn't great, and the energy there felt off."

"What do you mean off?"

"I don't know. It just didn't feel right, you know?"

"Hawaii has a powerful energy. The islands drift over a hotspot in the Pacific, where volcanic eruptions form new land. Over time, shifting tectonic plates create new islands.

Scientists believe that part of Molokai slid into the ocean and sent a massive tsunami toward the West Coast of the United States. They think the same thing will eventually happen with the Big Island."

"When do you think that will happen?"

"Probably not in our lifetime."

She gave me a look. "How do you even know all that?"

"Back in the day, we used to get stoned and watch *How the Earth Was Made*."

A couple hundred dollars in horse bets slipped away before we decided to check out the horses up close. Just before each race, they were shown in a small circular enclosure behind the grandstand, known as the paddock.

"The horses look so sad," she said.

"They're well taken care of, though."

Viewing the horses before they ran turned our luck. Mel picked a couple of winners over the next few races, recouping most of our losses. As the day stretched on, the bottomless mimosas fueled the rowdiness beside us, and she was ready to go.

We slipped away to a waterfront restaurant Sarah and Dave had recommended, where the conversation flowed effortlessly.

"We should go see some live music soon," Mel suggested.

"Portugal. The Man is playing at the Hollywood Bowl next Sunday."

"I love the Hollywood Bowl. Let's go!"

"I'll get tickets."

I told her about seeing them at Bonnaroo for my thirtieth birthday when they were still relatively unknown.

"Who else played?"

"MGMT, TV on the Radio, David Byrne, Citizen Cope, Gov't Mule, Hozier…"

"Hozier is one of my favorites. I did Coachella with Sarah once, but it was kind of a shit show. I didn't love it."

"Yeah, this was before DJs took over the music scene. The headliners on the final night were Snoop Dogg, Bruce Springsteen, and Phish. The only downside was the brutal heat. We slept in tents, and I woke up in a puddle of sweat at 6 a.m. every morning."

"Do they have hotels there?"

"Only one, and it's mostly occupied by the artists."

"I couldn't do it. I hate humidity."

"You might not like Bali, then."

"Is it humid there?"

"Oh yeah. The only other thing that sucks is you can't flush your toilet paper at most places."

"What do you do with it?"

"They've got a little garbage bin. Everybody is respectful about how they dispose of it."

"I don't know if I'd like Bali."

"You would. It's magical."

After dinner, about halfway home, she suddenly straightened in her seat.

"Wait. Where's my purse?"

We doubled back to the restaurant, my pace quickening as I felt her rising anxiety. Finding it quickly brought visible relief.

"I can't believe I did that. That would not have been good."

Forgetting her purse felt like a sign that she was enjoying her time with me. When we returned to Sarah's, I opened her car door for a goodnight kiss.

"See you Sunday?" I asked.

"Yeah, I need to figure out where I'm going to be, so I'll probably just meet you at your place, and then we can go from there."

The two-hour drive back to Venice Beach felt worth every mile.

That week, I moved with a different energy. Everything I was working for felt like it had a new purpose.

The following Sunday, we were in a box at the Hollywood Bowl for KCRW's show. Chicano Batman's opening set captured Mel entirely. She danced with an infectious joy that warmed my heart.

"Have you ever heard of these guys?" I asked.

"No, but they're pretty good. And I'm Mexican."

"Really? I always wondered where that exotic look came from. What else are you?"

"Mostly Mexican and German. What about you?"

"I'm Irish, Scottish, English, Welsh, and German. My dad thought we had some Native American blood, but I did *23andMe*, and it turned out to be bullshit."

Mel laughed. "I've only ever dated Italian guys."

Portugal. The Man took the stage as the golden sky gave way to show lights. She danced in my arms, and I stole kisses between songs.

On the way out, I bought her a Chicano Batman shirt.

"I'm going to call you Mexi Mel."

"Please don't call me that. You can do better than that."

I paused, thinking about everything she had worked through, the transformation unfolding before me.

"You were in a cocoon for almost thirty years. Now that you've cleared all this energy, you have these amazing butterfly wings and are ready to take flight. What about Butterfly?"

It landed with a smile.

"It's perfect. I love it."

Back at my place, as things heated up and clothes came off, that hesitation returned, paralyzing me with unexpected nervousness. There was a block that I couldn't get past.

"If you're going to go down on me, you've got to do it like you mean it."

"I don't know what's going on. I keep getting super nervous. It'll get better."

"Can I have a t-shirt?"

She slipped on the one I handed her before climbing into bed.

"You need a new bed."

The California king's custom frame was five feet off the ground, with corner pillars and steps leading up.

"My dad gave me this bed when I moved to LA. It's a custom-made antique."

"It takes up the entire room. How many chicks have you slept with in this thing?"

"Do you really want me to answer that?"

"How many?"

"I don't know. Too many."

"Anybody I know?"

"Maybe."

She gave me a curious look.

"Any Newport girls?"

I named a couple, including one Melanie knew.

"She's hot."

"That doesn't bother you?"

"Not at all."

Mel cleverly turned an awkward encounter into a playful conversation, which eased the tension after stage fright. It wasn't the ending I wanted, but having her beside me was enough.

Reading with Brandie

June 6th, 2024

Liz, Becky, Sarah, John, Katie, and I joined Brandie for the online session. Just before we began, Becky and Liz reacted simultaneously.

"Oh my God, do you guys feel that?" Becky asked.

"Earthquake," Liz confirmed.

There were back-to-back earthquakes in Newport Beach that day.

As the surprise from the tremors subsided, we settled into an uneasy quiet. Although I believed Melanie guided me to Brandie through Kia, I remained skeptical since this was my first experience with a medium. Brandie introduced herself after brief hellos.

"I'm Brandie Dingman. Despite trying to avoid medium work, it always seems to find me. So now I've surrendered. Here I am, a vessel for you. Sometimes, my body channels individuals, and you'll notice tone changes or inflections as if I'm speaking as them. I know she hasn't been gone long, and their strength or energy can vary during the transitional process. It often depends on them. For your daughter, your sister, your partner. God, seeing her beautiful face, she was so magnetic and charming. I can't imagine what you're going through, and I hope to offer some comfort.

The first question everyone asks is, 'Is she okay?' Yes, she's absolutely okay. She now sees there were other choices she could've made, but at the time, her filters didn't allow her to. She's more apologetic than anything else. '*I'm good. Please tell them I'm all good,*'" Brandie said, channeling Melanie.

"Beau had asked about everyone being on the call, and at first, I wasn't sure because group sessions work differently. You all have different spirit guides, ancestors, and people who've transitioned, and many will try to come through. But she was adamant: '*Please have them come.*'

She definitely feels sadness and disappointment because, in the transitional phase, things become clearer. You're no longer trapped in that vessel, feeling heavy, secluded, and alone. For sensitive souls like her, it often feels like no one can understand us.

My left ear is going crazy," Brandie continued. "When you're that sensitive, you feel the world's pain in ways others don't. It weighed on her heart constantly. She could see a homeless person and almost feel what they were going through at that moment."

Brandie cleared her throat.

"Well, I'm already feeling this tightness in my throat. I think she often held things in and didn't share them. She kept it all to herself because she didn't want to burden anyone with her pain."

Brandie began to shed some tears.

"She would pray in her own way for it to go away. But it baffled her that others didn't feel things as intensely as she did. As a fellow empath, someone who feels others' emotions, who knows their pain, and can literally feel it in my body, I understand. Sometimes, during these sessions, I'll experience their pain. It's just how energy works.

She loved people deeply, especially her family. She mentions a disconnect. I'm not sure what she means specifically, but I get the sense she feels you all know. It's like she wishes she could bridge that gap, whatever it was, and fix it.

For Beau, all I hear her say is, '*I loved that man. I loved that man.*'

She's so fresh in spirit that it's making my heart ache for all of you, which makes her sad, too. I've cried most of the day today; it's her expressing that she doesn't want you to feel sad. She wants you to be happy, to know she understands there could've been different choices, but she's okay and at peace with where she is now.

There's no dark spot or hell. She's far too phenomenal a soul for that. She says people talk about eternal damnation, but that's not true. She's saying, '*I'm freer now than I ever was,*' though it feels selfish for her to admit that.

This might seem random, but she says, '*If I could pick those purple tulips again, I would.*'

For Beau, I just saw this purple light. Purple usually represents unconditional love. She's saying, '*He's crying but sleeping in his pain, and I comfort him.*' She lays beside him, with her hand on the back of his neck.

She mentioned something about her sister and a kitty but said to table that for now.

'Can you just let them ask their questions? I know they have questions, and I want them to feel okay,' Brandie said, channeling. "That's very important to her."

Becky asked the first question.

"I wanted to ask, on behalf of the family, if you knew how much we loved you, Melanie. How beautiful we thought you were, even when you couldn't see it. And do you know we would've been there if you had asked for our help?"

"Yes, 1000 percent she knows now. When you transition, it's like being in a soft, floaty bubble, but there's also a movie reel you can tap into at any time. We all go through those reels as we transition. A million percent, she understands that now. She mentioned, *'I used to have my walls up. It was how I protected myself.'* She's acknowledging that there were times when people showed her love, kindness, and compassion, but in her human body, she couldn't receive it. Her mind wouldn't let her, which wasn't anyone's fault. But she knows how much you all loved her.

She wants you to understand that we all do the best we can with what we have at the time. She's very clear: *'Please don't take my leaving as anyone's fault. There's no blame here. This was a decision I felt I had to make in the moment, but in hindsight, I understand I could've made different choices.'* She understands that you genuinely loved her.

She mentions the saying, *'Sometimes love isn't enough.'* She was still working on loving herself, so it was hard to receive love from others," Brandie clarified.

"Why did she stop breathing?" I asked, not specifying that I meant breathwork, as skepticism still lingered through my tears.

"So that's the choking in the throat and not breathing... I never really know for sure. The response I'm getting is, *'I was ready to take my last breath, but there was something stuck in the back of my throat.'* It seems like there was some kind of asphyxiation. *'My air was cut off, and I had no more breath to take.'*" Brandie replied.

"I'm taking more along the lines of how she used to do breathwork a lot, and she stopped." I explained, still unsure if this was legitimate.

"I think, without fully understanding your question, she essentially said, '*I had no more breath to take. Breathwork only got me so far, but heavy energy was stuck to me.*' It literally felt like something was stuck in her throat. I get the sense that she was extremely sensitive but didn't always show it. She's saying, '*My throat was stuck.*' Almost like her throat chakra and breathwork couldn't give her the relief she was seeking anymore."

Now, we were getting somewhere, and my belief started to grow. I saw this as her inability to tell her story. The next step in her breathwork journey was to share her struggle and connect with other young women who had faced similar trauma, but she couldn't.

"For many intuitive or sensitive people, it can feel like you're suffocating every day. Other people's energy sticks to you like glue, and when you don't know how to move it through your body, it feels like you're trapped, just suffering." Brandie continued.

I asked, "She was doing so well when she was committed to breathwork, but at some point, she tailed off and started using Adderall again. Is there any way you can help us understand why she made that decision?"

"So, it's interesting. I got the sense there were pills involved. Did she ever have an injury or something like that? It feels like that might have interfered with her thinking or processing clearly. But with drugs like Adderall, sometimes your brain can move faster than your body, and for someone trying to regulate their mind, body, and emotions all at once, it creates constant highs and lows. Was she a perfectionist?" Brandie asked.

"Yes, in a lot of ways. You couldn't see it outwardly, but she put a lot of pressure on herself to make things perfect before sharing them," Sarah replied.

"That makes sense... the feeling of not being enough, always having to be hyper-vigilant, can consume you. I feel like she's saying, '*I was trying to do my best, and my best wasn't good enough.*' But now, she understands it was enough. Adderall gave her the clarity and focus she needed because her body was pulling her in all directions, making it hard for her mind to stay on track.

I can see the conflict between the beauty and power of breathwork and the feeling that it wasn't enough. It devastated her when things weren't perfect, whether it was work, business, or relationships. She needed perfection; it was the only thing that gave her a sense of control because she often didn't feel in control of her body or mind.

People who are that sensitive to energy keep it contained. When people don't accept your gifts, you feel like a curse, like a burden. Imagine walking into a room, inundated by everyone's energy, while still trying to have the clarity to shine, produce, and show up for the world. It's a constant state of trembling, of unsettlement, always longing for focus.

'*But I did love breathwork. I know now that it helped me*,'" Brandie channeled. "But it couldn't get her to where she wanted to be. Does that make sense?"

A text message came in on the family text chain: "*Wow, she's really good,*" Becky wrote.

"Does she want us to continue what she started with breathwork? Does she want her story told?" I asked.

"That's an interesting and funny question because, at my nephew's concert, the song 'Remember Me' from *Coco* played. I cried the whole time, thinking, '*Oh my God, she wants to be remembered.*' I would say that's an absolute yes, without a doubt. For each of you to finish what she started would be the greatest honor, a testament to her. It would make her feel like she can finally breathe.

And I'm sorry; I know this is your session, but I'm the most emotional one over here." Brandie apologized through tears.

Becky had another question.

"Brandie, I understand that Melanie, speaking through you, is saying her best wasn't good enough. She had the breathwork she was doing, but maybe it wasn't enough to heal her. I'm curious if you could ask Melanie, did your ex ultimately influence you in any way that led to these decisions? Did he say or do something that affected your mindset, making it hard for you to go back? She always said, 'I can't go back.'

For context, she openly talked about leaving him two and a half, three years ago, describing the relationship as very toxic. He was eighteen years older, and while not physically abusive, he was emotionally and possibly sexually abusive. She left him and dedicated herself to healing through breathwork, detoxing her body, and striving to purify her heart, soul, body, mind, and spirit.

She even stopped taking the Adderall medication. But starting in March, she felt drawn back to his spirit, like there was unfinished business. She didn't tell her family she was going to explore that, but ultimately, she did. I want to understand from Melanie, was he the one who weighed her down? The one she wanted to be good enough for, who made her feel like she wasn't good enough? He kept her down, and she realized, during her healing process, that he was really bad for her."

"The feelings of not being enough were genuinely hers, regardless of context. Most people experience that, so it's not uncommon. When you have that internal struggle, you tend to connect with people who may not serve your highest and greatest good. He was simply a mirror of her internal struggles.

We can have momentary addictions to coffee, to a person, or even to experiences of pain and suffering. There's a saying: *Pain is inevitable, but suffering is optional.* Often, we don't realize we're choosing suffering because we think pain is just part of the process.

She's very clear: there's no one to blame here. She's adamant about that. Was he good for her? Absolutely not. But was he a mirror that helped her understand what she was not? Yes, because once you understand what you are not, you can begin to see what you are. He showed her what she was not, and sometimes, even in the worst relationships or friendships, we learn valuable lessons. He was a valuable lesson for her.

Could he have made her feel more secure, confident, and beautiful? Maybe, but he didn't. He wasn't the reason she went back. In our healing journeys, it's not uncommon to backpedal a bit because it feels familiar, even when it's harmful. She wishes she had done things differently with him. She wishes she had found her voice... she kept so much in her throat," Brandie responded.

I dove in on the question that had been haunting all of us.

"Can you ask a specific question that we're all curious about? She mentioned to me on multiple occasions that she wanted to try doing Molly. She thought it could be exciting, something that could help us connect. The night before she passed was his birthday, and we think there might have been some MDMA involved. We won't know from the toxicology report for another three months."

Becky added, "And there's a history of experimenting with that during their past relationship. But they were together on his fiftieth birthday, at his party, the night before she did this. He said she woke up in a state of almost... like she called herself psychotic. So we believe she might have been under an additional influence that led her to make a bad choice."

Brandie paused to channel an answer before returning to us.

"Okay... so, the response was... '*I'm not gonna lie, there could've been MDMA. Let's just say drugs.*' There may have even been a bit of Fentanyl... so, okay... earlier, I was picking up on something with pills, something with opioids or opiates. I was wondering if she ever had an injury or if she was ever hurt. That brings me to this response: I'd say yes, it's very plausible. They may or may not find it in the toxicology report because, according to her, it was minimal. But your answer is yes... yeah. Those were the two things that came through earlier today at my nephew's concert," Brandie replied.

"To continue with the questioning, Melanie, do you feel that taking that drug, or whatever you took that evening or day, changed the course of events? If you hadn't taken it, would the storyline be different? Did it cause you to act abruptly?" Becky asked.

"She says, '*Did I make a rash decision? I did. My mind wasn't right... it hadn't been right for a while.*' She doesn't want you to think badly of her, but she does feel protective of that person, almost saying, '*It wasn't his fault. I made these choices. Were they the best choices? They weren't. I can see that now; I can feel that now.*'

She's asking for forgiveness: '*Please forgive me. I'm sorry I hurt you all, but don't blame him; it's not his fault.*' It's as if she's saying, '*He can do bad on his own, but I have to be accountable for my choices.*' Does that resonate with you, that she had a lot of integrity?" Brandie asked.

"Absolutely. She probably doesn't want us to carry hatred toward him or anyone because that won't help any of us. That's likely what she's feeling," Sarah confirmed.

"'*I'm accountable for this. It wasn't my best choice. But I promise you, I'm not far away. I'm right here. I've been to the sporting events, been on the water, seen the boats, looked at the flowers, smelled them, and been to the garden.*' She's saying, '*I know you won't forgive me, but please don't forget me.*' Not in a toxic way, but understanding that we're not all capable of unlimited love. She's asking for forgiveness for her choices."

"Can you ask her if she wants me, or anyone, to write and share her story?" Sarah asked.

"She's being a little funny," Brandie said, her laughter mingled with tears. "'*Well, they could write my story, but it would be a little messed up,*' in a weird, funny way. But yes, if you find it in your heart to do that, absolutely.

'*But I also want people to be proud of me… knowing that I didn't give up, even on the days I was struggling. Even though I didn't always make the perfect choices, I kept trying to choose myself, over and over, even when I felt like an alien on this planet and just wanted to give up.*'"

"Can you tell her we're proud of her?" Sarah said.

John added, "Yeah, I want to make sure we all acknowledge that. I've heard a couple of times, '*Do you forgive me? Are you proud of me? Do you love me?*' It's a resounding yes from this family, Melanie. You know that. We love you. I want to make sure she hears that clearly, that it's not just us trying to figure things out.

And I have one question for a sister who's struggling, who was very, very close and talked to her every day. Could she have done more? She's carrying a lot of guilt."

"'*There's nothing anyone could have done for me. I promise I got myself here. You have to forgive yourselves. You couldn't have called me more or told me I was better, prettier, more beautiful, or stronger. My mind was blocked, so my heart couldn't receive it. But I know you would have done anything for me. I know that completely.*

It's important for me to tell you: Please forgive me and continue to love me. I'm remorseful, but I'm at peace. I've never felt this kind of peace. It's beautiful. And now, I get to be closer to you all than I ever was because my body isn't in the way. Is it absent of breath? Yes. But am I in full existence? Absolutely. I'm everywhere, with every one of you, at all times.

That's all I ever wanted, but it was hard for me to be me. I know you called me at all hours, checked on me, and stuck up for me when I made bad choices or put myself in difficult situations. I know you loved me, and I need you to be free of any hurt or guilt. I need you to understand that I have now been set free, but that cannot happen with the chains of your guilt, hurt, and suffering. It cannot. Because that means I, too, am not free here,'" Brandie channeled.

"Is that why she feels like she's stuck? She needs us to be okay." I asked.

"But she's not stuck. She's in a beautiful place. When you transition, you don't go straight to the light. You flow back and forth, closer to Earth. The beauty is that she can choose. You'll feel her presence, whether touching your forehead, knocking something off the counter, her scent, a ringing or laughter in your ear, or a brush against your arm or foot. These are her ways of showing she's still with you.

You might sometimes wonder why you don't feel her or why she hasn't appeared in your dreams. It's because they, too, take moments of grace and peace closer to the light. But she's not stuck. She's okay, safe, and as happy as she can be in this early transition stage. She's free from the bondage of human flesh.

It's important to her that you go through your grief process, and she'll be holding your hand the entire time. That doesn't mean she expects you not to cry, to be angry, in denial, or sad, all the stages of grief. She understands that's the human process. But she's looking forward to the days when you smile and joke in her memory.

Right now, it feels like pins and needles every day. Everything is a trigger, and she knows that. She can already see the peace, the calm, the laughter, the beauty, and the light she brought. She's looking forward to those days for all of you. But she doesn't want you to blame anyone. Her ex can be miserable on his own... even pathetic, actually. Because he feels a little pathetic, but she doesn't want you to blame someone else.

Please know, '*I could have made different choices, but this was my exit, and I chose it.*'"

Becky asked, "Could you ask her if, when she made the decision, was she in a state of despair, or was she resolute and clear? Even if she now thinks it wasn't the right decision, was she certain this was her way to go, not in sorrow, sadness, or hurt? I would love to hear what Melanie has to say. I'm just so curious about her state of mind because I feel like this was her calling at this time in her life."

"She said, '*I was sad. I was heavy. I just wanted to be free. My mind didn't know, but my soul knew I had chosen this time. Given my persona and human consciousness, I could never have imagined making this choice. But we all make these agreements before we come here, and there are usually three exits. You can choose whichever one you want.*'

She realizes this is difficult, sad, and tragic, but she also understands that her transition will bring about beautiful things. None of you can imagine that right now, but she knows the beauty that will result from her passing will be unprecedented.

And there's that damn *Coco* song, 'Remember Me,' again," Brandie said.

"Is there anything Melanie wants us to know unrelated to her exit? Anything she's learned now that she's there that she wants to share with us?" Sarah asked.

"'*I want you all to live fearlessly. We put so much pressure on ourselves, following rules that aren't even society's, but ones we impose on ourselves.*'

She understands now that these are self-imposed restrictions. She wants each of you to live more freely and to stop putting so much pressure on yourselves. Bask in the small moments with family and friends. Give yourself the grace to take as much personal time as you need.

She says that money is beautiful, but it's just an energetic frequency. The real power is in moments of connection. She feels closer to each of you now in a new and fresh way. That's not to diminish her love and connection with all of you before, but it's different now. If any of you can take the time to experience that connection regularly, she believes that's the essence of life, and she wants that for all of you.

Is your mom living, or has she transitioned?" Brandie asked.

"She's living and on the call," Sarah said.

"And what's her mom's name?" Brandie asked.

"Liz," Sarah replied.

"So I think she wants to take the time to acknowledge you, to tell you that she loves you. She knows you gave her all of you and everything she needed. There's nothing that was missing..."

Brandie's dogs began barking, interrupting the session.

"Just know that she loved you very much, and she's sorry that she hurt you. She understands that no one should have to bury their child and that it feels unfair to you. I see a yin and yang symbol with you two. Does that resonate with you?" Brandie asked.

"Hi, I'm here. I'm her mom. Yes, a little bit. Yin and yang... correct," Liz said.

"That resonates... I know she loved the Yin Yang, but she'd always correct me and say, '*Yin Yan*,'" Sarah said.

"Yes, 'Yin Yan,' that's so funny. I was thinking, why do I feel silly saying it, but I do say 'Yin Yang,'" Brandie acknowledged.

"She and I would always shop for Yin 'Yan' items. She really connected with the meaning of that symbol," Sarah added.

"So I think she's trying to help you all take comfort in knowing she's here. She's really here. And as her mom, she's worried about you. She doesn't want you to see this as a failure or something you did wrong. Like oil and vinegar, you know, they don't mix but make the most amazing salad. She's just saying, '*Trust me, Mommy...*,'" Brandie said.

"As her mom, I do have a lot of guilt. I wasn't there for her. I should have been. I loved her so much, but she was very private. She was a private girl," Liz said.

"That makes sense with the walls, then," Brandie responded.

"Oh my gosh... the seas right now. Is there another earthquake?" Liz asked, from her boat in the harbor.

"She's just being very powerful, and all of this is divinely guided. Yes, that's the power of it. I want you to understand that when she talked about having her walls up and keeping things in, she never let you fully in because she felt you'd then have to bear the depths of everything she was feeling," Brandie said.

"And I would have... she should have," Liz replied.

"See, but that's where, as a mom, we don't get to choose their persona. That's the difference between nature and nurture. We can put so much into them, nurture them, but their soul essence, that's different. You and her had a soul contract long before this, and I get the sense that she was either your mother or grandmother in a past life. She felt a deep sense of responsibility for you," Brandie explained.

"Oh, she did," Liz agreed.

"She had to protect your feelings because she couldn't imagine you feeling the depths of her pain. And that pain wasn't anyone's fault. There are many beautiful, sensitive souls on this earth, and if there is one thing Melanie can give us, it is understanding how important breathwork and energy work are. How they help sensitive souls learn to protect their energy, cleanse it, and serve others without making their sensitivity a burden.

Your daughter tried to shield you, to keep you at arm's length, not because she didn't want you close, but because she had to protect you. That was her feeling, and she said, '*I would never change that in a million years. That was my job on this planet, my job on this Earth.*' She feels like you were an amazing, beautiful mom who gave her everything she needed. There's nothing more you could have done. You didn't fail her in any way. She needs you to hear that. '*You did not fail me in any way. If anything, you gave me my essence, a little bit of firecracker, sass, strength, and silly.*' She's acknowledging that you gave her that. Please take comfort in knowing she loves you and knows you loved her.

Honoring her means working on forgiveness, which is a big part of the grief process. We all have those *what ifs*. Even in friendship groups, we wonder, *What if I could have done more, made that one connection?*

But out of the greatest tragedies come the greatest triumphs. Somehow, all of us are here in this moment. Our souls wrote this in the stars before we got here. The lessons we will experience and embody from this tragedy, from such a beautiful soul, are unfolding. The helplessness is the hardest part, wondering, *What could I have done differently?* The truth is, we couldn't have done anything.

If the one thing she did was connect us today, then there's a purpose. She's already building connections in ways that were hard for her in life. And that's the yin and the 'yan'… I get a sense of duality from her. She was a sweet, sensitive soul but also very rigid and cut off from the world.

I want you all to know that we're not in control. We've made these soul contracts in advance. We've made these agreements, and we understand that our lives have a bigger purpose, and so does hers. Even though she's no longer in her physical body, her purpose is even greater now. This is just the beginning. We've seen nothing yet. It will transform into something magical, something that will save and serve so many people.

For that, I can pay homage to my soul sister in heaven, your beautiful earthly sister, for giving us that gift. It's going to be the gift that keeps on giving.

'I kept keeping on, for as long as I could. But now I'm here to do different things. And I'm going to do that every day, right alongside every one of you,' Brandie channeled.

"I have a question for Melanie. This is her sister, Becky, number two in the lineup. I've acquired a lot of her electronics. Regarding her personal papers and notes to herself, should we keep them sacred, or does she want us to see them? Would reading those things in a respectful way and not sharing them with the world give us more clarity on the pain and emotions she was feeling? Would it help in our healing process? I want to respect our baby sister."

"'Can you put those notes in a journal for me? Can you shine a light on my story? Don't think you're going to make me feel raw and exposed because now I'm closer to my higher self, and I understand that was part of my human ego. You can share whatever you need to share. Please don't fight over what's appropriate and what's not. I know there could be differences of opinion in the group, but I need you guys not to be selfish right now. I know I'm your baby sister, and this isn't easy, but this is bigger than us. By sharing

my story, you're going to help others, young people and older people. It's going to be such a blessing for them.

In my human self, I would have told you to burn it and not let anyone see it because I would have kept it all inside. But I'm very clear now. It's meant to be shared, shared with the world. Please don't haggle over intimate details or raw emotion because that's part of the vastness of the human experience. Maybe even turn it into a memoir. Make some memoirs for me,' she said. And she's really sorry you have to deal with all the legal stuff," Brandie said.

"I love you so much, Melly," Becky said in tears.

"She loves you to infinity and beyond," Brandie replied.

John had a question: "One thing I want to make sure we don't regret not asking goes back to the last conversation she had before she did what she did. We know, from talking to the individual, it was a twelve to thirteen-minute phone conversation."

Becky interjected, "There's some context from a text message that preceded that call; maybe Brandie should know this. She was apologizing to her ex, saying she was 'so sorry' and hoped they could 'do it better in the next lifetime.'"

"'*Promise me we'll be together in another lifetime,*'" Katie added.

Becky continued, "Then came the twelve-minute conversation, and afterward, she entered Beau's house and took her life with a shotgun. So, continue with that question, John. I just wanted to give a little context."

John continued, "In the context, we may never know what was said... we've been told what the conversation was, but we can't shake the feeling or suspicion that something was said that pushed our beautiful baby sister over the edge. Did that conversation drive her to make the decision?"

"It's interesting because I'm getting the song by Erykah Badu, '*I guess I'll see ya next lifetime, no hard feelings, so there ain't nothing wrong with dreaming, but don't get me wrong. Cuz my love is for my baby... but emotions just don't lie,*'" Brandie started singing. "It's beautiful in a way because I feel like what she's trying to say through Erykah Badu is that she loved Beau, loved him unconditionally, but she felt an obligation to her ex. She felt like she could save him, but knew she couldn't.

We all have soul ties, and soul ties don't mean it's your permanent person or the greatest love of your life. They're there to help you learn your greatest lessons. She felt a sense of obligation to that. She did have an old soul, and in different incarnations, her ex may have been someone amazing in a past experience.

In the same way, each of us can be family; mother, daughter, sister, best friend, lover, niece, nephew; because those roles change through different lifetimes.

So, to answer the question, is there anything he said that incited her to make that rash decision? She said no... '*I just couldn't stand that I couldn't make life different. I couldn't make him different. Some days, I felt like screaming from the rooftop, but I felt like even if I did, no one could hear me. Nor did I want them to. And I struggled with that on a daily basis,*'" Brandie said.

"So, would that mean she doesn't want us to expose his abusiveness, him being a predator?" Liz asked.

"Because in the limited things we've read, she expressed that it was a toxic, predator-type relationship. But she did love him," Becky noted.

Liz continued, "She loved him, but she went along with his BS. He took advantage of her, her vulnerability, her innocence. This man was a predator. He took advantage of this young girl's innocence in every way, mentally, physically, in every way possible. Does she want us to expose him? Because I feel we need to expose him for what he is so he doesn't do this to other women."

"He definitely falls into the category of a narcissist," Becky added.

"That makes sense," Brandie replied.

"He's also a Hollywood guy… a C-rated actor. Not even B, C, or D," Liz said, which made Brandie laugh.

"I love you for that," Brandie responded.

"I think she supported him during COVID," Liz said.

"The first thing I heard her say was, '*Mommy, let me make my decisions.*' There are two things. One is her wishes and desires:

'Please share my life, share my story. You can include anything and everything about my experience to help women learn, grow, and evolve, to help them understand that even if you go back to a toxic situation, it doesn't define you. You can still move forward.'

The other lens is the mom lens, the sister lens, the human lens; the question is, what would exposing him get us? What would it save? Was he a piece of shit? Absolutely. Let me say that one thousand percent; yeah, he's a piece of shit," Brandie explained.

"Oh, hell yeah, he was a piece of shit," Liz interjected.

"Having said that, her compassion made her feel obligated to him. I get this parent-child dynamic, where she was the parent and he was the child. Her sense of obligation was this caring, almost like, *'I'm the parent, you're the child, and I need to make sure you're okay and don't destroy yourself.'* That's true; it was the case. And I can say it's probably karmic, probably ancestral. I don't think it's rooted in this earthly plane. I think it's from a prior connection.

That's why, even though the relationship came with predatory behavior and all kinds of toxicity, your beautiful angel of a sister could still see greatness in him when he couldn't see it in himself. And yes, he was a piece of shit, guilty as charged. But it doesn't matter... you could go from the White House to the crack house, and I'd still see your higher self and all the beauty you possess.

But if I invest in your higher self and you can't acknowledge or embody it, there's nothing I can do in this human incarnation. That was the case with them.

With Beau, it was fresh, beautiful, light, and airy. For once, someone could see her, witness her, honor her, love her, respect her, and cherish her. But she needed to feel needed, and that protective pull towards her ex was strong. I want to be very clear; she does not want to negate what she had in her sacred union with Beau. That was its own thing and had nothing to do with anyone else. However, her ancestral need to protect and provide pulled her toward that other connection.

Can you destroy that man? You can, but how is that going to help anyone? That's the fine line. That's the tricky part. And honestly, I don't think I'm here to speak on that. I don't think it's my place. Predatory behavior... as someone who's experienced sexual trauma and survived, I think…"

"Melanie also experienced sexual trauma as a little girl," Becky interjected.

"Sometimes, I've thought about exposing them. But I think there's beauty in having hard conversations. There's beauty in communication, not destruction.

Right now, this is so fresh. Could you put an ounce of blame on him? Absolutely, you could. There's no denying that. But she is very clear in her stance... hell or high water, no matter what any of you feel or think...

'This was my choice. This was my reality. I made these choices, and this is where I was.'

Did her entanglement of emotions influence it? Yes. It's impossible not to have feelings for people who are connected to you. Do we burn that man at the stake? You could," Brandie continued.

"Yes!" Liz cut in.

"And I don't think it would make her feel relief or content. Allowing him to self-destruct would be the greatest gift, and that will happen. It's like Mother Teresa. She never went to antiwar rallies. Why? Because she said, 'I cannot put my energy where I do not want it.' So, she did pro-peace rallies instead. That's where she put her energy.

If anything, Melanie is saying today, *'I need you not to put your venom where your anger is, even though it's justified. Please put it where you want your energy to go. Pro love. Pro support. Pro community. Pro connection. Whatever it is, that's where we need to focus our energy.'*

Because if we choose the other route, anti-ex, anti-predator, anti-narcissist, anti-abuser, how is that going to serve us? How will it help us serve humanity? It won't.

That man is going to self-destruct because he is self-destructive, and she was trying to protect him all this time. And it's crazy because women often try to save them while destroying ourselves," Brandie acknowledged.

"You know what's interesting? She always said that she wished I needed her more. She said, 'You're so independent. I wish you needed me more.'" I barely managed to get the words past my tears.

"And she needed to feel needed. But Beau, that was not your fault. That was her brokenness, and when you have those feminine wounds… especially from sexual trauma, somehow you feel like if they don't desperately need you, or you can't protect them, then you feel like you're half alive.

But that's not true. That's just the trauma and getting to those next steps. She couldn't see how you needed her at the depths of your soul because she wasn't prepared for that yet. It was a different kind of need… a different kind of depth.

With him, he was blatant about it because he was fucking broken. So, it allowed her to feel wanted, needed, and purposeful because it filled the void that was absent in her. And she now understands what that purity is. It's a different kind of need." Brandie replied.

We took a bathroom break. When we returned, Brandie introduced her son, and Liz introduced Jim and Jimmy, who were in the room with her. "That's everyone except Melanie, who's not here."

"She's here, Mom," Becky replied.

"I know, but I can't see her," Liz said.

"And I think that's the part that sucks the most. I know I'm your first, but I'm sure I won't be your last in terms of connection. But when you really solidify that she's there, it just hurts your heart. How in the world is she not physically here? It's absolutely frustrating.

But the beauty is that this feels like a long time for us. For them, it's a hop, skip, and a jump because there's no time in that realm. Time is just a construct we use here," Brandie commented.

Becky shared, "I have a question for Melanie, or maybe you, Brandie. Melanie always sought guidance to find peace and understanding of her purpose while dealing with her emotions. There was no lack of support, even if she didn't turn to her family at the end, maybe because she was embarrassed about reconnecting with an old relationship. But right at the very end, she sought help from someone with talents similar to yours.

She had a session with an intuitive healer named Peggy. After an initial consultation, she contacted her again at the end of her life and recorded it on Zoom. It lasted about thirty minutes on May 7th. On May 8th, she begged for a follow-up, asking in an email, 'I would like a follow-up because I want to understand if I can undo the pact I made with my ex.'

My sisters and I watched the Zoom recording of her session, which was sent to her email. It brought us some understanding, and the healer was so encouraging. I felt she really tapped into Melanie's spirit, past lives and all. She seemed very talented. I don't have any experience in this, but I felt she was a very positive influence."

"We got the same feeling," John added.

"During the thirty-three-minute consultation, the healer tried to tell her everything she was doing right, but at a certain point, Melanie became agitated by all the positive feedback. Peggy talked about how her relationship with Beau gave her the freedom to blossom, and to regain her sense of self. She knew Melanie's attachment to her past relationship needed to be severed for her to be fully present and centered. She said that the only way it would be cut off was if Melanie or her ex decided to end it. Without that, it would always linger.

Melanie was scared to sever the tie, saying, 'It's something I can't let go.' The healer responded, 'You don't have to let it go; you can integrate it into your life, into your relationship.' Melanie understood that… it was reasonable and rational, and she was taking it all in.

But at minute twenty-two of the conversation, even though she hadn't mentioned corresponding with her ex, Melanie asked, 'What if I tried it one more time with my ex? What would you say?' The intuitive healer paused for a moment, and I saw it all. She responded, 'You would hang yourself.'

The camera switched to Melanie, who was stunned. Her mannerisms showed she was alert and wanted to know more, but then Peggy changed her tone…" Becky continued.

"She backpedaled," Brandie interjected

"She backpedaled and said, 'You would be so disappointed with yourself.' After watching the video, I felt she saw two paths: one where Melanie would literally kill herself, and another where she would grow and recenter herself.

Ultimately, Peggy tried to instill in her that she would do the right thing. She was warning her softly and subtly: if you need to have a conversation to close that chapter, 'I trust that you'll do the right thing.'

I called and left a message for Peggy but haven't heard back. What I'm curious about is this: the way Melanie took her life using a gun was likely quick and painless. But before that, on May 4th, she texted all of us her address in LA, which was temporary because she wanted to feel free and not stuck. She said, '*Hey everyone, this is where I live in case you ever need to contact me.*' After everything happened, we found two unopened ropes in her car.

Did hearing what the healer said stun Melanie because she had maybe already considered doing it on May 4th when she sent us that text out of the blue? Or did it give her some kind of direction, leading her to make that decision consciously? Or maybe she heard it, blocked it out, but knew deep down that's where it was going to lead her," Becky asked.

"I'm going to answer the question as clearly as I can. The moment that healer said what she said, she immediately backpedaled because she understood what she saw and what she shared.

I want to be very clear: people who are intuitive or psychic, everyone still has free will. Sometimes, you go to a psychic, medium, intuitive, or channeler, and they'll tell you one thing, but it may not manifest or come true. The reason is that we all have free will, so anything can change.

What I'm saying is that the moment that healer said those words, she said them because that was the vision she got. She saw it. 'That's it for you; life will cease to exist,'" Brandie explained.

"If you go down that path?" Becky asked.

"I'm all about love and light, as I'm sure that woman is too. Unless God or Source tells me I'm supposed to deliver a message like that, I'm never going to say it, period, unless it's for the highest and greatest good.

In that moment, it very well may have been for your sister's highest good to understand the choices before her. But in no way are they definitive of her exit because we have free will.

It's the same thing when people talk about things I'm not comfortable with, like possession or exorcism. That's not in my wheelhouse. But the key thing to remember is that those things can't happen unless you make a conscious choice to allow it," Brandie said.

"I understand Melanie had free will. Do you think it's possible for someone to see that bad path in such a way?" Becky pressed.

"Yes," Brandie replied. "She saw the path that wasn't good or healthy for her, and I think she tried to be very transparent in saying, 'These are your options.'

Whenever you have that protective notion around someone, like with her ex, it literally feels like a parent-and-child dynamic. It doesn't feel like a relationship to me. It doesn't feel like a man and woman passionately in love or anything like that."

"He used to always make her feel like the child, and I think that was frustrating…" Becky shared.

"Because she was the parent!" Brandie shot back. "A narcissist will reverse the reality, giving you a false narrative so you're disillusioned, even when you're clear. He could project that onto her all he wanted, but the reality was that she was the parent, and he was the child. Her obligation to him came from that standpoint. It wasn't about, 'Oh my God, I love this man,' it was more about caretaking, ensuring he was okay.

As I said, pain is inevitable, but suffering is an option. We often get addicted to that optional suffering. As messed up as it sounds, none of us are exempt from it when it goes on too long. It's like when chaos becomes comfort. If you grow up in a chaotic environment, chaos feels like home, and red flags start to feel like butterflies."

"She acknowledged that," Becky said.

I asked, "I've got a two-part question. The first part is about what Becky mentioned... the pact between them. Do you think that was a pact made in a previous life?

And then, you said Melanie was an old soul. I felt this overpowering connection the first time I met her, and it continued to exist every time I looked into her eyes. So, the second part of my question is, if you could ask her, 'Was this our first meeting, or did we meet in a previous life?'"

"So, the ancestral pact with her ex from a former life is a yes.

Was this the first time you two had ever met? Absolutely not. You guys have done this before. She refers to you as her 'knight in shining armor.'

That was the third thing that came through before my nephew's concert, and I hadn't remembered it until you just asked. But she's adamant; you are her 'knight in shining armor.' She felt like you were there to save her, protect her, and be there for her in ways she'd always been for others, but no one could ever be for her. And when I say 'knight in shining armor,' she's very clear about that."

"Peggy described him that way too, just so you know, you're on the same wavelength. She said he was on bended knee, her savior. I think she even said 'knight in shining armor,'" Becky added.

"When I was on the way to my nephew's concert, she said, 'He's my knight in shining armor.' She kept repeating it, and I was like, wow, I need to remember that for later, but I had to go.

And yes, is there an ancestral pact with her ex? Absolutely. Those soul ties are very ancient. I wouldn't even say within the last three incarnations; it's much older than that.

It might be a good idea to cleanse that karmic soul tie with her ex just to end it. This is the end of a karmic cycle, which means it won't continue into future generations," Brandie said.

"You mean the end of the karmic cycle between her and him?" I asked.

"She said those exact words, 'End the karmic tie.' Katie, didn't she say something like that?" Becky shared.

"She asked me if I knew what a twin flame was and if I understood karmic connections," I interjected.

"I can see why she'd be questioning twin flames. Often, a twin flame isn't someone you're meant to stay with or even be with. Sometimes, they're meant to teach you lessons, and that's what you get out of it. You're elevating your frequency in this human body. That's why there's yin and yang; some people you evolve with, and others just teach you.

The fact that she was on that path and communicating that with all of you shows that she was on the cusp of understanding this but didn't have the full context. Many of us don't until we reach a higher level of understanding and are dedicated to the ascension process with connection and commitment.

So, Beau, in terms of your sadness, your hurt, and the feeling that she connected with someone else more than you, the answer is no. You were her pure, free love.

Mel's experience with her ex was in no way triumphant compared to your relationship. If anything, it was a testament to the beauty you gave her: the freedom, the love, the safe space. And sometimes, when we're not used to that kind of safe space, we don't know how to cope with it because we're still learning. It was the first time she had felt that in a long time," Brandie said.

"The part that hurts the most is that we were just getting started, and in this life, at least, it's over. That's what hurts the most because I felt it for almost a decade, and we finally got our chance. Our first date was May 16th, 2023, and she passed on May 18th, 2024. So, I only got one year. And that's what hurts the most," I said, my voice cracking with sorrow.

"Yeah… because it feels very unfair. And it is unfair, but I think she would dance this life with you a thousand times over. A thousand times over, she'd choose this life with you," Brandie said, comforting me.

"I'd take a year if that's all I knew I was going to get, but my vision was so much bigger than that," I explained through tears.

"Right," Brandie agreed.

"Peggy said the same thing, 'Beau would dance with you all night long until the end of eternity, and you would join him.' It's insane, and I'm sorry, but it feels like everything is uniting. I truly believe Melanie is here, channeling her energy. Beau, Melanie loved you so much. She still loves you, and you two will have your chance again," Becky comforted.

"And I know that to be true. When she says, '*I would dance a thousand times over with you,*' she really means that and affirms it," Brandie said, wiping her tears away. "It's funny because you sent me that video of her dancing…"

Brandie was referring to the video of Melanie dancing to Bob Marley's 'Looking in Your Big Brown Eyes.'

Brandie continued, "I love that song. It's such a silly song. The fact that she's so adamant about doing this over and over, I feel like she wants to wrap you in a cocoon and help you understand that even though it was short, love is not beyond your reach or your grip.

You will have another love. It won't be the same, but it will be beautiful, and she'll witness it. It's a testament to her selflessness. Though it might feel like what she did was selfish, it was actually an act of selflessness because it has allowed so many things to blossom. I know people often think of suicide as the cowardly or easy way out, but sometimes it's not. Sometimes, you were born to do greater things, and I think this is one of those moments.

If anything is evident today, it's the purity of her love for you. It hurts her to know you feel like your time together was too short. But for her to testify that you are her 'knight in shining armor'… most women dream of that their whole life. The beauty is she got to experience that. You gave her that gift. Most women never get that."

We were three and a half hours into the call when we began to wrap up, sharing stories about how we felt her presence. Brandie explained that her spirit was omnipresent, meaning it could be in multiple places simultaneously. She offered guidance on where to look for her in nature, through birds and butterflies, emphasizing that while the animals themselves are not her, she can use her energy to send them to us.

"All of you are spiritually gifted. For you to communicate with her, to receive her nudges, and to be open to it while grieving, I can't say enough about you. You're building this little community to honor her. She says, '*Hey, write a memoir about me, put a journal together*.' She's really about that. In her human self, she wasn't like that," Brandie continued.

"Luckily, she has about ten or fifteen journals, day by day," Becky said.

"Women like that, who are so diligent in articulating their experiences, are incredible," Brandie replied. "And honestly, I feel like kicking her ass; if I can say that out loud because she knows now, there were other options. But the beauty of it is she understands that her selflessness will create something so beautiful. So many lives will be touched by your sister's story, her life, and her connections, even by this moment.

I'm sitting here thinking, holy cow, I'm witnessing someone's tragedy turning into triumph. And I know hers is going to be that. This is not the end of her story. If anything, it's just the beginning. I'm sorry, I get so emotional. It feels like it's her, me, and all of you," Brandie said, breaking into tears.

"She's really powerful. She always has been," Sarah added in tears.

"Maybe one more question," Becky asked. "It seems really important to Melanie that we tell her story. I know she lived 32 years, and her story is vast when you think about it. But are the takeaways from her story more about the end of her life, the struggles she endured, and how she healed from them? She was in depression, and she was coming out of it. I truly believe she was healed. Is that the focus we should have when sharing her story, or is it more about the time right before she died?"

"As she articulates it, '*I think it's a story of tragedy and triumph. You can't have one without the other.*' I don't think what you're going to write will be all encompassing; it will be sequential. It could be one piece, then another because her life was multidimensional... yet so simple.

You start with the stories and then connect them to the lessons. When you do that, everyone wins: '*the good, the bad, and the ugly.*' She understands you can't have one without the other. But triumph over tragedy, with lessons, is elevation. That's how you raise the frequency. I hope that makes sense," Brandie said, closing our four-hour session.

Would You Defend My Honor?

August 8th - August 10th, 2023

The first time I was in Ojai, in 2008, I was a sales rep for a startup vodka company. I rode along with Southern Wine & Spirits reps and ran my company card for case stacks in liquor stores. This visit was entirely different. I pulled into a gravel roundabout surrounded by desert plants and shaded by trees. After parking beside a sage garden, I stepped into the tranquil home of David Elliott.

"How was your session with Melanie?" he asked.

"It went really well, but I was overcome with regret during the middle of it. I felt like a failure, as if everything I had accomplished in my life had fallen short of my expectations," I said.

I shared the story of my first and only touchdown at the University of Colorado. "When I crossed the goal line and looked into the stands at the fifty thousand cheering fans, I thought, *This is it? All that hard work for this.* Looking back, I was upset at my lack of appreciation for everything I had put into the game. I took my talent and the opportunity to play at that level for granted. I could have had a better career if I had been more disciplined and sacrificed my social life."

David listened intently, pausing before responding.

"I don't think that was a lack of appreciation or you taking that experience for granted," he said. "I think that was your soul communicating you were meant for something much greater."

His words hit me. "I never thought about it like that."

David handed me two rocks as we moved into meditation.

"These are your rocks to help ground you. You can keep them for your personal sessions moving forward."

He saged the room as I began breathing deeply, sprayed a cleansing mist over me, and dabbed essential oil on my third eye.

Pressing a point on my knee, he asked, "Did you have any knee injuries playing football?"

"I've torn both of my MCLs."

"I want you to breathe into the pain," he said, applying pressure.

He encouraged me to breathe heavier, like during a workout, keeping the rhythm Melanie had taught me.

Toward the end of our session, he played an aboriginal horn called a didgeridoo. As the sound waves rolled over me, the energy coursing through me intensified.

"How are you feeling?"

"I feel like I could shoot lasers out of my fists."

As the energy continued to surge, a name repeatedly raced through my mind: *Michael Rupert.*

When the session ended, David asked, "How was it?"

"Intense," I replied, still dazed. "I'm super out of it."

"You don't need mushrooms, MDMA, or DMT to have a psychedelic experience," he said. "You can achieve it with the breath. You have powerful energy. Man, when I hit you with the Didge, your third eye exploded open. What was going on for you?"

"I kept hearing the name Michael Rupert," I said. "It was relentless, over and over in my mind."

David nodded, intrigued. I explained that Michael Rupert was the lead detective for LAPD in the Freeway Ricky Ross crack cocaine investigation in the 1980s. He later became an investigative journalist, diving into controversial topics like 9/11 and the 2008 economic collapse, warning of a larger crisis tied to peak oil.

I paused, still processing the significance of hearing his name. David watched me closely, waiting to see where this realization might lead. Mel had told me he was clairvoyant, and after a moment, he asked, "Are you a writer?"

"Yeah. I've written several screenplays and even turned one into a movie," I explained. "I had a passion project I wanted to write called *GOD*, a reference to Gold, Oil, and Drugs and how they are three elements that have shaped the world. I was going to base the lead character on Rupert. But after my last film, I lost faith in the process. Movies are just too expensive."

"A client of mine had an idea to write a book about a wealthy Asian family, but he didn't think there was an audience for it. I encouraged him to write it anyway. You know what that book was?" he asked. "*Crazy Rich Asians*. You have powerful energy, Beau. Don't be afraid to lean into it."

Leaving David's place, I sat in my car for ten minutes, still feeling hallucinogenic.

Mel called, eager to hear about my session.

"How was it?" she asked, excitement in her voice.

"I've got to call you back. I'm still pretty out of it."

"Are you okay?"

"Yeah, just way out of it still. I'm going to get something to eat."

"Okay. I can't wait to hear about it. I'll see you tonight."

Mel was heading to see David after me and then meeting me for a few days at an Airbnb in Carpinteria. I stocked the house with groceries and picked up some roses, hoping to spark some romance.

When she arrived, I was excited to share my experience with David, but I asked about her session first.

"How did it go?"

"It was okay."

"Did you have any crazy vibrations or anything?"

"Not really."

"Did David say anything about our session?"

"He said you're a good guy and that I should lean into the relationship."

It felt good to hear David was in my corner, but strange that Mel's curiosity about my experience had faded.

"I'd like to get outside before the sun goes down. You want to go for a walk at the beach?" she asked.

We followed a trail along the train tracks, passing through a patch of sunflowers.

Blobs of black tar were scattered across the sandy trail as we made our way to a cliffside bench, where we watched sea lions surf the waves below.

"Look at how much fun they're having. That would be such a cool life," she said.

"Except for all the tar on the beach."

"I know, so sad."

I noticed several oil platforms out in the ocean.

"Do you think the oil was seeping through, and they decided to drill here, or do you think the drilling is what's causing all of this?"

"I don't know."

As the sun set, I leaned in for a kiss but was denied.

"Can we just talk? I want to connect with you."

"I was excited to share about my breathwork session with David, but you didn't seem that interested."

"I'm sorry. How was it?"

"When he blew the didgeridoo over me, the vibrations were crazy. After the session, he said, 'Man, when I hit you with the Didge, your third eye exploded open.'"

She laughed. "I can totally see him saying that."

"Has he ever used the Didge on you?"

"He hasn't, but it's different for everyone. He goes with the flow, you know."

"And then I kept repeatedly hearing the name Michael Rupert in my head."

As I began explaining who Michael Rupert was, she interrupted.

"Is this some sort of conspiracy theory?"

"In his words, he didn't deal in conspiracy theory. He dealt in conspiracy facts."

"Can we talk about something a little bit lighter?"

It struck me as ironic that Rupert, who spoke about peak oil and its consequences, had come through during my session, and now here we were, watching the sunset on a beach covered in black tar.

For dinner, I grilled cod as Mel read about the Maui fires.

"Did you see what's happening in Maui?" she asked. "This is crazy. The fires are really bad. I told you the energy was off."

She seemed energized, as if the fires validated her decision to cut the trip short.

"I knew something bad was going to happen," she added.

After doing the dishes together, we snuggled on the couch watching *1883* with Tim McGraw and Faith Hill. I was eager for Mel to see it as it told the story of their move to Montana, a place I hoped to convince her we could call home.

I had forgotten about the attempted rape scene and quickly explained it was meant to reflect the harsh realities of the time. Melanie tensed beside me.

"Maybe we should watch something lighter," she said.

Moments later, Tim McGraw's character shot the man attacking his daughter.

"Would you defend my honor?"

"Absolutely," I replied. "As long as it was justified."

Mel raised an eyebrow. "What do you mean?"

"I had an ex that was a total drama queen who thrived on creating chaos," I explained. "She'd start shit just to stir the pot and then drag me into it, like some twisted test to see how much I cared about her."

"That sounds exhausting."

"It was," I admitted. "We broke up several times, but the final straw came one night at a St. Paddy's Day event I was hosting. She got wasted, so I dropped her off at home. When I told her I was going back to work, she slapped me in the face."

Mel's eyes widened. "Seriously?"

"Yeah, that was it for me. I couldn't do it anymore."

The question about defending her honor stuck with me.

"What happened when you were four?"

"It was a fifteen-year-old boy who lived in the neighborhood."

"What did he do?"

"He put his hand down my pants."

It was clear she didn't want to talk about it, and I respected her privacy, hoping she'd open up when she was ready.

As *1883* carried on, Mel was swept away by the music and cinematography. At one point, I got a little teary-eyed and sniffled.

"Are you crying?"

"Maybe, just a little bit."

She laughed softly. "You're so sweet."

We powered through three more episodes. That night in bed, I leaned in to give her a goodnight kiss and sampled a line from the show.

"Yep, way too pretty for me."

"Wow, you really like me," she said, shifting her hips into my lap as we fell asleep.

The next day, we drove to Santa Barbara to explore a hiking trail Mel wanted to check out. The sun beat down the overgrown path, but we pushed through the brush, eventually reaching a shaded stretch along the well-maintained ivy-covered mountainside.

Back at the house, we relaxed on the porch while I continued teaching her cribbage. She was nearly ready to play with her cards face down.

We stopped for ice cream after an early dinner in downtown Carpinteria that evening. Sitting on a bench outside the shop, a group of high school boys passed by. Mel licked her cone provocatively, her expression playful, igniting a rush of desire and hope for something later. I wasn't sure if I was the only one she was teasing.

"Easy on the ice cream cone," I joked.

The mischievous glint in her eye told me she found it amusing, but as my words settled, her eyes shifted. My look must've told her I felt it was inappropriate.

"Have you ever been sexually abused?" she asked suddenly.

"No."

"That's not true. Everybody has sexual abuse energy in them," she pressed.

"But I haven't been sexually abused."

"Really?" she said, sounding unconvinced.

"I mean, I guess there was one time in Tahoe. We were all partying, and I woke up to some chick having sex with me. I threw her onto the floor, and when she turned on the light, she said, 'Oh my god, you're not Kevin.'

We all laughed about it at the time.

And then there was this girl I shared a bed with in Big Bear. She wouldn't leave me alone about hooking up, and even though I didn't want to, I eventually caved so that I could go to sleep."

"That's different," Mel said. "I'm talking about abuse energy that gets stuck, like an entity your body needs to release. I've been doing David's entity release meditation to clear mine."

Ending the night on that note deterred me from pursuing anything physical beyond light kissing. Whatever energy she was struggling with had become a block for me, too, and I was growing sexually frustrated in the relationship.

While Mel ran errands the following day, I got ready for another breathwork session. *Maybe I had energy to clear.* I tried David's entity release meditation and reflected on toxic relationships from my past. Had my fear of messing things up with Melanie become a block? I was walking on eggshells, trying to make everything perfect.

As I neared the end of the meditation, I slipped into a transcendental state. Suddenly, I woke, gasping for air as though I were drowning. A paralyzing energy left my body.

When Mel returned, I was eager to share my experience, hoping she would appreciate what I had just gone through. Instead, she brushed it off for the second time on this trip.

I didn't understand why. Breathwork was her thing. I had leaned into it for her, let myself go completely, broken through something I hadn't even known was there. I wanted her advice on entity release, to hear what she thought, and to connect on what it had been like for her. But she barely seemed to care.

For a moment, I considered pressing her, asking why she didn't want to engage. But I let it go. I always did.

That night, we finished *1883*, sparking a conversation about a road trip through California, Oregon, Idaho, and Montana. I hoped Flathead Lake would help sell her on my dream of raising a family there.

Master Builder

June 9th - June 13th, 2024

I took Chris's advice and booked a 22-day trip to Bali, selling the tickets to the Chris Stapleton concert at the Hollywood Bowl to help fund the journey. Missing the chance to honor her with her family was difficult, but we all agreed her absence would have made it even harder.

Then came the voicemail from my dad:

"So, I wasn't able to get the song dedication done, but I ran into my buddy yesterday who was working on it. He told me his son also died by suicide with a shotgun. 22 days after his son passed, he spoke to a woman named Erin the Angel... said she knew things about him and his son that nobody else could have known. You need to call her." He ended the message with her number.

The number 22 kept surfacing. Chris's advice to get out of town for 22 days, minute 22 of Melanie's reading with Peggy when she asked about going back to her ex, and now my dad's voicemail regarding Erin the Angel. *What was up with 22?*

Before heading to the airport, I called Melanie's breathwork friend, Bear. David had mentioned that during their March retreat, she confided in Bear about being back on Adderall, so I wanted his perspective.

"At the New Year's Eve retreat in December, she told me she was having suicidal thoughts. Mornings were fine, but nights were challenging for her when the sun went down.

We made a pact that if she ever felt like she was going to do something, she would call me first," Bear revealed, clearly upset that she hadn't.

Finally, I understood her secrecy about their calls. She was hiding the depth of her struggles.

"I found out she got back on Adderall in February. That's around the same time I caught her unarchiving photos of her ex on Instagram. It's like the Adderall unlocked the door to the dark energy that led her back to him.

David mentioned she confessed to you that she was back on it at the retreat in March."

"She did, but I noticed a change in her personality during our phone conversations before then. I could tell she was on it again… her mind would get stuck on these loops. She'd ask the same question over and over until she got the answer she was looking for."

"Her psychic, Peggy, told her going back to her ex was a bad idea, but she fought that advice. The next day, she had a session with David, who told her he didn't think it was a good idea either, but if she wanted to see if there was anything there, she needed to do the right thing and cut things off with me. And that was the answer she was looking for. She called me right after and told me she wanted no attachments."

"I want you to know, Beau, that she had nothing but great things to say about you," Bear reassured me.

"I don't understand why she stopped breathing, though."

"She told me that when she was in the bathroom line at the firewalk retreat in December, she heard someone say, 'I think breathwork is making me fat.' Melanie took that thought and made it her own."

"She used to talk a lot about external validation. She was always asking me if she was pretty, if I thought she was fat, and my answers were always, 'What are you talking about?' She never had to work for that validation with me, but she told me her ex used to put her down a lot."

"I didn't know she was going back to him, but that would make sense. Like I said, she would get into these mind loops."

"She probably asked him if he thought she was fat. I wonder if him maybe affirming what she thought about herself was enough to push her over the edge."

"She knew he was no good for her…

She mentioned she had her own narcissistic tendencies that she felt she needed to break.

She was supposed to call me before she did anything. I can't believe she didn't call me," Bear lamented. "If you need anything, don't hesitate to reach out, Beau."

Signs and synchronicities appeared everywhere at the airport. In the check-in line, a woman with a butterfly tattoo stood in front of me, reminiscent of *The Matrix's* "Follow the White Rabbit" scene.

After checking in, I wandered into a bookstore. My eyes drifted from one magazine to the next as if being guided.

Ryan Reynolds, Mel's celebrity crush, was on one cover. A haunting headline about Gabby Petito read, *"No One Should Die Like She Did."* She was 22. Then a Grateful Dead magazine cover echoed Mel's words: "I appreciate you. I'm grateful for you."

I couldn't shake the feeling that I was being forced to walk this path.

I watched Dune: Part Two again on the plane, wrapped in Mel's scarf. Learning that *Lisan al Gaib* meant *"Tongue of the Unseen World"* in Islam, I remembered my vision in Lake Arrowhead of Melanie and me having a child that would change the world.

Unbearable guilt darkened my thoughts as exhaustion set in on my second flight. Just as panic took hold, violent turbulence shook the plane, knocking a woman to her knees and shaking the shotgun from my mind. I wondered if the accident had not happened in my room, would I still have been able to communicate with Mel? *Was all of this divinely orchestrated?*

After 22 hours of travel, my friend Made picked me up at the airport. When I got to my hotel, I collapsed into bed. Jet lag woke me a couple of hours later, at 3 a.m. I started my day scrolling through my phone and came across an RFK Jr. Instagram post: *"Pain is ultimately the touchstone of spiritual gifts."* Losing Melanie had unlocked something in me I didn't know was there.

At 8:30 a.m., I rode my motorbike to Bali Training Centre (BTC) in Bingin, an open-air gym specializing in Muay Thai and HIIT fitness. My hip was screaming from the long flight, and I was looking forward to getting back in shape. Jake, the owner, was writing the morning workout on the whiteboard.

"What's up, big boy? When did you get in?" he asked.

"Yesterday afternoon."

"Not wasting any time... No jet lag, huh? Are you on holiday?"

"More of a healing trip. My girlfriend committed suicide a little over three weeks ago."

"I'm so sorry, mate."

"I'm down 15 pounds from the shock, so I'm going to need you to go easy on me today."

"Fifteen pounds? What's that, almost 7 kilos? Wow, that's a lot."

I struggled through the class, missing multiple sets. I was mentally and physically weaker than I had ever been. There was a disconnect between my mind and body that I had never felt before.

Afterward, I went to Jake's other business, Santai Recovery Spa, an outdoor oasis with a sauna overlooking a pool plus cold and hot plunges. I powered through a five-minute ice bath, then scootered to Dynasty Hill for a $12, 90-minute Balinese massage.

That night, I tapped into David's 28-minute breathwork meditation. By 6 p.m., exhaustion hit me like a wall, and I passed out.

That night, a recurring dream haunted me. Mel and I flew back and forth between Amsterdam and Los Angeles, trying to meet up. Every time I landed, she did too, but in the opposite city. No matter how much we tried, we kept missing each other. I woke up frustrated. My first instinct was to call her, only to remember I couldn't.

It was my 45th birthday—another battle with grief.

At 4:44 a.m., my phone lit up with a message from Brandie: *"How are you?"*

"Every morning, I wake up to the same nightmare, and the first thing I realize is that Mel is gone. Still processing a lot of guilt."

She responded with a comforting voice note:

"You'll never be the same, but through this process, we learn that we are not in control. There is a greater scheme beyond anything we can perceive. There's nothing you could have done differently."

I realized Brandie was the soft-spoken woman Chris had told me to find. Her words felt like divine intervention. I questioned whether missing someone was merely an egocentric emotion and if a greater plan was unfolding behind the scenes, one that might help others. Either way, I had to start with myself. I had no idea how long it would take to feel okay again, but I couldn't start at the finish line. I had to follow the advice I had always given Mel: focus on winning each day, one day at a time.

As I settled into a corner at BTC to stretch, "Something in the Orange" by Zach Bryan played. I kept my head low as the class filled in, trying to conceal the silent tears sliding down my face.

Still severely jet lagged, I battled through Jake's HIIT class, improving on the day before. During the cooldown, I caught the lyrics of a song I had not heard before: something about being glad my last dance was with you. The somber words triggered more tears, which I quickly wiped.

I ended the day with a five-minute ice bath at Santai, losing myself in the clouds as the cold stole the pain from my mind. I closed my night with two breathwork sessions, one before dinner and another before bed.

Each morning, I woke up in a dark place, reminding myself to take one step at a time. That day, my first step was to text Erin the Angel to schedule a reading.

"Hi Erin, my dad referred me to you. I lost my girlfriend, Melanie, to suicide on May 18th. I'm currently in Bali, but I feel like I'm supposed to schedule a call with you 22 days after my trip. I don't know why, but the number 22 keeps coming up."

Cashew Tree was a restaurant collective that BTC was part of, along with a yoga boutique and daycare. The atmosphere was magical. Each morning, a local woman placed a Canang Sari offering in a banana leaf basket. The birds usually got to it, but the energy remained tangible. Over breakfast before my workout, Erin's reply came through.

"Hello, friend. I am so sorry about Melanie; there are no words. I hope you find time to 'be and heal' in Bali. 22 is a powerful number. It is the master

builder number and a sign of personal spiritual guidance. You are being shown your inner strength. Do sunflowers mean anything to you?"

"*Sunflower seeds, yes… in connection to Melanie.*"

I recalled how she got a kick out of me loading sunflower seeds into my mouth at her nephew's baseball game.

"*I see sunflowers around you, so I wondered how you relate… Our loved ones send messages in different ways. It is like a puzzle we piece together.*"

On my way to the bathroom, I noticed two sunflowers painted on the wall at the daycare. I snapped a picture and sent it to Erin.

"*Here are your sunflowers at the daycare next to where I am having breakfast.*"

"*Aww, those are beautiful.*"

We scheduled my appointment for July 2nd, after my return from Bali.

At BTC, I ran into Lucas, a friend from back home. After class, we settled into the poolside bean bags at Santai, where I shared my story. He felt the weight of my loss, and when energy healing came up, he suggested Reiki at Yoga Barn in Ubud.

I mustered up the courage for my ice bath while warming up in the hot plunge, where I struck up a conversation with an Australian couple. They raved about the sunset Yin Yoga class at Istana. Melanie had always loved the balance of Yin and Yang, and something about their enthusiasm made me feel like I was meant to go.

I followed their recommendation and rode my motorbike to Uluwatu. Perched on a cliff overlooking the Indian Ocean, the place radiated serenity. As I fought through each pose, the instructor introduced a breathing technique I had never tried before. I inhaled deeply, pushed the air through my body, held it as long as I could, then exhaled. With each release, the energy inside me grew stronger.

"*Melanie would have loved this,*" I thought as grief swelled inside me. I felt a profound sense of relief from the ache I had carried for weeks.

As the sun dipped below the horizon, casting an orange glow into the studio, I sat in quiet reflection. The gentle sound of the waves provided a soothing backdrop to my thoughts. I embraced the small victory. The pain of losing Melanie would never entirely disappear, but in moments like this, peace felt possible.

Suicide After Sex

August 17th - August 29th, 2023

Mel had raved about the Greek Theatre, so I took a chance on its next show: Cigarettes After Sex. As we crawled through rush hour traffic past the grand mansions near Griffith Park, we watched teenage girls in black mini skirts and Doc Martens race toward the entrance.

"What did we get ourselves into?" I asked, noticing we were the only ones not dressed in black.

"You bought the tickets," she teased. "I thought you had seen them before."

The venue erupted with deafening screams when the band finally took the stage.

"Oh boy," I muttered.

Mel burst out laughing, thoroughly entertained by the scene. "Let's give them a chance."

As the first song started, the crowd sang along at the top of their lungs. We looked at each other and started laughing. We could not have been more out of place; this band had a cult following.

By the fourth song, it was clear that every track sounded the same: slow, melancholy, and drenched in sadness. I leaned over, quoting a line from *1883*.

"'Don't you know a happy one?'"

As the song ended, I gave her a look that said, *I screwed up*. She burst into hysterical laughter.

"You want to get out of here?" I asked.

"I'm so glad you're not into them either. Yes!"

As we left our sixth-row seats, a few people glanced at us, surprised. We had spent more time waiting for the band to start than actually watching them perform.

Relief washed over us as we stepped outside.

"So, how was your date?" I joked. "Well, we sat in traffic for hours and saw this awesome band called Suicide After Sex."

"Suicide After Sex, that's perfect," she laughed.

We got home in half the time it took us to get there, which was another advantage of leaving early. Even though the music fell flat, the adventure brought laughter and closeness. We sank into the couch, still riding the high of our escape.

The playful energy continued as we began kissing. Things escalated naturally until, out of nowhere, she bit my lip hard. I laughed it off, but then she did it again, this time drawing blood as I pulled away. Before I could react, she growled and sank her teeth into my shoulder, clenching my skin between them. Instinctively, I pulled her hair, thinking she was in the mood for something rough.

"Don't pull my hair," she snapped, glaring at me.

"Then don't bite me!"

"Oh, come on, you're no fun," she said, leaning in and biting me again.

"I'm serious. You're going to break my skin," I said, showing her the indentation on my shoulder, already starting to bruise. "Don't bite me unless you're looking to turn me into an animal."

"Geez, I'm just playing with you," she dismissed.

"This isn't playful biting," I said, pointing to the bruise again.

"You're no fun."

"That's not fun for me," I replied firmly.

That was the end of her biting phase. Her reaction made it seem like this behavior was familiar to her, and I couldn't help but wonder if it was linked to the toxicity she had become accustomed to in her past relationship.

"Let's watch a movie," she suggested, trying to soften the mood.

We searched through options, with Mel always asking for something lighter. We eventually settled on *Past Lives*, a film about a Korean couple who seemed destined to be soulmates but struggled to make things work in their present life. As we watched, I couldn't help but notice the parallels to our relationship.

"What do you think happens when we die?" Mel asked.

"Have you read *Many Lives, Many Masters*?"

"No."

"I'll get it for you."

Lying in bed afterward, my mind wandered to the idea of Melanie being my soulmate. *Did she see us in them? Did she ever feel like we were pushing up against fate?* She already knew how I felt, and I didn't want to ask for fear of spooking her.

When Mel's workday slowed in the morning, she interrupted mine with some foreplay. After nine years of buildup, we had sex for the first time. The anticipation got the best of me, and I finished almost instantly, leaving me embarrassed.

"I promise it will get better."

"It's okay. I just want to connect with you," she replied.

"I know, but I want it to be enjoyable for both of us."

"Maybe we don't have any chemistry," she said softly.

"It will get better," I reassured her.

I wanted to believe that, but my performance eroded my confidence as the days passed. Her words about our chemistry haunted me. I needed another chance to quell her doubts.

I planned a hike into Christmas Tree Cove in Palos Verdes for our next date. During the drive, we passed through one of my favorite neighborhoods in LA, and I was excited to show her my dream home. I pointed to a wood Nantucket-style house overlooking the ocean.

"Which one is your favorite?" I asked.

"I don't know, yours is nice."

This was the second time I had failed to get her to participate in this game.

We parked in the neighborhood, grabbed our chairs, and began our trek to the cliff's edge. The lookout over the Cove was spectacular. The ocean teemed with seaweed, a rare sight in Southern California.

The hike down was steep. We traversed the dirt trail, then picked our way across the rocks to a secluded beach and set up our chairs overlooking the ocean.

Mel was in her element, soaking in the natural beauty. She loved being outside.

"It's so peaceful down here," she said.

"Look at how clean the water is."

"I love it. You know, my dad grew up in Palos Verdes."

"Really? Would you ever live here?"

"I want to get out of LA. It has bad energy. I'm telling you, I feel like something awful is going to happen right before the election. Like a major natural disaster or something."

"Wouldn't you miss your family too much?" I asked, sidestepping her ominous prediction.

"I would, but we could come back and visit."

"What about Ojai?" I asked.

"I could do Ojai."

"Let's keep our eyes open for a house."

"Would you leave your place in Venice?"

"For the right spot, I would, but it would need to make sense. I have a great deal on my place, and it's super close to work."

"I could pay like $2000 a month."

"Or you could move in with me, save that rent money to build your website and establish your business on the Westside. I can help fill your classes with my network."

"Can you help me get people to my classes in Costa Mesa?"

"That's a little far for my crowd. What about your family?"

"I've been trying to get my mom, Becky, and Jimmy to come. My mom's friend has been saying that she's going to bring a group."

"You should get a class pass and start pitching yourself to yoga studios in Venice and Santa Monica."

"I really don't want to be in LA."

"Starting over from scratch in Denver or Ojai would be tough for both of us. Let's build your client base here first, then consider moving."

"I can't work in finance anymore. I feel like it's killing my soul."

"You work remotely, and it only takes a few hours each morning. It's the perfect setup while you transition to a new career."

"What happens if Meryl fires me?"

"Why would they fire you? They just gave you an extension to work from home to continue focusing on your mental health. They're not going to risk a lawsuit by letting you go for something they just approved you for."

"You don't know that."

"I've heard you on the phone with your boss. He loves you, and your clients love you."

"You're right," she admitted. "They did just clear me for another year. Thanks for talking to me about this."

We packed up as the sun dipped, making our way back up the steep trail. On the quiet drive home, I brainstormed ways to get her out of LA without derailing our lives.

That night, Mel moved through her routine, saging the bedroom, applying essential oils, and slipping into breathwork. After her shower, I slid in beside her, kissing her neck, but when my hand drifted below her waist, she shut me down.

"I just want to cuddle. I'm exhausted," she said.

My desire for redemption continued to evade me until Mel finished her workday the next morning. She flirtatiously drew me away from my computer and began escalating our physical intimacy on the couch. As things progressed, she became critical again.

"What are you doing?"

I didn't know what to say as my frustration mounted.

"I need some foreplay." She demanded. "Maybe we just aren't compatible."

"Maybe you should tell me what you do like instead of critiquing everything I do."

"That was hot. I like it when you're direct."

Her response caught me off guard but gave me the confidence to flip her over and spank her firmly.

"Get the other side," she said.

For the first time in our relationship, she was genuinely aroused.

Midway through, she asked, "Would you mind if I grabbed my vibrator?"

She used it for the rest of intercourse, which helped her climax.

"Do you think I'm weird?" she asked afterward.

"Why? Because you wanted to use a toy?"

"Yeah."

"That doesn't bother me."

"That was really good. I don't know why I'm like that. I need to get better at letting things progress naturally. I'm just so used to a little chaos to spice things up," she remarked.

She was content, and for the first time, things had finally clicked for us. I was too caught up in the moment of victory for her comment about chaos to fully sink in. But at last, we could put the issue of sexual chemistry to rest.

As football season approached, my schedule intensified. In addition to running two weekly events and building my website, I was preparing for the third season of my football betting podcast, *Armchair Donkeys*. Tuesdays were for scripting, and Wednesdays were for shooting and releasing episodes.

I wanted to ensure Melanie felt prioritized while navigating the complexities of my increased workload.

"I've got my first podcast this week. It'll take up most of my time on Tuesday and Wednesday," I explained.

"You're already working Fridays and Saturdays. When are we supposed to hang out?"

"Thursdays and Sundays would be best for us. I'll be more present on those days."

"I only get to see you on Thursdays and Sundays?"

"I didn't say that," I replied. "I just want you to get the best version of me on date nights."

"You know my dad was a workaholic, and it took away from his time with us. I don't want that."

"Your dad did what he had to do to support five kids in Newport Beach."

"I need some spontaneity in my life."

Her idea of spontaneity often involved a four-hour hike on a Tuesday, a luxury my schedule rarely allowed. I wanted to see her using that time to build her career, but she kept hesitating.

"I want you to know that you are a priority in my life," I said. "But I also want to see your dreams come true.

We don't have any kids yet, and you have the perfect opportunity to build something for yourself so that when they're grown up, you have something other than your family that you're passionate about.

Then, when we come together, our time will be magical. But if you don't spend the time to build it now, when is it ever supposed to happen?"

"You're a really good guy. Thanks for believing in me."

Her eyes held mine with that familiar gaze.

"Are you using the computer on your desk? All I have is my work computer," she asked.

"It's all yours."

The next day, I took my old Mac to the computer store to get the hard drive wiped, so she could start creating content for her website.

When Truth Hides in the Shadows

June 14th - June 18th, 2024

My body was getting stronger, but I still sat at the edge of the gym, wiped out after my workout. Floyd, the massive Bali beach mutt and gym mascot, bypassed everyone that morning to seek me out. As his fist-sized paws landed on my shoulders, I heard Mel's voice: *"Give him some love."* While rubbing his belly, I recalled Brandie saying spirit could use animals to send messages. At that moment, I was certain Mel had.

The connection, a subtle but undeniable pull, left me feeling closer to her than I had in days. It was as though she was reaching out, motivating me to carry on the work she had started. I wanted to share the profound experience with her family but wasn't sure how it would be received, so I decided to check in on them instead.

Sarah replied that they were considering a wellness event for Mel's birthday.

"I love the idea of an event on her birthday. I'm also feeling drawn to putting together an event, picking up where Mel left off and sharing her story with the world to help people who are struggling with abuse, trauma, and addiction." I wrote.

"Beau, when you return, we will all discuss what will be Melly's story and how breathwork can help others. It's mental illness awareness, not addiction," Liz shot back.

"I love you, Liz. I would never tell her story without your blessing, but I do believe it is incredibly powerful and can help a lot of people, including all of us if we are brave enough to tell it. In our session with Brandie, she said to be bold and not to fight over it, which I'm not going to do. I love you guys," I replied.

Liz's text about us getting together to *"decide what Mel's story would be"* felt wrong, as if she were trying to shape her truth. It unsettled me enough that I reached out to Brandie.

Brandie's response:

"When truth hides in the shadows, it cannot help anyone. A light must be cast upon it to make a difference."

I re-watched the Zoom call with Brandie and was amazed at how much more I absorbed when I wasn't distracted by the questions I had wanted to ask. The entire session was packed with messages. I took a break halfway through, but one thing became crystal clear to me: *Melanie wanted her story told.*

Liz gave me her blessing to share Mel's story, but then she took it away. Frustration burned through me. I grabbed my pen and let it bleed onto the page.

"Sadness comes like a tsunami, especially in the mornings. Breathing, working out, and taking ice baths keep me from drowning. I feel like I'm understanding what she was going through. You work so hard every day to get to okay. I want to share everything I'm doing with her, and while she has sent some signs, I haven't been able to speak with her directly, which is the first thing I want to do when I wake up in the morning.

I held a lot of space for her and was always there when she needed me, loving her unconditionally even as she broke up with me. I would have been there for her on the last day, but I understand now that she was in such a state of despair that she was unable to ask for help. I failed to recognize how severe her struggles were. She took her life in my bedroom with my shotgun, which is the most selfish and devastating thing anyone has ever done to me.

I'm riddled with guilt, running the same scenarios in my mind over and over again, thinking about what I could have done differently.

She manipulated me into leaving a key. I trusted her.

That day, I was juggling three events and two businesses.

Everything I was building was for us.

There was a root cause of Melanie's mental illness that she identified through her breathwork practice. She knew she had an addiction. She went back anyway. She pushed me away to chase her destructive fix. She made a terrible choice, and it cost her her life.

I will be stronger next time."

I slammed my pen down, frustration twisting into something sharper. For the first time in this healing process, anger broke through, and I started thinking about giving up on her.

Why was I wasting my energy on someone who ultimately gave up on me? Her mom didn't want to tell her story, at least not the whole story. So why did I feel compelled to do so?

I needed to breathe on it, so I turned to David's 28-minute breathwork meditation. When the session ended, I remained in that stillness, Melanie's scarf across my eyes. A soothing song played, accompanied by a beautiful spoken word piece.

THE PHOTOSYNTHESIS OF HEALING
BY EMORY HALL

(Scan the QR codes to experience the music as it came to me through the lyrics, the visuals, or both so you can absorb each song with the emotional weight of how I interpreted its message.)

I was floored. This was a sign. Melanie was speaking through the lyrics.

At that moment, I decided to break my promise to Liz. Mel wanted her story told. I was going to turn it into a garden.

Honoring her meant more to me than protecting her mom's wish.

None of us are perfect. We are all beautifully flawed, and Mel's story wouldn't help anyone hiding in the shadows of a graveyard.

Brandie's channeling echoed in my mind again: *"The good, the bad, and the ugly."*

I sat with that decision for a long time. I had no idea where to begin. Then, as if on cue, inspiration landed in my lap.

My business partner Josh from the festival offered me a room while he was out of town. His fiancée, Tara, who was leaving the next day, helped me get settled. That night, I needed someone to listen as much as I needed answers.

She did. Then, after consideration, she handed me a book, *Between Death and Life,* by Dolores Cannon.

"You might find something in here."

I opened it immediately, and it consumed me for two days.

The book explored a hypnotherapist's sessions with patients who, while under hypnosis, shared insights from spirits about the afterlife. It was formatted similarly to *Many Lives, Many Masters*, which Mel and I found fascinating. I started reading and taking notes, unable to put it down, as I searched for answers to what had happened to her.

I came across a section in the book about elementals:

Elementals feed on emotional energy. Some are drawn to places of worship, absorbing the warmth of prayer and joy. Others thrive on darkness like hate, lust, and despair, gathering where those emotions are most intense. The book described them as mischievous forces that attach to people and sometimes influence their behavior.

This reminded me of the entities Mel often spoke about and our trip to Las Vegas when she saw them crawling up the wall. To this day, I have no doubt she saw something real. Whatever she encountered that night likely possessed her when she took her life.

Protection, it explained, was simple: Call upon a higher power, whatever form that may take, and genuinely ask for it. There were no specific words or rituals; only the intention mattered.
My dad once told me that he was visited by a spirit that would not leave, and he used the mantra, "By the power of Jesus Christ, I command you to leave this room." He encouraged me to use those words if I ever found myself in a similar situation, and this passage seemed to align with that.

The book also distinguished between evil spirits and negative energies. It suggested that those believed to be possessed were overwhelmed by accumulated negative forces. The possessing entities were not true spirits but warped energies, similar to what some might call demons. These beings were lower than human souls, twisted by interactions with other entities or even people, leading them toward malevolent behavior.

According to this perspective, these energies do not disappear immediately after death. Instead, those affected must undergo a cleansing process in the afterlife before finding peace.

Reading this, I could not shake the feeling that Melanie had been carrying something heavy that was not entirely her own. She had stopped her breathwork routine, which always began by her saging the room with protective intention and cleansing spray, followed by breathing to clear the energy that constantly clung to her sensitive soul. And she understood that what she was dealing with was energetic.

When asked where such entities originated if they had never lived human lives, the response pointed back to the Formation. According to this view, possession is not typically caused by a human spirit crossing over but by elemental forces that have always been part of the Earth.

These cases occur when a person's karma becomes severely imbalanced, creating a void in their energy field. This vacuum acts like a magnet, pulling in disorganized energies and loose collections of force often tied to nature, such as Earth, fire, or water elementals.

Despite the fear associated with possession, the book suggested that these entities do not enter with harmful intent. They are drawn in response to the imbalance rather than seeking to cause chaos.

Their influence can appear violent because their energy is unstructured compared to a human soul's. Without the ability to act with deliberate control, their presence leads to disorderly or extreme manifestations.

While some elementals might behave mischievously, actual possession is a natural consequence of cause and effect. These energies react to the imbalance they are drawn to rather than deliberately seeking to invade.

Again, this sounded a lot like Melanie. These energies were drawn to her imbalance, which stemmed from life events that happened when she was too young to control. It seemed like these energies existed on Earth for a reason.

I wondered again: was this divinely meant to happen the way it did?

The book explained that souls can become trapped on Earth, tethered by grief —either from their own attachment to life or from someone still living who won't let go. Each time someone mourns intensely, they unknowingly strengthen that tie, making it harder for the spirit to move on. While grief is natural, Dolores emphasized that most souls find peace after passing, but prolonged sorrow can weigh heavily, unintentionally keeping them bound to the earthly plane.

I thought back to my feeling that missing someone was selfish, and after reading this passage, I considered that grieving might be egocentric, too.

She did not need it in the spirit realm, but I needed it in my human experience.

Leaving on a high note—Dolores also explored perceptions of the afterlife, suggesting that an individual's expectations shape experiences of heaven and hell. Those who believe they deserve punishment may find themselves surrounded by negative energies after death, mistaking them for hell. But this is not a permanent state. It is a manifestation of unresolved emotions and fears.

Near-death experiences, according to the book, are filtered through personal beliefs, which is why some describe blissful realms while others recall terrifying visions of fire and torment. The book referred to the resting place, where souls can go to cleanse themselves of this negative energy.

It comforted me knowing that Mel was finally getting the healing she needed.

Betting with my Heart

August 30th - September 15th, 2023

Betting on football games was the only thrill that came close to playing in front of 50,000 fans. We had just wrapped the first episode of season three of *Armchair Donkeys*. My co-hosts and I had played for the Colorado Buffaloes, part of the last team to win a conference championship in 2001. This season felt different. Colorado had hired Deion Sanders as head coach, and the hype was real. Their opener against TCU would kick off the Coach Prime era.

On the show, I predicted Colorado would beat TCU. The previous year, TCU had reached the national championship, where they were dismantled by Georgia—and that team lost 11 players to the NFL. Colorado, meanwhile, had Coach Prime and a roster full of transfers, including his son Shedeur, who I knew was highly skilled.

With Colorado listed at +700, a $100 bet would return $700. It was a bold prediction, but I jumped on it. The day after our podcast aired, I flew to Las Vegas and placed a $3,000 bet. If Colorado pulled off the upset, the payout would be $21,000. A few hours later, I was back in LA, waiting to see how it would play out.

My dad was in town that weekend, so I invited him and Mel to Grunions, a Colorado alumni bar in Manhattan Beach, to watch the game. I had bought Mel some CU gear, and she was decked out for the occasion.

"My family was never big into football," she said. "My dad watches it now, but we didn't watch it growing up."

"But you have been to games before, right?" I asked.

"I have been to SC games, but mostly just to tailgate," she replied.

Knowing I had flown to Vegas to place a big bet, I wanted Mel engaged.

"I'll tell you what," I said. "If Colorado wins, I'll take you to Bali during my slow season in April."

"How about Italy instead?" she countered. "I have always wanted to go to Italy. It is on my bucket list."

"All Right," I agreed. "If Colorado wins, we'll go to Italy in April."

As the game kicked off, Mel was into it. She was unfamiliar with the rules, so I explained how teams had four attempts to gain 10 yards for a first down, which would get them four more chances to do it again.

"How come nobody ever told me that before? It makes so much sense now," she said.

She and my dad hit it off, bonding over their shared financial backgrounds. I watched her impress him with business knowledge, clearly earning his respect. During her bathroom break, my dad leaned over.

"She is the best girl you have ever dated, pal."

"I have been waiting for her a long time, pop."

Soon after, my dad left for a high school reunion, leaving Mel and me to finish the game. Italy had done the trick. She stayed locked in until the final whistle.

I went wild during Colorado's game-winning drive, high-fiving Mel and chest-bumping CU fans at the bar. She reveled in my excitement; I had just won $21,000.

"Do you know that guy?" Mel asked, referring to one of the fans I had chest-bumped.

"Never met him in my life."

"He has predator energy."

"I got you."

"I'm not scared. I was just letting you know he has dark entities attached to him."

I barely processed what she said, still caught up in the adrenaline of the win, thinking about the cash I would pick up.

"Do you want to fly to Vegas with me to pick up the money on Monday?"

"I don't really like Vegas."

"Come on, it will be fun. We will go for one night, have a nice dinner, pick up the cash, see a show, and come back the next day," I encouraged.

"Okay, sounds fun."

Mel went south for the end of Labor Day weekend to spend time with her family, so I booked flights out of Orange County.

When I parked outside her house, her dad was washing one of his cars.

"Jim?" I asked.

"Yes?" he replied, looking confused.

"Hi, I'm Beau. I'm here to pick up Melanie."

"Oh, hi, Beau," he said, relaxing. "I thought you were going to serve me for a second."

"Serve you?"

"Yeah, I'm a lawyer, and you never know in my business. You caught me off guard," he said with a laugh.

Just then, Melanie stepped out, visibly mortified. It reminded me of meeting her mom when she had rushed me out of the house.

"Do you want to come in?" Jim asked.

"Nope. We have a flight to catch," Melanie replied quickly.

"You guys are headed to Vegas?"

"Going to pick up some money I won on the Colorado game."

"Okay. Have fun. Be careful. The house always wins. They didn't build all those shiny buildings by giving their money away."

That was solid advice, but I was not planning to gamble. I was more excited to show Mel a good time.

"Are you embarrassed about me meeting your dad?" I asked as we left for the airport.

"I'm just not ready for you to meet the family yet," she said. "It's already enough that you met my mom. I was not ready for that."

"But you met my dad, and that went great."

"Your dad was great."

I did not love the feeling that she was keeping me from her family, but I let it go.

We checked into a complimentary suite at the Cosmopolitan.

"The energy in here is really intense," Mel said, grabbing my arm.

It was the tail end of Labor Day weekend, and lost souls clinging to their four-day benders spilled out of their swimsuits as they left the Marquee pool party. I understood what Mel was sensing, but she seemed to feel it on a deeper level.

Getting off the casino floor and into our suite offered her some relief. She let out a deep breath and relaxed as we settled onto the bed, watching the sunset over the Strip. I was still riding the high of being in Vegas. After a few brief kisses, she gently declined my attempt at physical intimacy.

Our Vegas adventure began at the cage to pick up my winnings, followed by dinner at Bouchon, a quiet escape from the chaos. When the oysters arrived, Mel let out a dramatic slurp, drawing a laugh from me.

"I am so excited for oysters!" she said, her eyes lighting up.

She had a beautiful way of finding excitement in life's simple pleasures.

"You know, I almost didn't make that bet. I meditated on it after a breathwork session, and I heard a voice say, '*Do it*.'"

Mel smirked. "You're not supposed to channel spirit to win football games, you know."

"I probably would have bet it anyway."

After dinner, we saw *Mystère* at Treasure Island. The opening featured a grown man dressed as a baby speaking gibberish. While some in the crowd laughed, Mel grabbed my arm.

"This is creepy. There is really weird energy in here."

"Do you want to leave?"

"No, I'll be okay."

She made it through the show, but I could tell it wasn't sitting well with her. The performers' makeup and eccentric personas leaned more toward unsettling than entertaining.

That night in bed, Mel wasn't feeling well. We did some breathwork, and then I rubbed her back, helping her get to sleep before drifting off myself.

Around 3 a.m., she shook me awake.

"We need to get out of here. There are entities crawling up the wall," she said urgently.

"What do you mean, entities?"

"I can see dark entities crawling up the wall."

"What do you want me to do?"

"We need to get out of here. We need to rent a car and drive back to LA."

"It's 3 a.m., Mel. No rental car spots are open right now, and flights don't leave until 6."

I doubted she would do any better at the airport.

"I'm freaking out. I can see them crawling up the wall."

"Give me a minute while I figure something out," I said, rubbing her back again.

Mel loved the desert.

"Okay, we're in the desert," I said, thinking out loud. "We just need to get you off the Strip. Let me see if I can find another room."

"Thank you so much. I'm really sorry. Please don't think I'm crazy."

I didn't think she was crazy. I had felt the energy all day, but Mel was different. She could see it. Still, watching her in full panic mode was jarring.

I booked a hotel near Lake Las Vegas, and we took an Uber out of the city.

"Thank you so much. I'm so sorry."

"It's okay." I was relieved to see her tension ease.

The silence of the desert felt different. The weekend travelers had cleared out, and we had the hotel to ourselves. After we checked in, Mel wanted to ground herself.

"I'm going to put my feet in the grass," she said.

She crawled into bed with me two hours later, and I held her for the rest of the night.

A little while later, she whispered, "Thank you for believing me. Nobody has ever loved me like that before."

"I do love you."

"I love you too. I feel so safe with you."

She loved me. My heart was whole, filled with warmth. In that moment, I understood just how sensitive Melanie was. Most guys I knew would've given up on her at the Cosmo. But I loved her unconditionally, realizing I would have to go out into the world—for both of us—to protect her from it.

The energy between us shifted after Vegas, and we were becoming a couple. Over the next few weeks, we settled into a daily routine. As she slowly began to take over my office, her suitcase became a permanent fixture. I wanted her work-from-home setup to be as comfortable as possible, so I worked from the living room. This arrangement gave her the privacy she needed for client calls, but I could still hear the growing frustration in her voice as days passed.

"I'm so over this job," she said.

"Your workload isn't that bad."

"I know, but it's soulless work."

"Is the money good?"

"Yeah," she admitted.

"Use it as bridge income until you get your breathwork thing going."

"I'm spending so much money on breathwork," she said, conflicted.

"But you're building something."

"I don't want to be in finance anymore."

"You could always use your dance background and get a job at the Spearmint Rhino," I joked.

"I'd kill it at the Rhino."

"Show me," I challenged.

"Right now?" She said, gauging if I was serious.

She could tell I was.

"Okay, let me wait for the right song," she said with a playful grin.

"Looking in Your Big Brown Eyes" by Bob Marley came on.

"This will work," she said, breaking into a full-on dance routine in the living room.

I hadn't seen her dance since she and Becky's epic dance battle in my garage years ago. Her moves were impressive, but her carefree, radiant spirit stole the show.

Mel was in her element, and watching her light up the room lifted my day.

(scan for video)

The Signs I'd Love Again

June 19 - June 24th, 2024

I dreamed Melanie was shot in the chest. Her naked, rotting corpse lay before me, her skin a morbid green. I cradled her against my bare chest, devastated, when suddenly the wound closed, and her body flushed with color. As life flowed back and she opened her eyes, I opened mine from the beautiful connection to the same painful reality I faced every morning—she was gone.

Sarah had posted a picture of Mel holding her daughter, with the caption: "*Miss you like crazy.*" Her pain was palpable.

After my daily HIIT workout and ice bath, I watched the rest of Brandie's session. When she started singing Erykah Badu's "I'll See You Next Lifetime," I pulled up the song on YouTube.

NEXT LIFETIME BY ERYKAH BADU

Once again, the song amazed me. Badu was one of Mel's favorites, and the lyrics, video, and message aligned. The song was about being taken in this lifetime, and I thought of the ancestral pact Brandie mentioned with Mel's ex. That motherly need to care for him was something she could not escape.

At one point, Erykah sings about being butterflies in the next life, and in the video, a swarm of butterflies surrounds her. I couldn't believe what I was seeing. Given Mel's deep connection to music, it made perfect sense that she would communicate this way.

The synchronicities continued. That evening, Liz texted a screenshot of a message from a family friend:

"*Later this summer, I plan to walk the Camino de Santiago, a pilgrimage. Along the route is a Catholic shrine where pilgrims leave simple rocks, shells, and the like to honor those lost. With your blessing, I would be honored to carry and place one for Mel."*

I wrote back:

"A couple of months ago, Mel and I watched 'The Way,' where Martin Sheen walks the Camino in memory of his son who died there. She was fascinated by the pilgrimage. Leaving one of her breathwork stones would be perfect... maybe even a journey for you, Liz."

It felt like a clear message, but Liz's lack of response suggested I was alone in believing the universe was communicating.

The next morning, another sign—a text from my first love, Molly Koch, checking in. The timing couldn't have been more significant. I was packing for a trip to Ubud for a Reiki session with a healer named Melani Koch— spelled like one of Mel's nicknames but pronounced Melanie. Her name carried both of theirs. *Another piece of the puzzle.*

The first thing I noticed when we started the session:

I am physically attracted to this woman.

I poured out my story, trying to help her understand the trauma I had experienced. She shared that she had lost her mother at thirteen and spoke about the metamorphosis of a butterfly.

"The death of a caterpillar is the rebirth of a butterfly. Her death created a rebirth in you, and you are at the beginning of a beautiful process. It is hard to appreciate fully because of the grief, but it is okay to acknowledge the beauty in what is happening."

"She was my butterfly... that was my nickname for her," I said, recognizing the irony.

"What is your intention for the session?" she asked, reminding me of my first breathwork session with Mel.

"I guess I'm looking for clarity on what is next. I have been in the nightlife business for a long time, but I don't want to go back to that now.

I have been thinking about continuing her breathwork journey to help people struggling with trauma and addiction.

Starting over means giving up my livelihood, but I have a database I can market to when I'm ready."

"There is power in introducing breathwork to your network," she said. "Okay, let's get you on the table."

I hopped up, and she covered my eyes.

"I am going to wrap you in a cocoon of safety, confidence, and clarity," she said, reminding me of when Brandie told me that Melanie wanted to wrap me in a cocoon and that love was not beyond my reach.

Wow... I am emotionally attracted to this woman as well.

At that moment, I knew I would be able to love again. I felt the warmth of her energy as her hands hovered just above my body, focused mainly on my legs. When the session ended, she asked how I was feeling.

"It felt like ants were crawling down my legs."

"As you may have noticed, I was working around your legs, trying to pull in extra grounding. That was your energy moving. Your crown chakra and third eye are wide open, but your root, sacral, and solar plexus chakras are not. Your chakras should be balanced."

I thanked her and went to the restaurant in Yoga Barn. The energy was incredibly calming, and I poured creativity into my journal for five hours.

"People are looking to escape the noise, the news propaganda and social media, the daily pressures of survival, and unfulfilling jobs. They use drugs and alcohol as an outlet, but deep down, they are searching for something greater. I can be the conduit to introduce them to that something."

Clarity struck. Retelling my story would be exhausting. Instead, I would let my written words speak for us. The book could serve as a bridge for those ready to shift from a place of heaviness to lightness and transformation. I emptied my head for five hours, and then the title came to me: *One Year with My Soulmate.*

The following day, I left Ubud early to avoid traffic and returned to Bingin in time for the 9 AM HIIT class at BTC. At Cashew Tree, I searched Instagram for my Reiki healer and found her post titled *Signs "Your Body Is Saying No."* One sign was being stuck in mind loops, which Mel often experienced. Another was feeling anxious, something I frequently was with her.

Brandie once said butterflies could be a red flag. *Had I missed the sign?* I was incredibly nervous when we first met, and that anxiety lingered for years. Even on our first date, I was attacked by fleas. Curious, I looked up their symbolism.

"Fleas appear as guides to remind us to care for ourselves and be vigilant. If we neglect self-care, we risk harm physically, emotionally, and spiritually."

I texted Brandie:

"Was Melanie a mirror for me, reflecting what I was not, just as her ex was for her? Was she my soulmate, or did our one-year connection serve its purpose?"

Brandie replied:

"Before I respond or attempt to tap in, I would love for you to do whatever practice you need to get into state. Ask these questions and write down the answers. I feel like I am here to support Mel's transition, but somehow, I am also here to help you lean into all that you are becoming."

I struggled as I left the Cashew Tree, questioning the book's title. My smoothie spilled all over my motorbike. Thankfully, a kind Australian woman helped me clean it up.

The spill felt like a message from the universe telling me to back off. At the hotel, I looked up its spiritual meaning.

"Spills challenge us to embrace the unknown with grace. As liquid flows without form, our lives are open to unexpected twists. Spilling can also be an unconscious release of inner turmoil, a sign that it's time to clear negative energy and regain clarity."

I took Brandie's advice and that passage to heart. It had been days since I last practiced breathwork, consumed by the book. I decided to breathe on it.

After my 28-minute meditation, I considered turning off Spotify to ask my yes-or-no questions, but my intuition said to let it play. This time, there were no commercials, just seven songs, each carrying a message.

My chakras buzzed as the first track started—Mel was telling me to pay attention.

BIRTH BY EMORY HALL & TREVOR HALL

Though our first actual date was May 16, 2023, Melanie did not consider us a couple until August, marking exactly ten new moons together. As a Scorpio and a water sign, she ultimately had my heart.

I was determined to help turn her dream into a reality, believing that doing so would bring her solace and purpose while helping others heal.

Then she stopped breathing.

When she started using Adderall again, her dream shifted. She longed to return to the chaotic codependency she mistook for love.

In the early hours of a spring morning, she texted to say she was coming over to pick up the last of her things. Neither of us had any fight left.

She left with my shotgun in her hands, shattering her earthly body, the sliding glass mirror behind her, and my dream of our future together. It left me in devastating pain.

I was reborn in her dying. The magic of our journey continues as she guides me from the spirit world, mending my aching soul as we build this mountain together.

BREATH BY ZACH WIRCHAK

The song had no lyrics, but the message was in the title. I hadn't practiced breathwork in two days. The song felt like a reminder:

"I know you're working hard on the book, but don't forget to breathe."

DARLING BY BEAUTIFUL CHORUS

The powerful lyrics left me weeping. *"Keep your head up, Beau."* She urged me to stay strong through the stormy weather, to embrace the energy of my beautiful soul, and to trust that the sunshine would return as long as I didn't give up.

ATTRACT BY EQUANIMOUS, RUBY CHASE, BLISS LOOPER, OPUS

This was a message of clarity, strength, and confidence, the cocoon Melani wrapped me in during our Reiki session. Mel encouraged me to lean into my gifts, reminding me I had all the tools to manifest my dreams. I envisioned lying in the grass, breathing with hundreds of people and butterflies.

OH LOVE BY AYLA NEREO

Oh, love was brutally honest for us.

I knew she was at peace, but she carried sadness, aware that those she loved were hurting, including me. I had been torn to shreds, rethinking my entire existence.

The song's final line, *"This is all you asked for,"* suggested that this may have been our agreement before coming to earth. This possibility was still difficult to fathom.

But Mel's messages kept coming, reminding me that the ripple effect of her death and my rebirth would leave a lasting imprint.

HEALING BY BLISS LOOPER - INHANA - EQUANIMOUS

This song had no words, but when I looked it up on YouTube, the image showed a butterfly in a field with purple flowers, reminding me of the ones Brandie mentioned.

It felt connected to the other wordless song, "Breath," carrying the message to keep breathing to heal.

Maybe she was creating a playlist for *Butterfly Breathwork*.

MOTHERS BY EMORY HALL & TREVOR HALL

I envisioned the sensation of butterflies, the same ones that made us dance with the idea of love and a life together, drawing us back to each other for nearly a decade.

Yet I was broken, carrying the weight of a thousand lifetimes of heartbreak after spending my life searching for her.

Now she was at rest, free from pain, meeting master souls and learning all they had to teach.

After "Mothers," the commercial that should have aired fifteen minutes earlier finally played, ending our communication. I fell into a deep sleep, cradled in unseen protection.

The next morning, I returned to BTC for my tenth HIIT fitness session in thirteen days. A young woman with a 444 tattoo on her ankle caught my attention. 444 had been showing up frequently, and 44 was my college jersey number. It turned out to be a fantastic session, my best yet.

After class, I saw Jake at the check-in desk and decided to ask him about the song I kept hearing.

"What's the name of that song you always play to start stretching at the end of class? It's something like, '*I'm glad my last dance was with you.*'"

Jake immediately knew what I was talking about. "Oh yeah." He pulled out his phone and added, "It's called 'Last Dance' by Montell Fish."

I thanked him and hurried to Cashew Tree, snagging the last table by the cashier. A line had formed, and at the end stood another Aussie with a *444* tattoo on his tricep.

"Excuse me, what does your *444* tattoo mean?"

I expected it to be an Australian area code, but he said, "Oh, it's just my favorite number, mate. But I've heard there's some spiritual significance."

I placed my breakfast order and went to grab my phone and wallet from my bike. As I approached, I saw the woman with the *444* tattoo on her ankle chatting with some friends.

"Excuse me, what's the significance of the *444* on your ankle? There's a guy in line with the same tattoo on his tricep."

"It means an angel is watching over you."

My heart skipped a beat. "Wow," I said. "Ah... my girlfriend committed suicide a month ago, and I feel like she's watching over me."

She stared at me for a moment. "I have goosebumps," she said. "Can I tell you something? I had a boyfriend who killed himself. I was working with mediums and having heaps of signs."

I felt my emotions welling up and asked her name.

"Bella," she replied.

I thanked her and made a quick exit before the tears could fall. Eating in silence, I realized my life would be so much different when I pulled through this. The experiences were multiplying, and I wondered who would believe me, but knowing someone else had been through something similar made it easier to hold onto.

After breakfast, I went to Santai. In the changing room, I played Last Dance.

LAST DANCE BY MONTELL FISH

The song transported me back to the last year of her life, and the two weeks we spent in Europe, fulfilling her dream of visiting Italy.

It ended with, "*And darling, how could you know me so well? That's where I, like, fell in love with her. Like, after the first moment I've seen her.*"

I loved her unconditionally from the moment I laid eyes on her, and that love never wavered.

I wiped my tears and spotted Bella across the grass. I had a feeling she'd be there—she usually was after the workout. Then I heard Mel's voice: "*Go talk to her.*"

She was talking to a friend, but I approached anyway.

"Hey, I wanted to finish our conversation and hear more about your experience. I had some strong emotions come up and had to step away."

"I totally got that."

She shared that after losing her boyfriend, she had set an intention to move to Bali to become a trainer and partner in a fitness business, which was now manifesting for her.

I shared my story with her and told her I was writing a book with a plan to create our *Butterfly Breathwork* Retreat.

"I'm not much of a reader, but I'm definitely going to read your book. Be kind to yourself, Beau, and keep coming back to class."

The breathwork at night amplified my ability to process all the signs. Before bed, I tried a session on my own—no electronics, no guide, no music. Just me, my breath, and Mel's scent on her scarf draped across my eyes. The singular focus led to a strong vibration. I slowed to a gentle inhale through my nose and began talking to Mel.

"You always used to ask me what love is and how I knew I loved you. I knew because whenever you needed me, no matter what I was doing, I'd put it down and hold space for you. And it was a lot for me. We spent so much time inside your head, searching for comfort, reassurance, and confidence, and we usually found it.

I didn't need much in return, but I was always there. And I would have been there on that last day if I'd known then what I know now. All you had to do was ask. You were my everything, the reason I was excited to wake up and face life every day. And even now, I continue to hold space for you after you're gone."

As I formed the next line in my mind, *I loved you so much, and I still do*; all my chakras lit up as strong as ever, and I felt an energetic shift in my voice box. Instead of *I loved you*, what came through was "*I love you*," in a low, raspy voice that was not mine.

But my original thought remained, and my voice carried on as I intended:

"…so much, and I still do."

She had used my voice box to communicate.

"I can feel you," I said as the energy continued to rush through my body. "I love you too!"

Can We Move Here?

September 24th - October 5th, 2023

Mel was ecstatic as the wheels touched down at Denver International Airport. A friend had raved about Crested Butte, and she was dying to visit. Her enthusiasm spiked when we picked up the Jeep Grand Cherokee I rented.

"You're so hot in a Jeep."

I laughed, appreciating the compliment while recognizing it as another jab at my Prius.

As we passed Red Rocks in Morrison, Mel shared a story about attending a concert there with friends.

"We took a party bus from Denver, and everybody was on Molly."

"Did you take any?"

"I didn't know them very well, and I'd never done it in public before. One time, I did so much with my ex in Joshua Tree, trying to keep up with him, that my eyes rolled into the back of my head, and I went into convulsions. Definitely didn't want to have that kind of experience at the show."

"Did you go to the hospital?"

"No, thank god, but it was really scary."

Passing through Evergreen, I told Mel that my Grandpa Marty had lived there and shared some of my oldest memories. The drive through the mountains was stunning, winding through old mining towns, rugged terrain, and wide-open high plains. Mel DJed, singing along to Ray LaMontagne, Hiss Golden Messenger, Hozier, and Chris Stapleton.

We followed a dirt road into town, packed with character and breathtaking views. Turning onto the street leading to our Airbnb, we looked down into a gulch where a stream ran through a meadow of golden Aspens, their leaves shimmering in the sunlight.

"Look at how pretty that is," I said.

"It's incredible. I love it here," she said, snapping a video and posting it to Instagram with the caption: *I'll stay here.*

The Airbnb was equally impressive. The back deck offered a spectacular view of Crested Butte.

"Can we move here?" she said, taking it all in.

While we made dinner, I put Chris Stapleton on Pandora. She prepped the salad while I grilled the fish.

A familiar song came on, "Keep The Wolves Away" by Uncle Lucius. Although Mel was the singer, I couldn't help but sing along to the parts I knew. As the chorus dropped, I slid into the kitchen where she was preparing the salad and belted out, *"He fought like hell to keep the wolves away."*

It brought a smile to her face. I was always hypersensitive to her energy and how hard she worked to stay grounded.

Before bed, we did a gratitude meditation. Mel saged the room, and we held hands as we eased into pranayama. A strong vibration coursed through me, almost as if her hand was an extension of mine. As I slipped into a translucent state, I remembered David's words: "you don't need psychedelics to have a psychedelic experience." While I didn't see the green goddess as I had the time we took mushrooms, it felt as though we were a singular organism, deeply connected.

The next morning, I asked Mel how she slept.

"You woke me up a bunch of times last night. I know you're a big guy, but if you could be a little gentler getting in and out of bed, that would be great," she said.

"I'm sorry. This altitude is kicking my ass, and I'm all stuffed up."

At nearly 9,000 feet above sea level, Crested Butte was no joke. While Mel seemed unaffected, she was tuned in to the fact that I was.

"You need to stay hydrated," she said, reaching for a packet of Liquid I.V.

Mel never went anywhere without water and was my electrolyte fairy the entire trip, always ensuring I was okay.

164

Our hike would show how differently we moved through the world that day. Mel liked to stop and greet the trees, and while the trail was adorned with beautiful wildflowers, I still wanted to push the pace.

"It would be nice if we could hike together," she muttered.

"You could pick it up a little," I suggested. "I'd like to get a workout."

"Can't you just enjoy nature?"

"I like to do both," I countered.

"Do you think we're compatible?" she asked.

"Why? Because we have different hiking styles?"

"What makes you so sure about us?"

"It's not always easy, but I want to be with you. Relationships take work, patience, and sacrifice from both partners. I'm willing to do that for you."

That seemed to reassure her.

"If you want to go ahead, you can."

"I'll wait for you at the top, and we can walk down together."

I jogged up the trail, working up a good sweat. When I reached the service road where the path ended, I turned back to reconnect with Mel.

"You know what I like best about this hike?" she said.

"What's that?"

"I haven't had to pick up any trash. I love it here."

On the descent, we crossed a herd of deer. They paused, watching us, and I locked eyes with the mother. In that silent exchange, we shared a quiet understanding and a respect for each other's space in the stillness of nature.

"Look at how beautiful they are," Mel said.

"How cool is this?"

That evening, we had dinner at an Indian restaurant with a stunning outdoor patio overlooking the mountains. It was the perfect setting for our first picture, a quiet milestone we shared with our families.

"I could really see myself living here," Mel said.

"I could picture you with a breathwork studio in town," I replied. "People would probably love it."

"That would be amazing. Would you ever move here?"

"The altitude is tough for me, but if everything falls into place, I'd be open to it."

We walked hand in hand through town to the Majestic movie theater for the Crested Butte Film Festival and watched *Biosphere*, a comedy about the last two men on Earth. We shared a bag of popcorn, stealing glances at the ridiculousness of the film as one of the men mysteriously transitioned into a woman so they could have a baby. After the movie, we drove back to the house and curled up by the fire pit under the full moon.

My walls were completely down, ready to cap off our most romantic day yet.

"Give me your hand," I said. She did, and I squeezed it three times.

"Now you squeeze twice."

She followed my lead; then, I gave her one last strong squeeze.

"What does it mean?"

"Three squeezes for '*I love you*,'" I said, "one for each word. Two for '*How much*?' and one big one for '*This much!*'"

"That's really sweet."

"My dad taught me that when I was a kid."

She sat with it for a moment, then said, "Hey... I don't think I'm ready for that yet."

My heart dropped. The warmth from the day was gone.

"No problem."

I wanted to leave. I needed space.

"I'm tired. I'm gonna go to bed."

"Okay. I'm going to stay out here with the moon a bit longer."

I locked myself in the guest bedroom and let out months of frustration. I had given her my best, but it never felt like enough.

Fifteen minutes passed before I heard her voice.

"Beau, where are you?"

"I'm down here."

She tried to open the locked bedroom door. "Wow, you're locking me out?"

"I need some alone time."

"I want to talk to you."

"I'm not ready to talk right now."

"Okay."

An hour later, I took a deep breath. I wasn't going to let this ruin our trip. I knocked on the master bedroom door.

"Mel, please open the door."

I got into bed with her and fell asleep.

Over breakfast the next morning, she asked, "Can we talk about last night? I don't like letting things linger like that, and I think communication is important in a relationship."

"I'm sorry, but I needed some time to process my emotions and didn't want to say something I might regret."

"Okay, I get that."

"What I shared with you last night meant a lot to me. After what I thought was an amazing day, I felt safe enough to teach you that. I wasn't asking for you to say you love me back, but dismissing it the way you did really hurt my feelings. I'm trying really hard here, Mel, but it makes me want to pull away."

"I'm sorry. I need to get better at receiving, and I don't want to push you away. I want you to know that I love what we're building, and I really do appreciate you."

"You tell me you appreciate me and are grateful for me, but I need to feel it, Mel. This relationship always seems to be about your needs, how you're doing, what's going on inside your head, and me working on issues that you have with me."

"You're right. You do hold a lot of space for me, and I'm grateful for you."

"Then show me."

A sensual look crossed her face as she approached me. She began kissing me, but when I leaned in to return her embrace, she playfully pushed me back and dropped to her knees. As I gazed out at the beauty of Crested Butte Mountain, we shared an unexpectedly magical moment.

Riding high on her affection, I carried that energy into leading our morning workout at the Elevation spa before unwinding in the sauna. Ready for lunch, we made our way to A Daily Dose, a charming coffee shop with an acoustic stage. The owner saw our CU gear and mentioned that her son went there.

"We're headed to Boulder tomorrow for the USC game," I said.

The talk about the game got me excited.

"I kind of want a beer," I told Mel.

"Do it! I think I'm gonna have a cappuccino today."

When it arrived, she lit up with childlike excitement, slurping the foam just like she did with the oysters.

We spent the rest of the afternoon shopping. Mel wandered in and out of stores while I turned the mountain backdrop into a playful photo shoot as we explored the neighborhood. She fell in love with a yellow Crested Butte sweatshirt, and after seeing how excited she was when she put it on, I offered to buy it for her. It would become one of her favorites over the next couple of months.

Crested Butte was great, but I couldn't help feeling excited for our weekend in Boulder. The city was buzzing, and the energy was contagious.

Friday night, we joined some college friends for dinner. My buddy Clark, with his offbeat humor and larger-than-life personality, had Mel in stitches the entire time.

On our way home, she mentioned that my friend's wife had told her she had never seen me with a girlfriend before.

"She told me I must be special."

"You are special," I replied. "I've been waiting for this for almost ten years."

"How can you be so sure about me?" she asked.

I locked into her eyes and smiled, seeing what I had always seen.

"I just am."

The next morning brought game-day excitement. I looked forward to sharing another first with Mel, the walk along Boulder Creek to the stadium for the tailgate.

I expected her usual morning cheerfulness, but something was off.

"Is everything okay?"

"I need to stop by a store," she said, her tone secretive.

I knew exactly what she meant. She had gone off birth control a year ago and hadn't had her period in months. Mel made a quick stop at Safeway before meeting me at the tailgate, where we had a quick hello with some of my teammates before heading into the stadium.

The atmosphere at Folsom Field was electric. The stadium buzzed with a sold-out crowd under the scorching sun. Mel was a trooper, fully engaged in the game's twists and turns. Even with the loss, Colorado had covered the spread, and I pocketed some extra cash, feeling lighter as I walked away. Riding the wave of good vibes, I hailed a pedicab to take us to Pearl Street.

This might have been Mel's favorite moment in Boulder. Her matinée smile lit up the entire ride, and I pulled out my camera to capture a video of her jo

(scan for video)

My gambling luck continued at a sports bar on Pearl Street. While I caught up with friends, Mel took a break from football to shop downtown.

We reunited for sushi and then returned to our hotel for an outdoor concert with classic rock cover bands. We danced in the grass at the foot of the mountain, its towering peak looming behind the stage. The night was filled with deepening connection and unforgettable kisses.

The next morning was Mel's day. We wandered Pearl Street for a cappuccino and then browsed the shops until she found a pair of cowboy boots she loved. Her new coffee routine seemed to energize her. When we got back to the hotel, she jumped into bed, turned on her vibrator, and invited me to join her. It was a refreshing side of her that I hadn't seen much of in our relationship.

The intimate connection fueled my excitement to show her Chautauqua Park for our best hike yet. We wound the rugged trails into the Flatirons, Boulder' iconic rock formations. This was her day to lead, and she had a pep in her step. Upon settling at a lookout point, staring out over town, she suggested something that caught me off guard.

"I guess I could move in." The idea made me nervous, but I was open to it if it gave her stability.

"It would give you a chance to build your breathwork business in LA."

"We'd need to get rid of that bed, though."

"You can do whatever you want with the bedroom. I want it to feel like your place, too."

Things weren't perfect, but they were progressing, and aside from the one mishap in Crested Butte, I settled into bed that night feeling good about what we were building.

Around midnight, Mel got up to use the bathroom.

"Someone's trying to break in."

I jumped out of bed. A strung-out homeless man yanked our door handle, then moved to the next room. I called the police and watched through the window as he tried every door on the property. When the officers pulled into the parking lot, he slipped into the shadows and disappeared from my view.

Mel sat up in bed, wide-eyed. "Is he gone?"

"Yeah," I said, but I wasn't sure I believed it.

She was too shaken to go back to sleep. I checked the door, double-checked the window locks, then scanned the parking lot one last time before climbing into bed.

Neither of us slept well. By morning, coffee was the only thing that made sense. Mel had been strict about avoiding alcohol and caffeine, but coffee seemed to be quietly slipping back into her morning routine.

After settling into our next Airbnb in Breckenridge, we went into town for lunch.

"I think I'm gonna get another cap," Mel said.

"Are you sure?"

"I'm on vacation; I can have a little fun."

It was just coffee.

Snow flurries began to fall, setting the tone for a romantic walk around town. We bought some free-range buffalo beef jerky from a street vendor, which we both agreed was the best we'd ever had.

As we passed a realtor's office, Mel suggested, "We should look at some houses while we're here."

I laughed.

"What?" she said.

"You're really pushing this Colorado thing, huh?"

"I'm just saying, it's so peaceful here."

We continued along the creek trail, but the snow was unusual this time of year, and we weren't dressed for the cold.

"It's a little chilly," Mel said. "We should head back to the car."

"Have you spent much time in the snow?"

"Not really."

"You sure you can handle the cold in Colorado?"

"There's only one way to find out."

"I just don't want to end up buying a house and starting a family out here, and then you decide you miss your family and the weather in California and want to move back."

"We'll cross that bridge when we get to it."

"I'd want to be fair to the kids. If we moved back, it would have to be a family decision."

"If there's enough love around them, they'll be fine."

I liked that response. It was genuine, and she was right. If there was enough love, it shouldn't matter.

"How do you see finances working out?" she asked.

"I haven't thought about that."

"I think it's an important conversation if we're going to have a family together someday."

"I guess it would depend on the dynamics of the relationship. Raising a family is a partnership, and I would view finances as a partnership as well."

"That makes sense," she said. "I'm glad we're on the same page."

That evening, as the snow continued to fall, we settled into the hot tub.

"What're you hiding under that top?" I joked.

"Some titties," she replied playfully.

"You should take it off," I suggested, moving closer.

"I just want to connect with you."

"Haven't we been doing that all day?"

"You kind of ruined the moment."

It was apparent she wasn't in the mood, but instead of being honest, she blamed me for ruining the moment. Frustration simmered, and suddenly, a hot tub was the last place I wanted to be.

"I'm getting hot. I'm going to get out."

"Me too," she replied. "Would you mind getting me a towel?"

I wrapped her up and took a cold shower before joining her in bed. There was a disconnect I hadn't yet figured out. Still, the trip marched on. After a solid night's rest, we let it go.

The next morning, I had a podcast shoot, so I booked Mel a spa day. When she returned, she was glowing.

"That was exactly what I needed. How was the shoot?"

"Perfect timing," I said, pulling it up on YouTube. "Clark was hilarious."

Still amused by his antics at dinner in Boulder, she settled in beside me, eager to watch. She was both supportive and genuinely entertained.

That night, we had dinner with my scholarship donors, Mr. and Mrs. Z, who had been like second parents to me in Colorado. Mr. Z and Mel connected over finance while she and Mrs. Z delved into wellness and breathwork. I sat back, watching her bond with two people I cared deeply about.

On the way home, Mel smiled. "I'm really happy about what we're building."

"I feel the same way."

"I'm so excited for Denver tomorrow."

The next day, we wandered Larimer Square, a charming pedestrian street lined with barrel flower pots and historic brick buildings. Mr. Z had recommended lunch on the patio at The Capital Grille. Mel was at home, soaking in the mountain sunshine.

"Do you think Mr. Z could give me a job if we moved here?"

"Probably, but I thought you wanted out of finance?"

"I mean, if it meant I could move to Colorado."

This was new. She was so desperate to move that she was willing to stay in finance—something she had spent months trying to escape. I didn't understand how running away from LA would fulfill her.

"How's your website coming along?"

"I haven't started it."

"Why not?"

"I don't know. I don't feel like I'm offering enough. I want to get some sound bowls and take sound healing workshops."

"You can add that later. Get the breathwork thing going first. Most people have never experienced it. There's a niche there for you to capitalize on."

"You're right. I'm going to work on the website next week."

I wanted to believe her, but was growing weary of her procrastination.

We checked into the Westin in Westminster. That afternoon, I realized our physical intimacy only ever happened during the day. It struck me as unusual, but I was grateful for it when it did.

That evening, we walked across the street to catch a movie. *Oppenheimer* was a mistake.

"This movie is really intense," she said, gripping my arm like she had during *Mystère* in Vegas. Each explosion made her squeeze tighter, and I noticed her eyes close during the nuclear tests.

This time, I suggested we leave before it was over. Sleep came easy that night, and I was starting to understand how to move with Melanie.

The next day, on our way to the airport, she looked over at me.

"Hey… Thank you for a great trip."

Her gratitude was always so sincere.

I smiled, reaching for her hand, the weight of the past two weeks settling in. I hoped it was the beginning of something concrete.

The Note She Never Left

June 25th, 2024

When I first heard "Darling" by Beautiful Chorus, Sarah came to mind, and something inside kept telling me to text her about it: *"I think Mel wanted me to share this with you."*

"That's our song. I told Mel I had Beautiful Chorus on repeat when I was pregnant by myself in the hospital."

"That's incredible. She always said, 'I want to connect with you.' Now we're connecting in a way I've never experienced."

"I'm so glad you're having these powerful connections and conversations with her. I miss her so fucking much."

"Love you, B. Have you tried breathing yet?" I asked, knowing that was how I had helped Katie, John, and her mom connect with her.

"No breathwork yet. No huge connection either. I know I should."

Guilt crept in. Messages came to me constantly, quiet reassurances that Mel was near. But Britt? She was grieving with a newborn and a two-year-old who needed her constant attention.

I wanted her to forge her own connection and sense of comfort—I believed Mel did too. I knew breathwork could help, but I also understood her fears. Melanie had spoken so often about dark entities, and Sarah worried about what else might come through if she opened that door.

Brandie had been guiding me, offering comfort in voice notes and texts. So, I passed on her words:

"You can set boundaries. Only messages of love and light, nothing else. Communication and breathwork are blessings, not burdens. We are far stronger than spirit."

I sent her Brandie's number.

"Amazing. Thank you for this comfort and support. Ugh... so sad."

I wished I could do more. My healing routine was working, but I only had to worry about myself. I could only imagine how overwhelming this must have been for her.

That morning, after a pre-workout smoothie at Cashew Tree, I stored my things in the moped. A white flower with a yellow center had landed perfectly in the slot between the seat and the body of my bike as if someone had placed it there.

As I walked into BTC, "Something in the Orange" played again. Another sign. Mel was showing off, ensuring I knew the flower was from her.

I recognized the next song but couldn't place it. It had that gravelly Chris Stapleton feel and looped through my workout, clinging to the edges of my mind. Even as I rode through the jungle, the engine's hum and thick island air couldn't shake it loose.

As I pulled up to Santai, my fixation momentarily broke. A mother hen with five baby chicks wandered toward me, four black and one white.

I immediately thought of Liz and her five kids. I recorded it and sent it to her.

"Mama hen looking after her five chicks. Four black ones for the girls. The white one for Jimmy. A lighter sign but so powerful."

She replied almost instantly.

"Thank you, Beau! I miss her so much, and it still seems unreal. We will never be the same. Love you."

"No, we won't," I wrote back. *"She was the most special person to ever come into my life. I miss her dearly."*

Liz responded, *"She was very special, and I'm so sorry you lost her. We all lost her."*

I left an exclamation point on her text, then paused. Something wasn't sitting right.

The white chick wasn't Jimmy.

That was Mel. She was still here even though we couldn't see her. She was the white angel chick now.

I thought about sharing my new discovery with Liz but decided to let it be. Instead, I dove back into my song search, determined to figure out the Chris Stapleton track I had heard at the gym. After listening to about twenty songs, I finally came across "Broken Halos." As it began playing, a rush of wind appeared out of nowhere. The moment it ended, the wind stopped.

It felt like something, though I wasn't sure what.

Still, I'd had enough. I stepped away for my ice bath, figuring the song would eventually come to me.

When I returned to the hotel, I put on Chris Stapleton's Pandora station while catching up on work, hoping the lingering track would surface.

What happened next was extraordinary. Time stood still as twenty songs played in succession, each one feeling deliberately chosen to spark a memory of our journey together or offer encouragement to keep moving forward through the pain. This was the beginning of the suicide note she never left. I began taking notes as they played, capturing the memories and meanings they evoked.

BROKEN HALOS BY CHRIS STAPLETON

Mel was announcing her presence—the white angel who had come down from the heavens during the windstorm to help show me the way. She had been a butterfly ready to take flight but chose to fold her wings on this life. I was not meant to ask why I lost her but to move forward with her angelic guidance.

LOSE CONTROL BY TEDDY SWIMS

This was the song I had spent all morning searching for. She used to sing it whenever it played, and more than once, I had mistaken Teddy Swims for Chris Stapleton, just as I did earlier that day at the BTC.

It marked the end of her life.

I always encouraged her to focus on the light shining through the forest, taking one step at a time. But the journey overwhelmed her. She wanted everything immediately: the breathwork career and to be madly in love.

She had attempted to pull me into the codependency she mistook for love, sinking her teeth into my skin, testing the limits of our connection like some learned behavior from her past.

She craved intensity. Her therapist's notes revealed she had gone back on Adderall in February. The pills dragged her back into a toxic cycle she could never escape.

She told me she needed no attachments, breaking up with me on May 9th to return to the familiar chaos.

I told her I couldn't promise I'd still be there if she came back. She was an addict when she was with him, and without me, she lost control.

I REMEMBER EVERYTHING BY ZACH BRYAN

She thought getting back on Adderall would ease her mind, but it didn't. It only made things worse. A rotten gut tends to show up as acne—and it did for her.

The night before she passed, on his birthday—they stayed up all night, likely sharing pictures and memories. But by morning, she told him she was psychotic. He was too self-absorbed to show up for her in the way she needed.

Her family had a strange suspicion he said something that pushed her over the edge. I'll never know what strange words came out of his broken mind.

But the cold shoulder I gave her at closing time that day haunted me.

SWEET HOME ALABAMA BY LYNRYD SKYNRD

It took her five days to move her things out of my house. She was conflicted about leaving, explaining she didn't love him anymore. When she woke up the Saturday after his birthday, I believe she wanted to come home to patch things up. But her weakened mental state weighed on her conscience, spinning her into a complete state of despair.

I was busy with work and distant that day. Instead of asking for help and forgiveness, she chose to end her life in our room.

A brand new pair of shoes arrived at my house a week after she passed.

TENNESSEE WHISKY BY CHRIS STAPLETON

She was shifting gears now, acknowledging my support in her healing journey. She loved being loved and always left our talks feeling better about life. But no matter how much she tried, she could never fully stay in that warmth. There was no love for her at the bottom of the Adderall bottle, and she chose to go back to that emptiness.

KEEP THE WOLVES AWAY BY UNCLE LUCIUS

Every day, I woke up excited about the foundation we were building together, with a plan to get us out of Los Angeles, a place I knew she didn't want to be. She was a hyper-empath, and the suffering in the city weighed heavily on her. We escaped whenever we could, traveling all over the world.

She viewed me as her "knight in shining armor," with an understanding that I *"fought like hell to keep the wolves away."*

MIDNIGHT TRAIN TO MEMPHIS BY CHRIS STAPLETON

The next day, June 26th, marked 40 days since she had been gone. I couldn't help but think of the 40-day judgment period, the belief that a soul lingers on Earth for purification, judgment, or preparation for its next destination.

The Chris Stapleton concert also fell on the 40th day.

When I typed *"Chris Stapleton"* into the notes section of my computer, autocorrect changed it to *"Christ Stapleton." Could she resurrect?* The last forty days had been filled with unimaginable moments, but that would truly be a miracle. *Could it happen if I believed?*

I journaled:

"If I believe in miracles,
can I bend space and time?

Can I wake up in a parallel universe?
Can I wake up, and it's all a dream?
Can I wake up, and she's next to me?

Can I wake up in LA without flying home?
Can I wake up in our bed so we can go to the show?

I will pray for this before I go to sleep tonight."

TRAVELER BY CHRIS STAPLETON

For the last three years of her life, she was nomadic, staying with family across Southern California and in Airbnbs. Even after she moved in and I bought her the bed she wanted, she said it was too soon. She always needed an exit.

She moved like a butterfly, landing for a moment, then drifting off again, searching for something she never quite found. Now that she was gone, she was calling back to me to sing her song.

This was also the song Sarah used to announce her service on Instagram.

GIVE ME ONE REASON BY TRACY CHAPMAN

This song speaks for itself. I wish I had called her that Saturday to check on her; it might have been enough for her to stay or ask for help. If she called, it must have been when my phone was dead because I had no missed calls.

She knew I loved her because I always showed up for her, but I held back from saying it, knowing it made her uncomfortable. My stance was clear, but I couldn't chase her.

Instead, I focused on creating a beautiful garden for my butterfly to return to, knowing she might never land for long. Butterflies are meant to be free, and I could only hope she would find her way back when she was ready.

MARY JANES LAST DANCE
BY TOM PETTY AND THE HEARTBREAKERS

Melanie grew up in a good family in Newport Beach. She did well in school, excelling in Dance and Crew. But she felt her dad wasn't around, and her mom made one critical mistake. She didn't know how to support Mel through the sexual abuse. Not as a child. Not later, when Mel tried to heal their relationship as an adult.

She didn't want to grow older. She was over Los Angeles. On her way out, she turned to drinking and partying again, chasing an artificial sense of fun she felt had been missing in recent months.

Her last call before walking into my house was to her ex, likely the worst person she could have reached out to in her fragile state.

She had grown tired of this town. In that moment, she made her exit.

RHIANNON BY FLEETWOOD MAC

Rhiannon was inspired by a novel called *Triad* by Mary Bartlett Leader. The story follows a woman named Branwen, who becomes possessed by a witch named Rhiannon. When I made that connection, all my chakras lit up once again.

Melanie wasn't herself during the last week of her life as she moved her things out of my house. It was as if something else had taken hold of her, pulling her away, one step at a time. She seemed lost to a force beyond my reach, like a woman taken by the wind.

COLD BY CHRIS STAPLETON

There was a coldness that grew between us toward the end of our relationship. I was tired of hearing about her ex. When she said she was going back to him, I told her I was going to sell the Chris Stapleton tickets. She asked what she was supposed to tell her family, and I said, "Tell them you broke up with me." But the line that *"cut her like a knife and put our love on ice"* came when she asked me to hold on to two tickets so we could potentially still go—and I told her, "I'm not sure I'm going to want to go with you after this."

I wasn't going to give her a free pass to explore her feelings for him while holding on to the comfort of knowing I'd still be there. I needed to know she wanted the relationship as much as I did—and she was going to have to work to get it back.

She came over the next day to try to fix things, but the timing couldn't have been worse. I was leaving for the USC graduation party I was hosting that Friday. We had plans to meet on Sunday and work through it, but that never happened.

In her weakened state, she was unable to make it through the weekend so we could talk things through. By Tuesday, when we finally got the chance to meet up, she was already back under his influence. After that, she didn't feel like she had the strength to rebuild the trust she'd broken—and I was distant. Through the lyrics, she was confessing that she didn't know how she was supposed to live without me.

Melanie didn't just break my heart. She shattered it like a rock through a window—with a self-inflicted shotgun wound to her chest. The shock left me reeling, and I'm still clawing my way back.

The hole she left in herself mirrored the one she left in me. And yet, I know this isn't the end. Though she's no longer in the flesh, she isn't gone. She reaches out to me almost every day.

In my fractured heart, I didn't just believe we'd find our way back to each other—I knew we would.

99 PROBLEMS BY HUGO

The devil came for her more than once. I had protected her from three homeless men and the dark entities in Las Vegas. Eventually, she wore me down, pushing me away just as she had feared. She found herself at the same crossroads as three years before.

Her dad called her "99." A perfectionist, she scored 99 out of 100 on everything in school. She graduated high school with honors, earned Magna Cum Laude at the University of San Diego, passed her Series 7, and landed a great job at Merrill Lynch in Santa Monica. Adderall worked for fifteen years until it didn't. Melanie had "99 problems."

In the end, she wasn't herself. When she ended her life, broken glass lay at her feet, along with everything she once held together.

FEATHERED INDIANS BY TYLER CHILDERS

As the song played, I watched two lovebirds mating on my patio—a fitting visual for the first few lyrics.

I always knew Mel had a sensitive soul, but I thought she had moved past her demons. Early in our relationship, my sports gambling was light, but that chaotic energy eventually sank its claws into me. I tried to shield her from it, but gambling had the ability to steal my presence.

I wondered if it made her feel lonely, if the chaotic energy seeped into her, triggering her Adderall addiction. She told me more than once she thought she could control it if she started again—just as I told myself when football season started. When she went back on it, she hid it from me.

I stood by her every step of the way, right up until the day the bullets flew. She left my protection for another man's. I had no choice but to let her go, hoping she would return. And she did. But when I found her, she was already gone.

SIMPLE MAN BY LYNARD SKYNYRD

When we were together, I produced a podcast, built a website, and juggled three events on weekends. A simple life in the big city was no longer affordable, especially if supporting a family was the goal. It demanded constant hustle, which I had. Mel wanted to stop to smell the flowers and greet the trees. I admired her for that.

I wanted so badly to get us out of LA, and I would have, but I was waiting for consistency from her before taking that leap of faith.

She once asked me what I would do without her. I told her I would probably move to Bali and live a simple life. And that was exactly what I was doing.

I woke with the sun to train HIIT fitness, took ice baths daily, wrote, and ended each night with breathwork. It was my healing routine, and it worked for me just as hers once had.

RECKONING BY WHISKY MYERS

This brought me back to my house before I left. I envisioned sitting at my desk, staring into an empty closet where her clothes had once hung, thinking it was what she saw when she went back to my house on the last day. Her empty room and remnants of our relationship sitting on the picnic table.

She was not coming back to me in this life, and that was the only thing I wanted. The thought crossed my mind more than once that I could reunite with her in death.

But there were too many people in my life who loved me. So I chose to move forward, believing that one day, in another life, we would get another chance.

Mel was hiding on the other side, waiting until we could lie next to each other once again.

AND IT STONED ME BY VAN MORRISON

When explaining where the idea for the song came from, Van Morrison recalled an experience from his youth during a fishing trip. On their way home, he and his companions walked through a village and asked an elderly man for some water.

The man gave it to them, stating it came from the stream. After drinking it, Morrison described slipping into another dimension for about five minutes.

It sounded as though the water was laced with LSD or a similar substance.

This narrative could have symbolized various experiences related to substance use, but it had me thinking that she drank some Molly water the night of his birthday.

The come down from MDMA was always tough for me, and if Mel did some the night before, I imagined it only amplified her despair that day, which would have made the "Reckoning" of her empty room and seeing the knickknacks from our relationship on the picnic table even harder for her.

THE COAST IS CLEAR BY DRAKE WHITE

Like the song's title, Mel waited until the coast was clear—for me to go to work so that she could do what she did.

The lyrics were a nudge to live fearlessly, take risks, stay true to my roots, and embrace the unknown.

Mel admired my writing, and it felt like her way of encouraging me to take a leap of faith to tell our story. To do it justice, I had to drop everything else and commit completely.

COLD LITTLE HEART BY MICHAEL KIWANUKA

Mel used to sing this song whenever it came on and the lyrics could not ring truer for what I think she was going through that day. She was too proud to ask for help, not wanting to burden anyone with her pain. She had a strong moral compass and I believe she was riddled with guilt.

Her heart was cold and as she sat next to the bedside table where her things were, the thought, *"I could live or I could die,"* played in her mind. And without knowing that I still believed in *"her and I,"* she chose her exit.

BLUESIDE OF THE MOUNTAIN BY THE STEEL DRIVERS

Her soul then continued on to the resting place described in Dolores Cannon's *Between Death and Life*, a space between worlds where spirits go to release the burdens of their past.

This was also her way of telling me the communication was done for the day as she was ready to return to healing. Before bed, I slipped into breathwork and stayed in that stillness.

"I understand why you did what you did, and I forgive you. If you had reached out, I would have been there.

I should have been there anyway. But I was hurting, too. So, I buried myself in work and took space after five days of emotional exhaustion.

I know you are at peace now. But this is the hardest thing I have ever been through."

Building a Home

October 8th - October 29th, 2023

When we returned from Colorado, Mel was excited to move into my house. We spent the day at Room & Board in Culver City, where I sat back and watched her pick out our new bedroom set with the designer.

"What's the budget?" the designer asked.

"Whatever she wants."

"That could be dangerous," Mel replied.

"I trust you."

She selected a bed with elegant rose gold legs, a stunning white headboard, matching pale wood bedside tables, and an off-white rug. As the bill came to $6,000, Mel's excitement wavered.

"Are you sure?" she asked. "What if this doesn't work out?"

"Then I've got a new bed," I said, brushing it off. "It was time for one anyway."

When we got home that night, we were both in high spirits. I felt like things were turning around for us, so I started dancing around the living room, much to Mel's delight.

As I began to wind down, she urged, "Keep going."

When "Something in the Orange" by Zach Bryan played, I took her hand and helped her off the couch for a slow dance. Lost in the moment, it felt like we were exactly where we were meant to be.

Our bed arrived a couple of days later. Once it was assembled, she met my eyes with a curious intensity. These soul-searching gazes often stretched on for minutes at a time.

"You really do love me," she affirmed.

Her familiar stare was a quiet comfort.

"You're a cute guy," she added.

I wanted to be the hot guy, but I let it slide.

"You're a safe guy," she continued, verbalizing her thoughts.

"I don't want to be the security blanket, Mel," I replied softly.

"It's not that. It's not a bad thing. I just feel really safe around you."

Her affirmations were heartfelt and unfiltered.

"How can you be so sure that you love me?" she asked.

"Because your struggles are mine. Because whenever you need me, I show up for you. Because I believe in you, even when you don't. Because this relationship isn't always easy, but I'm still here. And because I want you to be the mother of my children. I know you're going to be an amazing mom."

Her eyes glistened. "That was really good. What do you need from me?"

"I want you to be happy. When you're sweet, you're really sweet, and it's perfect. I wouldn't mind a little more physical intimacy, but I'm sensitive to your history."

"The sex is getting a lot better."

"I told you it would."

"Thank you for being patient with me."

"Come here," I said, rubbing her chest, my other hand steady on her back as she relaxed into the pressure. Mel loved a good chest rub to settle her nerves it was how we ended most of our long talks.

That night, after her meditation and shower, she tucked herself into our new bed for the first time and let out a joyful yelp. At that moment, everything fe right.

But by Sunday morning, the weight of Saturday's gambling losses had settled in, and I was chasing them. I'd be down five figures if my NFL bets didn't hit. The stress was palpable, and the drinks from the night before weren't helping. When Mel walked in at halftime of the morning games, she studied my face.

"What's the matter?"

"Nothing, I'm just really hungover from yesterday."

"What'd you drink?"

"I got carried away with the espresso martinis."

"Something else is wrong."

Her intuition cut through my facade.

"What's going on?" she pressed.

"I lost a lot of money yesterday."

Her expression almost reflected relief. I was frustrated that I had gotten into this situation, especially on our day together.

"Is the gambling going to be an issue?"

"I'm still up big on the year," I said. "I just hate losing."

"Okay, just making sure it's not something I need to worry about. Thanks for telling me," she said. "You know you can't hide anything from me."

"I know. I just need to sweat it out in the sauna and finish these morning games."

Both my bets hit, turning my Saturday losses into a weekend win and setting a positive mood for date night.

We celebrated our new bedroom set with a meal at Scopa Italian Roots. The restaurant had fantastic oysters, and Mel was thrilled to slurp them down. She even ordered a glass of wine to mark the occasion, though she only took one sip and left the rest for me.

"We still need to get a new comforter," she said, eyeing the room with a vision for change. My navy comforter was nice, but Mel wanted something brighter.

"It would be great to get a matching dresser and a mirror for my makeup, too," she added. "But let's hold off on that for now."

The highs continued as we settled into our seats at the Orpheum Theatre for Ray LaMontagne, whose music was a staple in our house. Mel's favorite song, "I Was Born to Love You," often inspired her to serenade me. When the song began, she excitedly grabbed her camera to capture the moment.

Between songs, Ray told stories. One was about his wife and how she had saved him, which was a lead-in to "Trouble." Mel squeezed my hand and leaned in as the opening chords filled the theater.

"That's the kind of love I want from my husband."

I wasn't looking for someone to save me. I let the thought drift away.

Days passed in a quiet rhythm. Mel settled in, and we fell into step with the little routines that made it feel real. On a rare free afternoon, we set out for a hike in Temescal Canyon.

The trail was littered with trash, and Mel, as always, picked it up as we walked. Flies swarmed my ears and neck, but I brushed them off and tried to stay positive. Afterward, we rewarded ourselves at Moku Sushi in the Palisades.

"This was such a great day," she said with a smile. "We should do this more often."

"I don't love that trail," I admitted, "but it's almost worth it for the sushi."

"The Toro is so good!" Mel exclaimed.

My comment about the hike gave her another reason to mention moving out of LA. The ocean views were beautiful, but we both agreed that the crowded trails made them difficult to enjoy. Still, I wasn't quite ready to make that leap.

My plan to leave the city was still taking shape, and in the meantime, I introduced Mel to my sauna and ice bath routine. In the garage, I had a one-person sauna, and on my patio, I filled an ice barrel with a hundred pounds of ice, chilling the water to 40 degrees. Mel always had me go first, letting my body heat warm the water to a more forgiving 48 before she stepped in.

I aimed to get her to do three minutes in the barrel.

"It's hardest in the first ninety seconds," I said. "Once you get past that, the pain goes away."

Mel let out her cutest yelp as she plunged in.

"It's so cold. Oh my God. Talk to me."

"Imagine yourself floating in the clouds," I advised. "Lose yourself in the purple flowers. Pretend you're that butterfly, flying with the birds."

"How much time do I have left?"

"You're at ninety seconds. How are you feeling? The pain should be wearing off."

"It's still really cold," she said, letting out another playful cry.

I counted down from ten to zero and wrapped her up in a towel as she let out one last triumphant scream.

"That was awesome," I said.

"Are you proud of me?"

"You did great."

Still buzzing from the ice bath, Mel went straight to the kitchen for a snack, meticulously washing and soaking her berries in vinegar to kill mold spores. Her commitment to health went beyond breathwork. She worked with a somatic therapist and an herbalist to heal her nervous system, frequently did juice cleanses, and was now on a rigorous detox after our Colorado vacation, eating only steamed vegetables, nuts, and berries. She ate in small portions spread throughout the day, each meal beginning with a prayer.

"We really need to be mindful of our gratitude toward Mother Earth." I loved this innocent side of her, always showing grace and excitement for the little things.

When her new crystal bowls arrived, she eagerly unpacked them and started practicing.

"I want to take some sound healing courses," she said.

I still sensed she was procrastinating on her website.

"How's your bio coming along?" I asked.

"I'm struggling with it."

"Your story is really powerful. You should be proud of all the healing you've done. It's time to take that next step."

"I just don't feel like breathwork is enough."

"Does David offer anything other than breathwork?"

"No."

"There are so many people who don't even know what breathwork is. You could be the one to introduce them to it."

"I know, but if I do get something going and someone wants private sessions, where would I do that?"

"Do them here. Set up a yurt on the grass the backyard, and if you want to offer additional services, you can use the sauna and ice bath. Then, when you're comfortable with the sound bowls, you can incorporate those as well."

"Maybe," she said. "But we would need a bathroom."

"There's a bathroom in the house?" I countered. "David has clients use the bathroom in his house."

"You're a really sweet guy."

"If you pick up little wins every day, your confidence will grow and the big wins will follow," I encouraged her. "You don't need to build this business overnight. Just make a manageable to-do list before bed. You've got this."

"Thanks for talking to me. I really appreciate you."

I couldn't tell if I was getting through to her. I desperately wanted her to get her business off the ground. Despite a handful of breathwork classes in Costa Mesa, it felt like she was treading water, and I couldn't figure out why.

As we grew closer, Mel let me deeper into her world. On October 22nd, she invited me to her nephew's baseball game in Malibu, a big step for her. It was my first time meeting her oldest sister, Katie, and John, who were like second parents to her. When she wasn't at my place, she often stayed with them.

John offered us sunflower seeds, which I promptly loaded into my mouth. Mel laughed at my impressive stash, which took me back to my Little League days.

Her nephew hit a line drive down the right field line. He beamed, seeing his Auntie Melly in the stands. After the game, we all went out for dinner.

"Please don't let them pay," Mel asked quietly. I slipped my card to the waitress before the check arrived. Mel and her family's appreciation was clear when they saw I had already taken care of the bill.

As we said goodbye, her nephew gave me a big hug. He was a genuinely sweet kid, and I was pleased that he seemed to like me, hoping it would score points with Auntie Melly.

The drive home along PCH was peaceful.

"Thank you for picking up the check."

"They've been really good to you. Today was great. Thanks for inviting me."

"You're a really great guy."

The warmth of the day lingered as we settled in at home. Mel turned to me with a soft smile.

"Do you want to breathe together in our new bed?"

193

After saging the room and using her cleansing spray, we began David's 28-minute meditation. As we held hands, that singular energy rushed through our bodies again. When we finished, Mel said, "I really enjoyed that."

The next morning, I opened my eyes to find her studying me with curiosity.

"How did you get me here? I friend-zoned you so hard."

I laughed at the irony of it, the smirk on her face telling me she was happy to be there.

"Maybe I kind of was a 'douchebag promoter' when we first met. I've changed a lot since then."

"How so?"

"I probably had some narcissistic tendencies, but after the music festival, I experienced what I'd call an ego death," I replied. "I got sober and gained a fresh perspective on life. I no longer care about my image the way I used to, and my circle got smaller. Now, all I want is to build a solid foundation for a family."

"I think I might be going through a bit of an ego death myself."

"Maybe you are."

I felt this was something she needed to navigate on her own.

With her birthday weekend approaching and the Buffs set to face UCLA, the focus turned to celebration. We had dinner at Water Grill on Thursday night with my college teammate Bobby. His drunk friends took over the evening, but Mel handled their rowdy energy gracefully, even finding their antics amusing.

In bed that night, Mel shifted uncomfortably. "Would you be upset if I didn't come to the game on Saturday?"

"Why don't you want to go? We've been planning this for months."

"Football isn't really my thing. Tonight was overwhelming, and I just got invited to a breathwork event that I really want to attend."

I had sideline passes that were impossible to come by, and Mel's pass couldn't be transferred.

"It would mean a lot to me if you came."

"You always take off work for football games. When are you going to take off work and come to a breathwork event with me?"

"When football season is over, I will."

"Okay, I'll come, but just know I'm missing something I really want to go to for this."

"I promise the game will be a lot of fun. People are offering a lot of money for our tickets. They're impossible to get."

During our drive to the Rose Bowl, I buzzed with excitement. Mel was in great spirits, feeding off my energy and fueled by her morning coffee.

"I just want to let you know how much I appreciate you," she said. "I'm excited for today and sorry for being a brat yesterday. I know how much these games mean to you, and I'm glad I came."

After a quick hello to some of my closest college friends, we hit the field. The game was a sellout, rare for the Rose Bowl, and the Colorado sideline was star-studded. I noticed a spark in Mel's eyes as she sensed the significance of the moment.

"Keep your eyes on the field. You never know when the action might come your way," I advised.

Mel stayed engaged throughout the game. I continued to explain the nuances, and she was clearly getting the hang of it. When UCLA pulled ahead, we left early to avoid the notorious Rose Bowl traffic from spoiling her experience.

"I had a lot of fun with you today," Mel said, giving my hand a squeeze.

"Tomorrow is your day."

We listened to the end of the game on the radio, where Colorado scored a late touchdown to cover the spread. I explained to Mel that I had just won my bet, and she was excited for me.

It had been a perfect Saturday. Sunday was Mel's birthday, and we had plans to celebrate in San Diego.

We started early at Sarah's house in Carlsbad, where her husband Dave made us cappuccinos and surprised Mel with an espresso machine, both a birthday gift and thanks for helping with their dogs.

Mel's mom, Liz, arrived and eagerly invited me to an event at her Yacht Club in December, where she was being named commodore.

"That sounds like fun."

"I told Melanie a while ago. You both should come," Liz added.

"Why do you always do this?" Mel asked, clearly annoyed.

"What? It's a big deal for me, and I want all my kids to be there."

"Let it go, Mom," Sarah chimed in.

"He has to work on Saturdays," Mel said, still irritated.

"With this much notice, I could take it off."

"It's going to be a lot of fun," Liz repeated, trying to keep the mood positive.

The tension lingered as more family members arrived. I met Mel's grandmother, who told me a fascinating story about traveling from the Netherlands to Los Angeles through the Panama Canal on a cargo ship with Mel's two-year-old father and his baby brother.

On the drive to downtown San Diego, I asked Mel about her resistance to the yacht club event.

"She's so annoying. I already told her I wasn't going."

"It seems like it means a lot to her."

"The parents of the boy who abused me are going to be there, and I don't want to see them," she replied tensely. "The dad has this really dark energy, and you can see how it's affected his wife."

"I'm sorry, I didn't know that." She was clearly upset. "Did anyone ever confront them?"

"No, and I wasn't the only one. There was another girl, and her family moved to Laguna. I don't understand why I had to live with it. Why wasn't I important enough for us to move? Why couldn't we start over somewhere else?"

"Does she know why you don't want to go?"

"I've told her so many times, but she doesn't listen. She just keeps pushing. I'm trying really hard to heal my relationship with her, but she expects me to just get over it."

I didn't know what else to say. I wanted her birthday to be special, but the conversation fueled some deep-rooted wounds.

"Please keep this between us, okay?" she insisted.

We checked into the Hilton in San Diego, which had a gorgeous bay view. While waiting for our Uber to dinner to meet my sister Kaylie and her boyfriend Josh, I noticed something was wrong.

"What's the matter?"

"This is all moving too fast," she said. "I wasn't ready for this."

"It's just dinner with my sister."

"I wasn't ready for you to meet my family. I'm not ready to meet your sister. I wish we would have waited."

"Waited for what?"

"It's just a lot."

Mel struggled with overwhelming fear and doubt. The best approach was giving her space, though it was challenging at the moment as we were on our way to dinner and the Hozier concert with my sister and her boyfriend.

"Kaylie is great," I said. "I think you're going to like her."

At dinner, I noticed a new tattoo on Kaylie's arm that read, "*Fail Fast.*" She shared a story from one of her surf trips to Costa Rica with *GrlSwirl*. She was struggling to get the hang of surfing when one of the girls, a New Zealander, told her, "You just gotta fail fast, mate."

"That's such great advice," I said.

"What's *GrlSwirl*?" Mel asked curiously.

"It's a women's skateboard collective that hosts surf and skate trips," Kaylie said.

"That sounds so cool. I would love to do something like that!"

"Yes, girl, come to the next one," Kaylie added.

We wrapped up dinner with Happy Birthday and dessert before heading to the show.

"Kaylie is so cool. I love her." Mel's whole mood had shifted.

"She's pretty rad. I love that '*Fail Fast*' tattoo. Such a great mantra," I added.

"I love how she says 'yes, girl.' She has really good energy."

The four of us were fully immersed in the Hozier concert until an intoxicated woman nearby killed the vibe with her obnoxious singing. We quickly found a better spot. Mel sang along sweetly as we swayed to the music, turning the night into another magical musical experience.

Despite another great date, I found it increasingly difficult to gauge where Mel stood. Whenever I felt we were growing closer, she seemed to pull away. It was confusing. I was fully invested, but I knew patience was essential. I kept hoping for the moment when everything would shift—when she would commit as I had.

(scan and click arrows for chapter photos)

The Songs She Couldn't Sing

June 26th & June 27th, 2024

The previous day's song exchange had been intense. Mel needed me that Saturday. I should've checked in. I should've been stronger. Tracy Chapman's "Give Me One Reason," Chris Stapleton's "Cold," and my "*cold shoulder at closing time*" gutted me. It could've been as simple as asking, "How are you doing today?" Maybe she would still be here if I had.

Guilt turned to anger at myself, then towards her, fueling an endless carousel of questions. *How could you do this to me? How could you do this to your family?*

I put on "Last Dance" by Montell Fish and cried out the pain. New songs continued to come through, telling her side of the story and offering support from the divine.

I DESTROY MYSELF JUST FOR YOU
BY MONTELL FISH

She had destroyed herself. That much I knew. Had we made some kind of agreement before this life? The timing felt too perfect. It was the middle of my work weekend. The night before, her ex's birthday. The day before that, she had learned my dad's heart procedure had gone well. And then there was the "*All you asked for*" line from Ayla Nereo's "Oh Love."

Two psychics confirmed her despair. Chris said her serotonin was depleted. Brandie mentioned a little Molly or other drugs may have been used the night before her passing.

Some things weren't meant to be understood, but if this was our soul agreement, her sacrifice had to mean something. My heart pushed me to keep going, to bring her story to life. Her death could not be for nothing.

DRIVE BY INCUBUS

Melanie's journey and my own grief mirrored each other in this song. Fear sat heavy as I thought about starting over at forty-five. It would be so easy to slip back into my old life just as Melanie had. The alternative was to choose water over wine and step into the unknown instead of drowning in comfort.

I had encouraged her with the same advice so many times. "Just wake up and win today." With discipline and hard work, you could shape something new. Now, it was my turn to believe it for myself, knowing she would be with me every step of the way.

SCAR TISSUE BY RED HOT CHILI PEPPERS

The opening lyric cut deep as tears welled up from my soul. It felt as though Melanie was channeling her sadness and the emotional scars she had left behind.

I knew she had a troubled past, and we spent a lot of time navigating her thoughts. I believed she wished she had let me see more than just a glimpse of her struggles, but the depth of her pain was reserved for people like Bear, who lived in Kentucky and was far removed from her circle. She had confided in him about her suicidal thoughts as well as her belief that breathwork was making her gain weight, an idea she got in the bathroom stall.

I didn't realize she was in this much pain. I never thought it would end like this.

UNDER THE BRIDGE BY RED HOT CHILI PEPPERS

Anthony Kiedis wrote this song while battling loneliness and depression during three years of sobriety. While his bandmates kept partying, he struggled to adjust, missing the false comfort of his addictions.

Melanie was two years into her sobriety after quitting Adderall, watching the people around her continue to party. She felt the same loneliness and depression Kiedis did.

The opening line stung—the thought that she sometimes felt she didn't have a partner.

I worked constantly, always telling her it was for us. I wanted her to pursue her breathwork practice so she had something in her life she was passionate about beyond her family and me.

She needed her family's blessing to share her story openly, and she lacked the confidence to build her business on her own. I kept encouraging her, believing it would give her real fulfillment, something lasting, unlike the false excitement her medication once gave her. I laid out a plan for her that I believed would have worked, and I was there to support her on her journey.

Now, all I could think about was how I had not gone all in as her partner.

"I Destroy Myself Just for You," "Scar Tissue," and "Under the Bridge" wrecked me. I turned off the music and threw myself into work, grinding so hard I lost track of time. By the time I left the hotel, I wasn't sure I would make it to the workout in time.

I showed up a minute late, and the class had already started. I expected to see Jake teaching, but it was Bella.

"Today is my first class, guys."

I almost missed it. Afterward, we took a group picture before stretching, and a familiar song played.

SAY YES TO HEAVEN BY LANA DEL REY

I still had reservations about going against Liz's wishes and sharing Mel's story. I knew her family was litigious. But Mel was telling me to let the fear I had fall away—she had her eye on me. And so did God. His court of law carried far more weight than the court of man.

I was witnessing Bella's dream manifest into reality. I reminded myself that sharing Mel's truth was defending her honor, and there was nothing to be afraid of. She would be there to guide me every step of the way.

On the way out, Floyd was playing ball with an Italian guy. He spit his tennis ball at me, which rolled across the grass and up to my feet. I kicked it back to him. The Italian popped the ball into the air with his foot, and Floyd caught it in his mouth.

"Nice catch, Floyd," I said.

"*If you fall, I will catch you. I will be waiting, time after time.*" The lyrics in the gym called back to me through another familiar song.

I was floored by the synchronicity as my eyes welled up.

The music was relentless. It found me in the gym and crept into quiet moments when I wasn't expecting it. I woke up the next morning with Cyndi Lauper playing in my mind like a broken record.

TIME AFTER TIME BY CYNDI LAUPER

The song pulled me back into Mel's world. The mind loops she was trapped in, the memories she couldn't let go of, and the confusion that weighed on her, twisting everything until she no longer knew what was real.

The second verse spoke to our relationship in life and my efforts to help her move forward when she fell behind.

Then, in death, it spoke to the recurring nightmares where she was just beyond my reach, and we were unable to connect.

She vowed that everything would be exposed like a drum beating in time, including the secrets she was forced to keep, tied to the innocence that had been stolen from her.

She was letting me know she would be with me every step of the way, guiding me from the other side.

I was curious what song would come next.

THANK YOU BY DIDO

She fought so hard, but the pain never let up. She didn't want to burden me with how deep her struggle went.

I wept as the chorus played—she was thanking me for giving her the best days of her life. It hit me like she was speaking directly to me.

I worked hard to make our lives easy, fun, and romantic. I wanted loving me to feel like a refuge, not a struggle. Even though she wasn't always able to receive my love, she always made sure I knew how grateful she was.

Hearing those words was exactly what I needed. I was struggling to start the day, and it felt like she was lifting me up at that moment.

BEAUTIFUL LIES
BY TANNER USREY & ELLA LANGLEY

The opening line hit me like a promise. Mel wanted to come back to me.

The song's theme cut deeper. She had been disillusioned by the chaos she mistook for love. She was not in love with him. She was addicted to his darkness. She lied to herself about what I was to her. My love was unconditional, something she did not know how to receive.

She lied about getting back on Adderall in February. She lied about unarchiving photos of them on Valentine's Day.

She said he found her grandmother's ring and reached out, but it was a lie. She showed up at his house unannounced.

She lied when I asked if she had told him we were going to Italy. She lied about practicing breathwork at her sister's.

Then, just like she always said she would, she pushed me away, and I wasn't going to beg her to stay.

She shattered the vision I had for us, making a liar out of me. I believed she was my person. I believed we would have a family and grow old together.

She lied to herself about loving him. That morning, the weight of it all was too much to carry.

THINK I'M IN LOVE WITH YOU
BY CHRIS STAPLETON & DUA LIPA

This song was released the Tuesday after she passed as if it were meant for us.

I asked my dad if he could get it dedicated to her at the Hollywood Bowl, the show I had planned to attend with her family.

Now that she was on the other side, free from the filters that once clouded her view, she could finally see what we shared.

I WAS WRONG BY CHRIS STAPLETON

I had been waiting for her to apologize. I never thought I would receive one, but this was it.

CHRIS STAPLETON'S GREATEST HITS

It was 8 AM in Bali on June 27th as the gates were opening for the Chris Stapleton concert in Los Angeles.

I began this YouTube musical journey with the Cyndi Lauper song she had sent me the day before. Through Dido, she thanked me. Through Dua Lipa and Chris Stapleton, she told me she loved me and apologized for her beautiful lies through Tanner Usrey and Ella Langley.

She made a point of letting me know she was here, giving me Chris Stapleton's greatest hits. It was the closest we could get to attending his concert together.

I was running late and had to give the greatest hits a rest after a couple of songs. I thought class began at 9:30, but it was actually at 9, and I missed it. Cashew Tree was full, so I drove toward Uluwatu to find another spot for breakfast.

On the way, a big green leaf floated down in front of my bike at the parking lot entrance to Alchemy, prompting me to turn in. The property featured a stunning outdoor vegan restaurant, multiple yoga huts, and gravel pathways winding through lush gardens. Next to the restaurant was a great coworking space that had me thinking I'd found a new home to work on my book.

On the way home, I saw a villa with a single word painted on the wall: "Breathe." I heard Mel's voice instantly. When I returned to the hotel, I took it as a sign—it had been a few days since I last practiced breathwork. After my session, I let Spotify run, and our communication continued.

I HAVE BEEN A THOUSAND DIFFERENT WOMEN BY EMORY HALL

The song was a tribute to a woman who had walked through many lifetimes, encouraging her to pay homage to the journey. Everyone who knew Melanie believed she was an old soul. It brought hope that we would get another chance.

EASTERN SUN BY AYLA NEREO

The next song carried the theme of rebirth.

Then came "Darling" by Beautiful Chorus, a song I had only heard once before. It was Mel and Sarah's song. Britt's pregnancy song.

Then, a commercial came on, ending the communication.

Through these three songs, the message was clear. She always said she knew I would be a great dad. Maybe this was how. Maybe Mel would come back to me as my daughter.

The message led me back to Erykah Badu's "Next Lifetime," setting off another chain of songs. Mel hijacked the YouTube algorithm once again, guiding the story in her own way.

DIDN'T CHA KNOW BY ERYKAH BADU

Mel lost her way, caught between emotions that were pulling her in different directions.

Brandie once told me that setbacks are part of healing.

She made a wrong turn, and we'll never know what could have been if she had just made it through that day.

NINE BALL BY ZACH BRYAN

Mel's dad avoided the subject of Adderall.

I could see the weight of unspoken guilt pressing down on him. He used it for work sometimes, but he didn't want to believe it had played a part in losing his daughter.

She started taking it when she was 15. He called her "99" and never stopped betting on her to win.

After being clean for two years, she went back to it. Three months later, she was gone.

THE GOOD I'll DO BY ZACH BRYAN

She always needed reassurance, constantly asking if I was proud of her and revisiting the same pep talks.

She wished I needed her more, often searching my eyes for the truth that I had been looking for her my entire life.

There was no way I could do this without her. I know there were people talking shit about the way she left me, but I didn't care. With her guidance from the other side, she had a chance to create something great with me, bringing her dream to life and giving hope to others who wanted to fight.

SHE'S ALRIGHT BY ZACH BRYAN

Zach Bryan wrote this song wishing his mom were here to see his success.

There was a disconnect between Melanie and her mother, as Mel's vision for breathwork didn't make sense to Liz. Mel wanted her to come to her classes in Costa Mesa, but Liz never did. She even asked me, "Was her breathwork thing a cult?" Liz didn't understand it or Melanie's pain. She needed her mom's blessing to free her secrets from behind the family image so that she could move forward with her new career and tell her story.

Mel was exhausted, and she tried to go back, but ultimately, she gave up.

Now she visits with the moonlight and city lights. Any success I find in this life will never feel the same without her by my side.

I can feel her at times, but I can't look into her eyes anymore. I can't hear her words. I can't rub her chest to calm her down.

And the only lips I get to kiss are behind the glass of a picture frame.

Why did my best friend have to die like that?

SHE TALKS TO ANGELS BY THE BLACK CROWES

When this song came on, I felt like it was meant for my upcoming call with Erin the Angel. I had started writing down questions for her in my journal earlier in the week, but I believed Mel was already answering some of them through the music she was sending me.

Then I heard the line about refusing to talk about addiction in certain company, and I realized we were still on her mom.

I have a good relationship with Liz, but she wants to tell Mel's story as one of mental health rather than addiction. Framing it that way is the safer choice, one that protects the image she wants to portray. But it doesn't peel back the layers to help people understand how it all began. If we choose to let her true struggle remain in the shadows, it won't help anyone, and her death will be for nothing.

THE DAY I DIE BY CHRIS STAPLETON

These lyrics were painfully clear.

She broke up with me on May 9th. By May 13th, she was back with her ex. On May 18th, she came to pick up the last of her things and took her life.

"Chris Stapleton's greatest hits" played again. It felt like Mel was asking me to finish our concert experience.

After a couple of songs, the pain was unbearable. I slammed my computer shut, needing to breathe through it before I could even think about sleep.

To Land a Butterfly

October 31st - December 4th, 2023

My thumb hovered over the *Purchase* button as the clock struck 10 AM. Chris Stapleton at the Hollywood Bowl—Mel's favorite artist. I didn't hesitate. Within seconds, I had six tickets, the maximum allowed, enough for her to invite four family members.

When I told her later that day, her eyes lit up with that unguarded joy I was always chasing, the perfect way to cap off her birthday.

I continued to nudge Mel to start assembling content for her website.

"I need to get some pictures taken," she said.

"Do you have a photographer?" I asked, ready to make a recommendation.

"My friend is going to shoot them. I really want to do a photo shoot in Joshua Tree."

"Let's go out there for inspiration," I suggested, booking us an Airbnb for two days in early November.

As we pulled into town, Mel pointed out the street to a friend's place where she and her ex used to stay. It was another return to memories of late nights on MDMA.

"Would you ever do Molly with a therapist?" Mel asked.

"If you really wanted to, I would. But I don't think it's a great idea for you. I've always had tough comedowns from MDMA, and watching you go into convulsions doesn't sound like fun to me."

"That was only one time, and I took way too much."

As we continued down the dirt road to the Airbnb, I noticed tears streaming down Melanie's face.

"What's wrong?" I asked though a sinking feeling told me I already knew.

"I'm sorry, I'm still grieving my last relationship."

"Maybe Joshua Tree wasn't the best idea," I said, knowing it carried mixed memories of their time together.

That night, we saw Drive-By Truckers at Pappy & Harriet's. I'd heard great things about the place and was excited to check it out. We had barbecue in the sandlot picnic area, but conversation was light. Mel was still in her head.

Inside, the venue was standing room only, packed to capacity. Mel edged closer to me.

"This guy is crowding my space," she muttered.

It was loud, and suffocating.

"Do you want to get out of here?" I asked, already knowing the answer.

The drive home was quiet. Mel stared out the window into the pitch-black desert, the kind of darkness that made the road feel endless. By the time we got back, the night still felt heavy. I made a fire, hoping to ease the tension.

"We should take some mushrooms," Mel suggested.

I still had the chocolate I'd brought to Arrowhead, but I couldn't shake David's words. They stuck with me, feeling like a direct warning.

"Don't you want to go hiking tomorrow?" I asked, hoping to dismiss the idea casually.

"We can do a little bit. Last time was so fun."

"David mentioned in my session that the psychedelic experience can be achieved through breathwork alone, without the side effects. I'm really proud of you and the healing work you've done. I want to keep supporting you on that journey."

"Where is the excitement supposed to come from?"

"Do you not have fun with me?"

"No, I do. I don't know what's going on with me. I'm really struggling right now."

I didn't know what to say. I sat with her in silence, feeling guilty about the beer I was sipping, wanting my presence to be enough.

"I'm going to go breathe."

"Do you want me to join you?"

"Not tonight."

The next day, we took Mel's car into Joshua Tree National Park, giving her the chance to play her music.

"Do you like Erykah Badu?"

"I don't know much about her."

"She's one of my favorites."

Mel continued to DJ, singing along to Janet Jackson, Whitney Houston, and Paula Abdul. Her dance background had shaped her love for their music.

It was my first time in the park. The rugged desert landscape stretched endlessly, with the park's namesake trees twisting along the horizon. The contrast of sharp desert sunlight and the shadowy silhouettes made it one of the most unique places I had ever seen.

"I love the desert energy," Mel said. "It's so peaceful out here."

We caught a stunning sunset at Keys View, surrounded by international tourists speaking various languages. It felt surreal that people traveled from around the world to experience a place just two hours from where I had lived for twenty years, yet I had never been there.

As we watched the sky change colors, Mel turned to me and asked if I had ever been in a relationship dominated by physical intimacy.

"I have, yeah."

"Is that something you think we can develop?" she asked.

"I've been waiting for it," I replied. "I'm just not sure what you need to get there. Are you not attracted to me?" I asked.

"I am. It's not that," she said. "Everything just feels so boring. When I was on Adderall, everything was exciting: work, workouts, sex. Now it's all just blah."

"Is the sex not enjoyable?"

"It is. It's just not the same."

It dawned on me that I might be the first guy she'd been with without the heightened stimulation that Adderall had given her.

"My dad once told me there are two types of love: Eros and Agape.

Eros is the initial attraction, where you can't keep your hands off someone. It's easy to find but quick to fade. Most people who experience Eros first never move on to Agape, so they get stuck bouncing from one physical relationship to the next until the excitement wears off.

Agape, on the other hand, starts as a loving friendship. If that bond is strong enough, Eros can blossom from it, elevating the relationship to much greater heights."

"How long does that take?"

"We've only been dating since May."

"May?" she responded. "We've only been dating since, like, August."

"Wasn't our first date in May?"

"Okay, well, fine, but I wouldn't consider us as a couple until August."

"Based on your timeline, we've only been together for a couple of months," I said. "I'm pretty sure it takes longer than that."

"You're so chill," she said.

"Is that a bad thing?"

"No, I'm just used to more excitement."

I understood that by excitement, she meant chaos. Her heightened sexual arousal often came from pushing me to the brink of frustration, only to apologize afterward. I didn't believe she did this consciously, and I usually diffused the drama quickly. Still, I wanted our intimacy to be built on something deeper than that. I didn't need petty fights to ignite my desire.

On the way back to the car, Mel was visibly disgusted by the empty beer cans littering the walkway. True to form, she took the lead, picking them up and tossing them into the trash.

"I'm telling you, Mother Earth is not happy with us. Humans are so gross. I'm so sick of people ruining the planet," she said, expressing her frustration.

"Mother Earth has been around for 4.5 billion years. It's not her we need to worry about. It's us."

The weight of that thought ended our conversation and seemed to spin in Melanie's head during our quiet drive back to Venice. Something was wrong. After unloading the car, she asked if we could talk.

"I think we're moving too fast. I wasn't ready to move in."

"Is this you breaking up with me?"

"No, I just wasn't ready for this. I wish we would have waited."

"Waited for what?" I asked, trying to understand.

"Until I had a chance to fully heal," she replied. "I think I'm going to get an Airbnb in Topanga."

"Do what you need to do, Mel," I said, my voice steady. "If you want to pack your things into a suitcase and put your bags back in the car, that's your call. But I've already cleared out space in the office closet. You're free to treat my house as a home base. You already come and go as you please, so I don't really see how things will be any different unless this is you wanting to break up."

"I don't want to break up. I really like what we're building. I just think I need to work on myself for a little while," she said, her voice tinged with uncertainty.

"Then do it." I was supportive.

It felt like I was juggling two versions of her: the fractured side that pushed me away, trying to provoke a reaction, and the tender, affectionate side that wanted to be close. Maybe some time apart would help us both appreciate what we had.

I knew I had to respect her need for space, even though her decision to move out couldn't have come at a worse time, right in the thick of football season. To distract myself, I threw myself deeper into my sports gambling habit, betting on games from Thursday through Monday. I was painfully aware of how easily this obsession could spiral out of control, tightening its grip on me.

I was tired of trying to win her over. I waited for her to make the first move.

When Mel finally asked me to go with her to the Nathaniel Rateliff concert at the Orpheum, I felt a genuine spark of excitement. She liked him, and it seemed like a good sign that she took the initiative and bought the tickets.

But she caught me off guard on the drive there with a familiar question.

"Do you think we have any fun together?"

"Why do you always do this?"

"I don't know," she said, clearly confused.

The frustrating part was that she really didn't know.

I pushed the thought aside as we found our seats. Shortly after, the guy next to me cursed under his breath.

"Are you kidding me" he muttered to his girlfriend, tapping his shoes in the mess. An usher was quick to help clean it up.

Mel's coat must have caught his beer in the cup holder.

"Can I get you another one?" I asked.

"No, it's fine." But he kept grumbling. "Unfucking believable." He wasn't going to let it go.

"You sure? Let me grab you one so you can enjoy the show."

His girlfriend let out a quiet laugh, nudging him. He exhaled, finally dropping it. "Nah, man. Don't worry about it."

Mel seemed pleased with how I handled the situation. She leaned into me for the first time all night, wrapping her hands around my arm.

She needed to feel something solid. And maybe she needed to be reminded that she felt safe with me.

Mel was always at peace when she was lost in music. By the time the show started, things felt back on course.

A few days later, she invited me to her parents' house in Newport for Thanksgiving. This was our biggest step yet. On the drive down, I resisted the urge to bet on the Thanksgiving NFL games; I wanted to be fully present and make a good impression on her family.

Initially, I felt a bit nervous, but as the house filled up, I began to relax. Once everyone had arrived, we walked down to the yacht club for family photos. Liz introduced the significant others to the photographer.

"This is my son-in-law John, My son-in-law Dave, Becky's fiancé Ray, and hopefully my future son-in-law Beau."

It felt good knowing Liz was rooting for me, but at the same time, she barely knew me. Her endorsement came far too easy and left me wondering why.

After the family photos, everyone suggested Mel and I take a picture. It turned out to be the best photo we captured during our time together. I thought about posting it to Instagram but hesitated, not wanting to spook her. Instead, I kept that moment private, though I would use the photo to show friends who asked if I was seeing anyone.

I bonded with Ray and Becky over Ray's Lemon Drop martinis, with Becky insisting, "Ray makes really good cocktails." After the second, I switched to water, as Mel wasn't a drinker, and I wanted to stay sharp.

I shared the shifting dynamics in my business and the growing challenges in hospitality. Dave spoke about similar struggles he faced in commercial real estate since COVID.

Once again, Liz pushed us to attend her commodore event at the yacht club in December.

"Mom," Sarah interrupted, cutting off the pitch, aware it was a sensitive subject for Melanie.

Everyone seemed excited to have me there, including Mel. After several comments about my size during dinner, I made a joke.

"I want to thank you, little people, for letting me join you tonight." It got a laugh at first, but then the room fell silent.

"Awkward," Mel's niece said, breaking the tension.

Mel laughed, sharing an inside joke with her that lightened the moment.

A verbal altercation broke out between Dave and Katie over a joke Mel made about his daughter being a pill that day.

"I told you my family was different," Mel said.

"This is nothing," I replied. "When I was sixteen, I saw my dad's cousins get into a full-blown fistfight on the Fourth of July."

Mel's dad, a fellow wine connoisseur, offered me a glass of wine, which I gratefully accepted as a nightcap.

After dinner, we played an eventful game of *Heads Up*. Ray joined us with another Lemon Drop martini.

"How many is that?" I asked.

"Six or seven." I figured he might be hitting his tipping point soon.

Not long after, Ray and Liz got into a verbal spat.

As I tried to calm him, Ray snapped, "You don't understand, Beau. You haven't been around it."

He was right; I was the new guy, and whatever was happening was between him and Liz.

That night in bed, everything felt right.

"I had so much fun with you today," Mel said.

"I had a great time. Thank you for inviting me."

"I told you my family was crazy."

"Dave and Ray were a little loose, but nothing I haven't seen at family functions."

John was the only one who seemed secure in his relationship. Liz clearly wanted the best for her daughters, and I could feel the pressure Ray and Dave were under. It only fueled my drive to work harder, hoping to secure Melanie's hand someday.

The next morning, Mel got up early to grab some things from her parent's house before rejoining me for breakfast at the hotel.

"My parents really like you. My dad said, 'We could use another peacemaker in the family.'"

I felt a renewed sense of security in our relationship.

Mel had the Airbnb in Topanga but spent most of her time at my house, which I was okay with. I didn't understand why she was wasting money on her place, but I didn't question her decision, as she seemed more comfortable knowing she had somewhere to go when she needed to be alone.

I hadn't started drinking coffee until I was thirty-nine when I first took a break from alcohol. With our new espresso machine, Mel taught me how to make them, and they became a morning ritual for us.

She enjoyed interrupting me while I was working, which, as an entrepreneur, happened often. I think it excited her to know she was important enough for me to drop everything and give her my full attention. Setting aside my work to hold space for her led to some of our most intimate moments.

"The sex is starting to get really good," Mel said.

"There's been a noticeable shift in your sex drive since the espresso machine showed up," I teased.

"Really?" she asked, seeming both amused and self-conscious.

"You do realize we only have sex during the day," I said. "Shortly after your morning coffee."

"I'm always so tired at night."

"Not that I'm against a good nooner."

"You better not be," she laughed. "Also, you need to stop trying to have sex with me without a condom. I know it feels better for both of us, but I'm telling you, I've got this baby circling me, so unless you want a kid…"

"Definitely not ready for that yet." I loved her but wanted to build a stronger foundation first.

"You're going to be a really good dad. How do you feel about Grace for a baby girl?" she asked.

"I love it. You know that's actually my sister Brittany's middle name after my dad's grandma, Mami Grace," I replied.

"Sarah was thinking about using Grace, but I wouldn't let her," she laughed as her mood shifted. "I hope I can have kids. I really don't want to have to do *in vitro*."

"Why would you have to do that?"

"The vaccine, and all the birth control. My period hasn't been regular for like two years."

"You only took one shot and are still so young."

"I'm not that young," she countered.

"You've been cleansing yourself of toxins and spent a lot of time healing. You're going to be fine."

"You're probably right. I just have this uneasy feeling in my chest. Like a tightness, you know."

"Come here."

The daily chest rubs continued, and Mel got better at busying herself while I worked. One afternoon, as she wrapped up her own day, she curled up beside me on the couch with my latest screenplay, *Molly*—about a DJ that signs a management deal with twin brothers who bankroll his rise by selling MDMA at his shows.

"You're a really good writer," she said. "It makes me want to do some Molly."

"You won't feel that way once you finish it—you're still on the fun and games part."

She laughed, then got distracted by her phone for what felt like an hour.

"What are you doing over there?" I asked, glancing up from my laptop.

"Scrolling," she said playfully, a nod to her Instagram habit we both knew too well.

"You know that's not good for you."

"I know," she said. "I'm going to delete it again until I finish my website."

"Good call."

A moment later, she let out an excited cry.

"What?" I asked.

"My breathwork photos came in!"

"Let's see them." I set my computer aside and slid closer on the couch.

218

Mel protected the photos, showing me only the ones she liked.

"There are eight hundred of them," she said.

"Eight hundred?" I replied. "You only need a couple for your website."

I knew this would open up a whole new can of worms for her. As Mel sifted through her photos, I saw the wheels turning in her head. Perfectionism had a way of slowing her down.

Meanwhile, I was dealing with my own spiral. December 3rd was a Sunday, a date day for us, but my mind was weighed down by a brutal four-figure loss from Saturday's college football games at The Victorian.

I nailed the first leg of a two-team parlay during the 10 AM games, leaving a massive bet riding on the 49ers during brunch with friends. My guilt sunk in as my mind spun on the potential swing that could pull me out of the red if they won. I snuck off to the bathroom three times in an hour to check the score on my phone, struggling to stay engaged at the table.

Though I felt she knew what was happening, Mel didn't say a word. When the 49ers pulled through, it felt like a boulder had been lifted off my chest. Gambling was cut and dry. There was no second-guessing, no mixed signals, no in-between. You either won or you lost.

After brunch, I took Mel to my favorite spot in Pacific Palisades, a hidden gem I discovered during my COVID biking adventures: the Point at the Bluffs. Perched on a cliff, the park offered breathtaking views of the Pacific Ocean.

"This might be my favorite street in LA," I said, admiring the stunning houses.

"It's nice, but if I were staying in LA, I'd rather be in Topanga or Malibu," Mel replied. "I'm telling you, I feel like a big natural disaster is coming this year."

"Malibu and Topanga aren't exactly the safest spots for that; easy to get trapped, and both are fire hazards," I said. "But I'd like to get out of LA before the election. If we stayed in California, Ojai might be a good option. The Santa Barbara mountains protect it, and the valley is pretty open."

"Would you actually move to Ojai? You keep talking about it," she asked.

"I've looked into it. Rent's pretty steep, and I'd rather wait until I'm ready to buy," I said.

"When do you think that'll be?"

"I've got enough in crypto for a down payment, but I'd rather hold out for the next bull run."

"That makes sense," she nodded, understanding the financial angle.

"Do you have any savings?" I asked.

"A little, but I've spent a lot on my healing journey. How much do you have in crypto?"

"Well over six figures," I replied with a grin.

"That's a pretty big range. How much is that?"

I just smiled. Things between us were improving, but I wasn't ready to start disclosing numbers like that with her.

Mel joined me on the couch the next day, beaming with holiday cheer.

"Katie loves Christmas. They already have their tree up. We should go get one," she exclaimed.

"You know, in my twenty years in L.A., I've never had a tree at my house. How sad is that?" I replied.

"Really?" she asked, surprised.

"I'm always home for the holidays. Never bothered to get one. Should we order one online?"

"No," she said, her voice edged with frustration. "I need a little spontaneity. You're supposed to say, Let's go get one."

"Let's go get one," I offered, trying to match her enthusiasm.

"Too late. You already ruined it."

The words landed heavier than they should have.

"It's Monday, and I'm in the middle of my workday."

"You could make an effort to be a little more romantic. That's all I'm saying."

"Do you enjoy putting me down all the time?" I asked, having reached a breaking point, feeling as though my efforts at romance had gone unnoticed throughout the course of our relationship.

"I don't put you down all the time," she replied defensively.

"Something is always wrong with me, Mel," I said, the tension rising. "I could sit here and nitpick all the little things about you that I don't like, but I don't want to do that."

"Like what?" she asked, challenging me.

I didn't want to say it, but the tension left me nowhere to hide. "The way you chug your water and make a scene with that 'ahhh' afterward. It's annoying."

"I've had people say it's cute; what else?" she shot back, clearly offended.

"Sometimes you talk like a valley girl. You're smarter than that. You don't need to say 'like' all the time."

I saw the hurt in her eyes.

"It doesn't feel good, does it?" I pressed, regretting the words as they left my mouth.

I softened. "Have you seen *Good Will Hunting*?" I asked, hoping to bridge the gap.

"No," she replied quietly.

"In that movie, Robin Williams' character talks about losing his wife to cancer. He tells Matt Damon's character, Will, that the things he misses most about her are her little idiosyncrasies.

I don't want to judge you for the little things that bother me, so I let stuff go, often asking myself, 'Is this a me issue?'

I put a lot into this relationship, and I feel like you judge me so harshly on everything I do. It has me walking on eggshells half the time and makes it really difficult for me to open up."

"I'm sorry," she said, her voice softening.

"I'm sorry too," I replied.

"I really do appreciate you, and I want you to feel like you can be yourself around me."

"I'll try to get better at surprising you to keep things spontaneous. I just get so excited to share everything with you. Should we go get this tree?" I asked, hoping to lighten the mood.

"Can I have a hug first?" she said, reaching out before the subdued tension between us turned into something more, an unspoken pull we gave into before heading to the Christmas tree lot.

The lot in the Marina wasn't much of an adventure, but we quickly agreed on the perfect tree and picked out a few special ornaments.

That night, as we decorated, Mel put on Mariah Carey's "All I Want for Christmas Is You" and serenaded me.

Her favorite ornament was a ceramic piece with an eye in the center of a golden sun surrounded by pink flower petals. On the back, she wrote, "*B + M —First Christmas—2023.*" The gesture moved me, suggesting it would be the first of many.

When Mel suggested a Christmas movie, I pushed for *Good Will Hunting*. She seemed to enjoy it, finding calming solace in the moments that brought me to tears and a smile to her face. Things were moving forward, even if the destination remained uncertain. This was the warmest my house had ever felt. My first Christmas tree in L.A. was with Mel; I thought I saw the future.

Against The Wind

June 28th & June 29th, 2024

"Somebody That I Used to Know" by Gotye played during the final stretch at BTC. The refrain felt like a spike to the heart, and I barely held it together. I spent the rest of the day at Alchemy, trying to write, but made no progress. My focus kept circling back to one thought: *Mel wanted to come back as my daughter.*

Procrastination took over. On Instagram, I found her ex's eulogy.

He barely waited for her family to post before making his tribute, framing their love as intense but fragile. A fire that burned too hot to last. He said they had met on March 31, 2018, at a child's birthday party, not even crediting his daughter, who was friends with her niece. I realized he was the "it's not serious" guy from our date at the Penthouse.

He then described how they had unraveled and parted ways but never fully let go, portraying their time apart as three years of silence and a slow, inevitable return to each other. He could not decide if their story was about lost time or a lingering connection, so he shaped it into both.

He made it sound like she had fallen back into something familiar and soft while acknowledging the chaos of their past. He described those weeks as a quiet, tender reunion, hiking, talking for hours, slow dancing in the kitchen, and her listening to him sing.

He made it sound as though they had spent all of April together. But that was not true. She had been in Europe with me for two weeks after their brief meetup, which she had told me about.

His words were not just misleading; they were hollow. He had not spoken about who she was, what he loved about her, or even what losing her meant. They were only about him, his version of the story.

And then he presented her reconnecting to say goodbye on his 50th birthday. Maybe that was how he needed to remember it, but even in his last words to her, he had not honored who she was, nor did he bother to spell-check his final farewell.

I played the song again, which had gutted me earlier that day at BTC, and realized it was never about me.

SOMEBODY THAT I USED TO KNOW BY GOTYE

Mel had built an illusion around her ex, not of perfection but of significance. Although she knew he wasn't good for her, their karmic ties kept her clinging to him.
Eventually, she blocked his number. He was bitter, and she wanted to move on.

Still, she struggled to accept who he really was, erasing the bad and romanticizing the good. When she went back, it didn't take long to see the truth. It wasn't love, only the sadness she was addicted to. Brandie called it the end of their karmic pact. Mel was glad it was over.

I was gaining clarity in the healing process, but the guilt was relentless. I replayed alternative endings on a loop, tormenting myself for not being there on her last day.

Brandie carried me through the rest of the night as I processed my guilt. She channeled Mel, who said her reincarnation could happen in a few different ways and that she would likely return to me as a daughter. Brandie also shared that she had experienced a miscarriage, and twenty years later, her baby came back with her sister.

Then she gave me a song that Mel wanted me to listen to.

A THOUSAND YEARS BY CHRISTINA PERRI

Mel was constantly afraid she would ruin what we were building. She marveled at my independence, often looking to me for guidance and reassurance. And I always encouraged her to just take that next step—the one that would bring her closer to all her dreams.

Now I was the one with doubts, and she was doing the guiding like she always wanted to. She was encouraging me to be brave—to tell her story. As

I continued my daily breathwork practice, I could feel my intuition—and her guiding light—growing stronger as I ventured into the unknown.

In *Many Lives, Many Masters*, Dr. Brian Weiss learned in a hypnotherapy session about seven planes of existence before a soul becomes a Master Soul —though we're not allowed to know what the planes beyond Earth look like while we're still here. Dolores Cannon described Earth as a school where souls come to learn. Both spoke about advanced souls having the ability to return to a lower level to help others evolve.

The line that suggested she had died every day waiting for me had me wondering—maybe Mel had already graduated from what Dolores called *Earth school*, and part of her purpose in returning was to help me graduate too. *After everything I'd been through, was I one step closer?*

My heart beat fast every time I saw her. I could still see that look in her eyes. I still believed she was my soulmate, and this song only deepened that certainty—a love that had spanned a thousand years and would go on for a thousand more. The lyrics confirmed our bond across lifetimes, promising we would find each other again—whether in this life as my daughter, or the next.

"Beautiful Lies" by Tanner Usrey and Ella Langley played again. It was the second time I had heard it, and considering it played shortly after I read her ex's Instagram post, I knew it was a response to his eulogy. She told me she wasn't in love with him anymore and had told him the same.

The next three songs were all repeats. As I reviewed their titles in my journal, the message for her ex became even louder. "Time After Time." "Think I'm in Love with You." "I Was Wrong."

The next morning, I woke up with "I Remember Everything" by Zach Bryan racing through my head. I couldn't shake the line about strange words coming out of a grown man's broken mind. It had me wondering what he might have said or done to her the day she passed.

AGAINST THE WIND BY BOB SEGER

Seger played next. Mel had been going against the wind her entire life. First, she grappled with the buried trauma of childhood sexual abuse. Then, an Adderall addiction took hold, driving her relentless pursuit of perfection. Next came a four-year toxic relationship.

She managed to break free from the turmoil for two and a half years, but when she returned to Adderall, it pulled her back into his orbit.

On his fiftieth birthday, she was surrounded by strangers she had once thought were friends. She drifted further away from home. And then, she lost her way.

I sent "Against the Wind" to Brandie with a message: *"This song is about the storm she was caught in her entire life."*

"Wow, your musical palette has so much depth and breadth. I'm stunned. Also, I can absolutely see how that would be fitting for her. The wind takes her energy, so I could see her running against the wind."

"It feels almost as if there was nothing I could have done to prevent this from happening. Like it was the perfect storm… And as I type that, a gust of wind blows through Cashew Tree, and my chakras light up."

"And that is absolutely true. There was nothing you could have done in this scenario. It was the perfect storm."

"It feels like it was meant to happen the way it did that day, an agreement we made.

Man, she sure took the easier path on this one, but I would never let her walk this path alone. Now I gotta activate the master builder inside of me."

"That is all you can do," Brandie said. *"And since we are on this nonstop music train, this one has been stuck in my head all day."*

She sent me "Voilà" by Barbara Pravi. It was in French with subtitles. I set it aside to catch my morning workout at BTC. While stretching at the end of class, I found myself lost in the lyrics of another new song. I settled into Cashew Tree for breakfast and pulled it up.

YOU'RE SOMEBODY ELSE BY FLORA CASH

The lyrics opened with her vision of my future, the part I wouldn't understand until I was older. The video showed a butterfly emerging from a broken heart. Tears flowed again as I texted Brandie the song link.

"She held the better cards… I can't believe I'm seeing these lyrics right now after the text I wrote about her taking the easier path."

"11:11," Brandie responded.

"Crazy, it's 11:11 AM in Bali too," I replied, my chakras firing again as I continued interpreting the lyrics for her:

"'It's like you told me… go forward slowly' was me telling her to take it one day at a time. And then, 'Well, you talk like yourself. No, I hear someone else, though. Now you're making me nervous'… She wasn't herself. I didn't recognize her in the last five days of her life. These lyrics are basically the text conversation we just had… my mind is blown."

As I was closing out my check with the waitress, I looked up and saw a caterpillar floating in the wind.

"What is that?" I asked, surprised.

The waitress pulled up a translation on her phone: *"Caterpillar."*

"How is it flying in the air like that?"

"Not flying," she said.

"It's floating," I pointed out.

She tried to figure out how to translate what I was witnessing. Then I saw a second one floating next to it. She called her coworker over to translate, who smacked the caterpillar out of the air with her service tray before I could stop her.

"And I shit you not. I just saw a flying caterpillar… The waitress said it's not flying… it was literally floating in the wind," I fired off to Brandie.

"Wtf?" Brandie replied. *"Talk about metaphor."*

"Maybe it was on a string or something… I've never seen anything like it."

"Ditto."

"Then the other waitress came over and smacked it out of the air."

"Wth."

"I know. Maybe that was the metaphor. It was beyond our control. Outside forces intervened and took her when they were supposed to. I've never in my life seen a caterpillar floating in the wind, and now we're back to going 'Against the Wind' by Bob Seger."

"Most definitely, going against the wind."

"What's messed up about the waitress knocking it out of the air was that I didn't see it coming. I would have stopped it if I had known she was going to do that. It was the universe reinforcing that there's nothing I could have done."

"What a beautiful example of not being in control and the unpredictability of life. However, tell Shorty if she does it again, I'm a come-and-pop-off LMFAO."

I looked up floating caterpillars and discovered a breed called *"Oak Skeletonizers,"* which hang from trees by silk strings. *Pretty cool.* Those caterpillars can create the sensation of flight before developing their wings, though it's not actual flight like butterflies experience.

This was a multilayered message. Mel couldn't go back after clearing her toxic energy, yet she was afraid to take flight with her new set of wings. Instead of embracing the transformation, she retreated into her cocoon, clinging to a silk crutch until an outside force knocked her from the air.

Gambling with Love

December 12th, 2023 - February 4th, 2024

My dad visited for a friend's gig at The Baked Potato, a renowned jazz club in Studio City. Mel had been looking forward to seeing him. When he arrived after his five-hour drive from the Bay Area, he raided our kitchen, flinging open the fridge and scouring the cupboards.

"You guys don't really have a whole lot of snack options here, do you?" he remarked.

"I tell him that all the time," Mel responded.

"Dad's nickname is 'The Snacky Guy,'" I grinned.

"How did that happen?" Mel was amused.

"We were at Disneyland when my sisters were little, and Dad snuck in a bunch of snacks. He had trail mix coming out of his ears. That's when I started calling him 'The Snacky Guy,' and the name stuck."

Mel laughed, "I'll make sure to have some good snacks ready next time you're in town."

"We taking your car, Pop?" I asked.

"Nope, we're in your town. You're driving," he shot back, our playful banter brightening Mel's day.

We arrived at The Baked Potato just as the show was starting. The place was packed on a Tuesday night, but some of my dad's pals had saved us a spot at their table. We were right next to the stage, which made the show feel even more intimate.

"Are you guys hungry?" my dad asked, eyeing the menu.

"I feel like we have to try the baked potato," Mel suggested.

These were the biggest baked potatoes I had ever seen. We ordered a couple to share, and "The Snacky Guy" was in heaven. The marinated steak topping was a hit with all of us.

Another successful planned date, but Mel's words about needing some romance lingered. Later that week, I planned a surprise. I'd pick her up in Topanga at 5 p.m., leaving the rest a mystery.

Her curiosity was palpable. She kept asking what to wear, fishing for clues. I could tell the suspense excited her.

The questions didn't stop when I picked her up.

"Where are we going?"

I smiled at her anticipation.

"Are we going to the Inn of the Seventh Ray?" she continued.

"Wow," I laughed. "That was supposed to be a surprise."

"I knew it!" she yelped. "I've always wanted to check it out. Where are we going after?"

"I'm trying to create a little mystery here."

"This is fun. You're doing a good job."

The restaurant's soft lighting cast a warm, intimate glow.

"This place is super cute," she said. "It would be a great spot for a wedding."

I envisioned it as a possibility for us.

Over dinner, we shared a piccolo of wine. For the first time, I watched her finish a whole glass.

Dinner wrapped up, and we hit PCH for part two of the surprise. As we drove toward Santa Monica, Mel asked, "Are we going to The Victorian for Salsa night?"

I shook my head in amazement.

"We are, aren't we?" she said, clearly enjoying the guessing game.

"You're impossible to surprise."

"I told you, you can't hide anything from me!" she laughed. "Thank you for trying, though."

While I handled the daytime programming on Saturday, The Victorian had a different promoter for salsa nights. The first part of the class had us switching partners every five minutes to learn different dance steps. I noticed Mel drifting to the other side of the room, and it hit me that this wasn't exactly ideal for a date night. It felt more like a singles event.

After dancing with a dozen strangers in the initial round, we were asked to find a partner. Mel turned down multiple invitations before making her way back to me. She was a little grossed out by the physical contact with randoms and suggested we wash our hands before pairing up.

Mel laughed as I fumbled through the steps, struggling to keep up. Not long after that, she decided she'd had enough.

"It's a little stuffy in here. Let's take a break," she suggested.

We gave up on salsa and wandered upstairs, where we stumbled upon a couples bachata class. This was where we should have started, but by the time we found it, the lesson was too far along, and Mel was tired.

"Thank you for a great night. I really appreciate all the effort you put into everything," she said.

I loved planning things for her, even when they didn't go exactly as expected.

The holidays were coming up, and while we were both eager to spend Christmas together, I missed Thanksgiving, and my dad wanted me home. He invited Mel to join us on Christmas morning, but the logistics weren't ideal. She was looking forward to her sister's Christmas Eve party, and a quick trip didn't seem worth the flights and hotel.

Even though we missed the holiday together, we had our own celebration before she left for her New Year's Eve retreat in New Mexico. In the warmth of the house, we exchanged gifts. Among the clothes and slippers she gave me, I surprised her with a 90-minute massage from our favorite therapist and a six-week pottery course at Good Dirt LA. She was excited to get her hands into clay, always searching for another creative outlet.

The new year rolled in with its promise of fresh starts. While I hosted two events, Mel reset in New Mexico. When she returned, refreshed and full of stories from her fire walk, she suggested we shop for new bedding to brighten up the room.

Shopping wasn't really my thing, but I let her take the lead as we browsed Brooklinen on Montana Ave in Santa Monica. She picked out a cream-colored comforter and white sheets while I grabbed some new pillows. Mel fell in love with a silk pillowcase and couldn't resist.

After browsing boutique shops and indulging in chocolates from a local chocolatier, we ended the night with a cozy dinner, wrapping up a perfect little adventure. As her head hit the pillow that night, she released that familiar little gasp of excitement, the one I loved. "I love my new silk pillowcase."

January was slipping by, and with the holidays behind us, we were both ready for a change of scenery. Our next adventure was already lined up for the end of the month. My best friend Pat, his wife Ola, and their daughter Barrett lived in Portland, and I was eager for Melanie to meet them. I'd been telling her stories about them since we started dating, and now she'd finally get to experience their warmth firsthand.

As we waited on the runway at LAX, I struggled with the urge to bet on the NFL wildcard games. I wanted to be fully present that week, but work was slow, and I couldn't shake the thought of hitting a bet to cover the trip. I went against my better judgment and placed a two-team parlay on the Cowboys and the Rams right before takeoff.

When we landed in Portland, we were met with cold and snow. I had booked a charming farmhouse in Vancouver, but it was freezing, and the heater took forever to kick in. Mel bundled up while I checked the end of the Cowboys game, the first leg of my parlay.

"I didn't fly all the way to Portland to watch football," Mel said, irritated.

"It's the playoffs. They only happen once a year."

"When does football season end?"

"Just a couple more weeks."

"Fine. But I get to pick the movie after," she said, settling into *Many Lives, Many Masters*, a book I had gotten her.

The Cowboys got crushed by the Packers, killing my first bet. Frustrated, I decided to chase it with a bet on the Rams, who lost by one point. Just like that, I was down a significant amount of money, not where I wanted to be at the start of our vacation.

I needed to lighten my mood after the losses. I tried the record player, but the needle was broken. I grabbed a deck of cards for cribbage, but some were missing. I asked Mel if she wanted to breathe together, but she declined, still cold and caught up in her book. With nothing else to do, I settled into a breathwork session to clear my frustration, promising to cut my losses and not let them ruin the week.

By morning, I was determined to reset. We tried to make the most of the winter conditions, scouring the town for a sled Barrett could use on the snowy hill in our yard, but we had no luck.

I could feel the weight of the day settling in, and the voice that wanted to win my money back grew louder. I turned to the betting lines, breaking my promise to myself. I knew I shouldn't, but I followed the plays of a college basketball handicapper I had subscribed to.

We wandered through Portland's neighborhoods, the cold creeping in as we passed through shops. At Levi's, Mel tried on clothes while I checked scores on my phone, the anxiety in my chest growing. When she stepped out in a baggy vest, she asked my opinion.

"What do you think?"

"It's a little big on you."

She smiled softly. "I like it like that."

"Why? You've got a great figure."

"I need to get in shape for Italy. Are we still going in April?" Her hopeful tone made my stomach drop.

The question couldn't have come at a worse time.

"I've lost a lot of the money I won in September, and work's been pretty slow," I confessed, the weight of it sinking in.

"You promised."

"I did. I'll book it when we get back," I reassured her.

That night, my gambling hit a low as I lost my final bet on the Eagles' wildcard game against Tampa Bay. Pat brought his family over for a sleepover, and while he made dinner, we caught up in the kitchen over red wine—a much-needed distraction from my losses. Meanwhile, Barrett had our ladies running around the house.

Over dinner, Ola shared a fascinating story about hiking Mt. Kilimanjaro, which Mel found intriguing.

"I would love to do something like that," she said enthusiastically.

I was thrilled that the four of us were getting along. Ola then proposed that we go hiking after dropping Barrett off at school in the morning.

Mel exclaimed as we got ready for bed that night, "I love them. They're so cool."

Hearing how much she had enjoyed their company made my night.

We woke up to news that Barrett's school had been canceled. Portland was under an ice storm warning, which shattered our plans for a hike.

"This is the worst weather we've had since we moved here ten years ago," Pat said. "They're saying the roads are frozen over. We better get back while we can."

As ice encased the roads outside, I retreated into the virtual world of my phone, watching scores of college teams I didn't even know. The numbers blurred together with my mounting losses. When Melanie finally ended her workday, I pulled myself away from the screen, determined to shift my focus back to where it belonged.

"How are the photo selects coming together?" I asked.

"I still need to figure out which ones I want her to edit."

"Why don't you pick a few of your favorites, and let's start piecing together your website? You can always swap the pictures later. They're really not as important as the written content."

She set a few aside, and I began to put things together for her on Squarespace.

"What do you think about *Butterfly Breathwork*?" I asked.

"I want to keep it simple," she replied. "Just my name, like all my friends use."

"It's super brandable. You can come up with all kinds of cool ideas for merch like butterfly eye pillows."

Her eyes lit up at the possibilities. "That's actually really good. I'm going to get both URLs," she said.

She was so excited about finally moving forward that she cooked dinner. I continued building the site, creating a bio about her transformation: how she had been like a caterpillar in a cocoon, carrying the weight of sexual abuse trauma and a fifteen-year Adderall addiction before emerging through breathwork as a butterfly ready to take flight.

She read it quietly, then said, "My family is going to hate this."

"This isn't about them. This is about you. You're thirty-two years old. It's time for you to be your own woman."

"I don't know if I can do this," she replied.

"If you want to help young girls overcome trauma and addiction, you have to be vulnerable. Sharing your story is how they'll connect with you."

"Maybe I should focus on couples healing or something."

"You don't have any experience with couples healing, and your track record with healthy relationships isn't great."

At that moment, I sensed something was holding her back. She seemed caught between her own truth and her family's expectations, but I couldn't fully grasp why it stopped her.

The next day, we made the most of day two of the ice storm with a couples sauna and massages at a spa in town. I still had a handful of basketball bets riding, clouding my presence, though my stress dissipated as they all came through, chipping away at the financial mess I had gotten myself into.

After the spa, we drove into Portland, looking for something to do. The adult arcade was closed, so we tried our luck at a bowling alley. However, the entire town was shut down because of the ice storm. It was one of those trips where nothing went right, no matter how hard we tried.

We settled on meeting Pat in his neighborhood for a quick slice of pizza before heading back to Vancouver. The drive home was the most treacherous I had ever experienced. Sleet pounded the windshield, and the car slid on the icy roads as we crossed the bridge. All I could think about was the precious cargo I was carrying. My hands gripped the steering wheel tightly, and I was laser-focused on getting us home safely.

"How are you doing over there?" Mel asked, sensing my tension.

"I'm alright," I replied, trying to keep my voice steady, though my white-knuckled grip revealed my fear.

As we pulled into the driveway, I finally confessed, "That was the gnarliest weather I've ever driven in."

"You were concentrating so hard," she laughed.

"The car was sliding all over the place!"

"Thanks for getting us home safely."

In hindsight, leaving the house that day probably wasn't the best idea, but we were on vacation. Despite the circumstances, we did our best to make the most of it.

My gambling balance fluctuated wildly all week, climbing well over five figures. On our final night, as we walked into OX, a fantastic restaurant that Pat and Ola were excited to show us, I hit a big bet that brought me back to even for the week, which was a huge relief. My gambling on this trip was a complete waste of time.

I knew Melanie was sensitive to energy. No matter how hard I tried to mask the gambling stress, I could feel it seep into our time together. I couldn't help but feel that she sensed it, too. I was disappointed in myself, knowing it could have been avoided entirely.

The night we got home from Portland, Mel attended a pottery class. She was over an hour late returning home when I asked if everything was okay. She texted that she was outside in the car, talking to Bear. I looked out the window and saw her parked in front of the house.

I found it strange that she and Bear would spend hours on the phone and that these conversations always took place in the car. I wondered if she was hiding something, but I wanted to respect her privacy.

When Mel finally came inside, she was excited about a couple's breathwork class she was hosting in Costa Mesa right before Valentine's Day.

"Do you want me to come down for it?" I asked.

"No, that's okay," she replied. "But we should do a couples session in Ojai with David."

"That sounds like fun."

"You should book it before his schedule fills up," she added.

As I thought about Valentine's Day, my financial situation weighed in. I was growing weary of my job as a nightlife promoter. The average spend per person was way down, and for the first time in my fifteen-year career, I genuinely worried about the business. On top of that, I was twenty years older than the crowd at my events, and keeping up with their party habits, which had always been my way of connecting with them, was no longer possible. Worse, I couldn't bear spending Sundays hungover with Melanie.

To entertain myself at work and avoid alcohol, I continued betting on college basketball. If my commission for the week fell short, I figured I could make up the difference with a few strategic bets. I was still riding high on house money from my Colorado win against TCU and remained confident in my ability to turn a profit.

But that confidence quickly unraveled. I found myself in a familiar situation: down a significant amount of money and chasing losses on a date day with Mel.

We left for the farmers market late because I was glued to a basketball game I desperately wanted to win. When we arrived at The Victorian parking lot where my event had occurred the day before, vendors were already packing up. Mel was clearly annoyed.

During lunch at Urth Café, I discreetly checked my phone under the table, watching another bet slip away. This would be the last time I let sports gambling disrupt our time together.

Aside from my lack of presence, an obnoxious homeless man's overwhelming body odor contributed to the unpleasantness.

We closed out and strolled down Main Street, trying to salvage the gloomy day. "I'm so over LA," Mel exclaimed.

While touring a coworking space, she suggested, "Maybe I should consider going back to work in the office."

I was taken aback. Mel had always complained about her job and couldn't wait to leave it.

"What would you do if I moved to Colorado?" she asked, her thoughts seeming to scatter in all directions.

"I can work from anywhere during the week. We can make it work if that's what you need to do. I just want to wait until EventReply gains more traction before I move permanently."

"Do you really think Mr. Z could get me a job?"

"I can ask him, but what about breathwork?" I countered, genuinely puzzled.

"I don't think I'm good enough to make a career out of it," she admitted, her confidence faltering.

"That's not true. Remember our first session? You helped me uncover so much, and EventReply is coming to fruition because of you. And don't forget the woman in Costa Mesa who thanked you for the incredible class, or your friend Grace, who said it was one of the best sessions she'd ever had."

"Nobody has signed up for my couples class next week. I'm going to have to cancel it," she said, her frustration mounting.

"Marketing is tough, but I can help you once you finish the website and get a class on the Westside. Your business will grow through word-of-mouth from people who've had great experiences. You've got to believe in yourself," I said, trying to encourage her.

"I know you're trying to help, but sometimes I just need you to be my boyfriend," she said, her tone soft but firm.

"You challenge me all the time, Mel. I just want the best for you, and I know how happy you'll be once you get this going," I urged.

"I don't need you to over-coach me," she shot back.

"Okay."

I hated seeing her lose faith in herself. But if she didn't find her purpose, I couldn't shake the feeling that things would become more complicated for us. I didn't know what else I could do.

Weeping with the Rain

June 30 - July 2nd, 2024

I woke with sharp hip pain. As I stretched to ease it, I heard Mel, telepathically: *"Text Sarah."*

I sent the Mama Hen video to the family text chain.

"Mama hen with her four black chicks and the one white chick. At first, I thought the white chick was Jimmy, but it was Mel. She's an angel watching over all of us. It's heartbreaking that she's not here in the flesh, but she's with you."

Everyone loved it.

"That is the most touching and perceptive story ever, Beau. Thank you. I think you have it totally right," Becky wrote.

"That's so beautiful. Thank you, Beau," Liz replied.

Hoping to realign my hip, I attended BTC's booty, legs, and core class. There were about thirty women and me. The old me would never have considered it, but I was glad I went. Jake introduced a new hip mobility exercise: standing on one leg, raising the other to the side, kicking it back, bringing it down to the center, and repeating.

This could be the key to rehabbing my hip.

After a quick ice bath at Santai, I returned to the hotel. The French song Brandie had sent me was still on my list, so I played it. As the first notes filled the room, I felt her again. Another five-song communication had begun.

VOILÀ BY BARBARA PRAVI

Her ex, the lead singer of a band, had paraded her as arm candy. Now, here we were, quietly writing her story. Two men from different worlds, one loud, one calm. Mel was caught in between.

The lyrics captured her self-doubt and longing for connection. She wanted to be truly seen and understood, even though the thought of it terrified her. It reminded me of what Brandie had once said. She hadn't understood why others weren't as sensitive to the world as she was, yet she didn't want to burden anyone with that.

The line that said look at what's left of me before I hate myself, brought me to tears.

It sounded a lot like our "Last Dance" in Italy.

Mel had people in her life, like Bear and Kia, with whom she revealed her deepest insecurities. She shared pieces of herself with me, but some things stayed locked up as if she feared saying them out loud would have pushed me away. She ached for love to prove she was enough but couldn't bring herself to lower her walls, still waiting for me to truly see her.

The third verse hit hard. This was the call she never made. The cry for help that begged me to stay, admitting she didn't know how to exist without me. She couldn't stand her own reflection and needed my love to hold her together. I tormented myself just as much over not being there as I did over the shotgun. This was the closest she came to asking for help that day: "*If you wanted me to come by while you're there, I can try, but evening is just better for me.*"

HOME BY DEYAZ

The moment I saw the video, any doubt I had that she was communicating was gone. I was amazed by what I was experiencing.

Deyaz had *99* tattooed on his neck, right over his throat. The nickname her dad had given her was staring back at me, inked over the place that had kept her silent. Her issue with perfection was locked in her throat chakra, forcing her to keep everything inside.

Adderall gave her the precision she was searching for, at least for a while. But when it came time to be vulnerable and share her story, she couldn't. Her "99 problems" silenced her.

"My family is going to hate this," the words echoed in my mind. She was committed to protecting their image, even at the cost of her own truth, so she tried to go back.

The song itself was a beautiful cover of a track by Edward Sharpe and the Magnetic Zeros.

The lyrics were simple, repeating one truth: She wanted to come home. And the only way I could see that happening was as my daughter. The message kept coming through.

I thought back to our troubles with sexual intimacy at the beginning of our relationship and how the construct of time did not exist in the spirit world. I wondered if my nerves stemmed from a subconscious understanding that I would be her father one day.

SILICONE HEART BY DEYAZ

Melanie's silicone heart was incapable of receiving true love, sealed off by her trauma. When she broke up with me, her moral compass left her riddled with guilt, and she didn't have the strength to try and rebuild that broken trust as I pulled away. She chose instead to bounce back into the toxicity of her past, finding herself in that familiar, lonely place.

During her healing journey, she gained clarity about the relationship's negative impact. When she returned, she quickly saw the broken reflection of herself that she didn't want to be. Feeling suffocated, weighed down, and convinced she had ruined things between us, she ultimately chose to end things on her own, rejecting the hand of the person who had caused her so much harm.

DYLAN BY DEYAZ

The still image that appeared when the song played showed a young child cradling a baby. I felt it was a message but did not quite understand it.

CIGARETTES AFTER SEX - LIVE IN PARIS

An entire Cigarettes After Sex concert played next, instantly pulling me back to when we jokingly called them "Suicide After Sex." It felt like her way of telling me she had slept with him on his birthday. Whatever substances they had partied with the night before, combined with her guilt, seemed to have amplified her despair when she woke up that Saturday.

I wondered if the image of the child holding the baby in the Dylan video was Melanie's way of showing me her thoughts—her ex's daughter holding a baby, and the fear that he might have gotten her pregnant on his birthday. I couldn't shake the feeling that he saw this as his last chance to tie her to him, trying to impregnate her to keep her from leaving.

The string of songs began to feel like her way of telling me that my distance that Saturday, her fear of being pregnant, and the crushing realization that life with him was not what she wanted were her reasons at that moment.

The heaviness of that morning's communication had me struggling to write at Alchemy. I needed to ground myself. My favorite sunset was on the cliffs in Bingin, but I had yet to take one in, weighed down by the dark thoughts I was carrying. Then I heard Mel's voice urging me, "Go." And I trusted myself.

As the sun dipped below the horizon, Zach Bryan's line from "Something in the Orange" told me we weren't done.

I immediately pulled up the song when I arrived back at the hotel. It kicked off another communication.

SOMETHING IN THE ORANGE BY ZACH BRYAN

This brought me back to the wood creaking during our first dance in my living room. It was the song I played repeatedly after her service, along with "Keep the Wolves Away," trying to release my pain. It kept finding me during stretching at BTC. I could still feel her hand in that familiar spot between my collar and jaw, where she always let it rest in photos.

I was hesitant to tell her how much I missed her or how deeply I loved her, afraid it would push her away. But the line I held onto every time was the one that told me we weren't done.

Although Melanie had moved into the light, I held onto hope that our soul exchange was far from over.

UNTIL I FOUND YOU BY STEPHEN SANCHEZ

Mel had been searching for love her entire life. Only in the afterlife, beyond the fear and darkness that once plagued her, did she see that she had found what she was looking for in me. She promised to cherish and honor our love in the next life and never let me go again.

SOMEWHERE ONLY WE KNOW BY KEANE

I had been deeply immersed in my uncovered musical connections for the past few days. These moments helped me piece together parts of Mel's story while I worked on the book. This focus had temporarily pulled me away from my nightly breathwork routine, but the song served as a gentle reminder to return to the quiet place only we knew and take time to breathe before bed.

The messages coming through the music brought healing to my mind, while my fitness routine at BTC rebuilt my physical strength. I was amazed by how many songs I continued to connect with at the gym, Melanie seemingly taking control of the Spotify algorithm on Jake's iPad. During my Monday morning HIIT class, as we transitioned into stretching, another song came on that tugged at my heartstrings, sparking more messages through music when I returned to the hotel.

TO BUILD A HOME
BY CINEMATIC ORCHESTRA FEATURING PATRICK WILSON

I reassured Melanie that she was the driving force behind my excitement to build a foundation and start a family. My priority was getting her out of Los Angeles, which I knew she desperately wanted.

The house in the song represented a life built with love and dedication, much like the one we had dreamed of. The line "*Until it disappeared from me, from you*" mirrored how our dreams unraveled with her loss, the vision of hope, love, and family vanishing, turning to dust.

The garden and the tree symbolized our growth over time as I gained perspective on why I lost her and what she left behind. The song spoke to the fleeting nature of life, but while all relationships were temporary, the connection between our souls remained. Our love endured.

RIVER BY LEON BRIDGES

This had been one of Mel's favorites. The vision of her singing it in our living room watered my eyes. I fully embraced the feeling that she was with me.

Mel was conveying the guilt she had left behind, surrendering to the good Lord and cleansing herself in His river of purification, a place where she could wash away her sins and emerge renewed. The repeated plea to be taken to the river emphasized her desire for deep healing, forgiveness, and a fresh start.

LETTING SOMEONE GO BY ZACH BRYAN

This message carried layers of meaning. She admitted that our love was real, unlike anything she had ever known, leaving a lasting mark on both of us, even after she was gone.

She knew I wouldn't support her getting back on Adderall, so she hid it from me, slowly losing herself to the very thing she feared. She missed the uniqueness of our relationship but, in the end, turned that pain on me, pushing me further away and somehow making me the villain in her final days.

Now, after her passing, the message shifted to me. She asked me to take it slow as I moved forward, warning me not to rush into someone else's arms just to fill the void she left behind. At the same time, she was urging me to release my grip on the past, trusting that she would find her way back to me in time.

The next song was "Something in the Orange," again, which I recognized as a good stopping point to dive back into writing.

My journal entries covering my time in Bali had all been entered into the book, so I focused on linking the day I lost Melanie with the moment I first began journaling.

I struggled to relive the trauma of that day, my words locked beneath the weight of *The worst day of my life*. A deep pain boiled within the depths of my soul. As my tears began to fall, the sky opened into a torrential downpour.

Since arriving on June 10th, I had only seen a light sprinkle on the way back from Ubud—nothing close to real rain. While heavy rain is typical in Bali during the rainy season, a downpour like this was unusual for July.

I cried with the rain, watching the golfers scramble for shelter. Mel was weeping with me as we relived May 18th together.

Backpedaling

February 14th - February 22, 2024

David had us sit facing each other, knees almost touching, clasping hands.

"Look into each other's eyes," he said. "Now, share this statement: One thing I find really attractive about you is… Melanie, you go first."

Mel's eyes held mine, steady and warm. "One thing I find really attractive about you is that you're tall and handsome, hardworking, and I love your beautiful blue eyes."

"One thing I find really attractive about you is how hard you've worked to heal yourself. And your eyes and smile are the most beautiful I've ever seen."

"Now Melanie, one thing I need to work on in the relationship is…" David prompted.

"One thing I need to work on in the relationship is letting my walls down and being patient with what we're building."

"Now, Beau, if you let your walls down, I will…"

"If you let your walls down, I will be more comfortable showing you my true self."

"Now, one thing you need to work on in the relationship, Beau."

"One thing I need to work on in the relationship is letting go of everything else and making sure I'm fully present when I'm with you."

"Now, Melanie, if you're more present, I will…"

"If you're more present, I won't be as afraid to let my walls down."

"Now, I know I love you because…" David said. "Melanie, you go first."

"I know I love you because I feel completely safe when I'm with you."

"I know I love you because every time I look into your eyes, since the very first day we met, I get lost in them as if I've known you forever."

"Don't ever forget that look, Beau," David said. It felt like a message, a reminder not to forget why I chose the relationship.

We held hands as David guided us through a breathwork meditation. I hoped for visions of a future together with kids, a dog, and a lake house somewhere but all I got was a sense that she had come into my life to introduce me to breathwork.

And yet, as my breath deepened, something else surfaced. A quiet thought. *Am I being taken for granted?* I didn't like what I was getting out of the session, but I kept it to myself.

We went for lunch at a cozy outdoor restaurant on the main drag, where we had amazing barbacoa Tacos. Mel talked about how great the session was and thanked me for booking it.

"Have you ever done therapy before?" she asked.

"My second-grade teacher once sent me to a therapist," I said. "The doc told my mom the teacher might be the one who needed help after just one session."

Mel laughed.

"Other than that, I saw a hypnotherapist when I was struggling after a bad mushroom trip. It only took her one session to fix me."

"Would you be open to couples therapy?"

"If it's something you want to do, I would."

"I think it would be really good for us. I'm going to look into a couples therapist."

After lunch, we checked into the Ojai Valley Inn.

"I've always wanted to stay here," Mel said.

We took a golf cart through the hotel grounds along the course to our room. I had arranged for a huge bouquet of flowers to be delivered.

"Wow, those are pretty," Mel said, assuming they were part of the room display.

"Check the card."

She let out that excited cry when she realized the flowers were for her. I leaned in for a kiss, wanting to seal the moment, but she pushed me away.

"What do you want?" she asked, her tone sharp.

"Nothing, I guess."

Whatever mood she was in, I wasn't about to push it.

That evening, we toured the grounds before heading back to the room.

"I think I want to take a bath," she said.

"Would you like me to draw one for you?"

"That would be nice."

I filled the tub for her. After ten minutes, I asked if she wanted some company.

"I'm okay."

The intimacy I hoped would unfold continued to elude me. Dinner at The Oak, a restaurant exclusively for hotel guests, was a seven-course experience I thought might improve her mood. I was wrong. The night ended with a routine goodnight kiss, but I knew by now my luck after the sun went down was nonexistent.

Maybe things would change after our morning massages. I went first, and Melanie followed an hour later. When I returned to the room, I noticed photos of her and her ex-boyfriend reappeared on her Instagram page, pictures that hadn't been there before.

When she returned, I confronted her.

"How come pictures of you and your ex are on your Instagram?"

"Those were always there."

"No, they weren't," I said, daggers in my eyes.

She went quiet, searching for something to say. The air between us thickened.

For Valentine's Day, the only gift I received from her was a Yoda card with a heart that read, "*May the Force be with you.*" Inside, she had written, "*Looking forward to seeing where things are headed for us.*"

It wasn't enough. After everything I had planned, my efforts felt completely unappreciated. In less than twenty-four hours, the thought of being taken for granted from our breathwork session had become a reality.

"I can't do this anymore, Mel."

Her eyes widened. "What?"

"This relationship. It's not working for me."

"No, no, no," she said, panicking. "Please don't do this. I can't lose you."

"Then things need to change. Because right now, I feel like I'm being taken for granted. I put so much into this, and I don't feel like I'm getting much in return."

"I know you hold a lot of space for me. Please just give me another chance. I really don't want to lose you. I promise things will change."

I wanted to believe her.

"You tell me I'm not romantic. Then, when I plan something special for you on Valentine's Day, you unarchive photos of your ex and lie about it."

"I want to be with you. I'm so sorry. It won't happen again. I made a vision board, and I found everything I asked for in a man in you. I manifested you, and I really like what we're building. I can't lose you. Please give me another chance. Can I come make dinner for you this week?"

I exhaled, exhausted. "That would be really nice."

While the magnetic pull remained strong, I was ready to walk away if things didn't change.

Mel's efforts improved after Valentine's Day. Following a weekend in Newport, she brought back her grandmother's famous tamales, a family tradition she was proud to share. They were incredible, and I could see why she raved about them.

"My grandma sent me home with some extras, just for you."

That small gesture reinforced my belief that Melanie's family was rooting for us, and I believed that Melanie was, too.

A few nights later, she got us tickets to a comedy show at Aviator Nation in Malibu. I sold two major crypto positions just before I left to pick her up.

Traffic was a nightmare. I spent two hours crawling down PCH, watching the value of those projects continue to climb. Selling early had cost me a lot of money. By the time I reached Topanga, my head was spinning.

When Mel got in the car, I was in a hurry, hungry, and already stressed.

"It'd be nice if you greeted me with a kiss," she said with a bite.

"I'm sorry," I said, kissing her.

"I want you to be excited to see me!"

"I am excited to see you."

"Then show me when I get in the car!"

"Why is it always about you, Mel? Instead of attacking me when you get in the car, maybe ask, 'How was your day? Is everything okay?' Because the last couple of hours have sucked."

"I'm sorry. What's going on?"

"I sold some crypto before I left, and it kept climbing. Then PCH was a mess, and I sat in traffic for two hours. Now I'm hungry and stressed because we might not have time for dinner before the show."

"I'm sorry about the crypto," she said. "Did you at least make money?"

"I did, but selling early cost me twenty grand."

"You can't look at it like that," she said. "You made money. Let it go."

"You're right. I just never would have sold if business wasn't so shitty," I said, exhaling.

"Hey, come here." She pulled me into a kiss.

Talking it out helped, and we had a great time at the show.

"How'd you hear about this?" I asked.

"I met a promoter who works for them on a hike in Topanga the other day. He invited me. He's from Austin and also does events for them there. Maybe he can help with EventReply."

"I'd love to meet him. Is he here?"

"I don't see him," she said.

The comedy show had lightened the mood. On the drive back to Venice, Mel asked to stop by a store to pick up some snacks for my dad, who was coming to stay with me. She left a cute note on the counter:

"Dear Snacky Guy,

Thank you for my Christmas goodies. Enjoy the snacks this weekend.

Love, Mel."

"Thanks for doing that," I said.

"Your dad is really sweet."

"I'm worried about him. He used to have so much energy, but he's been dealing with heart issues."

"What's going on?"

"A couple of years ago, he had what they call the widowmaker. They put in a couple of stents, and I talked him into giving up alcohol. Out of everything he's done in his life, I'm most proud of him for that.

After his second booster shot, he started having trouble catching his breath. They found out his heart was out of rhythm, so they put in a pacemaker. Then he had a cardiac ablation, but that didn't fix it either. He's still in AFib.

Now, he's seeing a specialist for a second ablation."

"When's his surgery?" she asked.

"Sometime in May, I think. He's lost a lot of friends to heart problems since COVID, and now he keeps talking about where he wants his ashes spread. It's hard to hear him talk like that."

Sleep didn't come easy that night as the recurring thought of what I might say at my Dad's funeral replayed in my mind. My thoughts then shifted to his upcoming procedure, hoping it would help elevate his energy levels. At some point, I must have drifted off because the next morning, Mel made a strange accusation.

"Please don't put your hand down my pants while I'm sleeping," she said.

"What are you talking about?"

"You put your hand down my pants in the middle of the night last night," she replied.

"Are you sure that wasn't a dream? I'm pretty sure I'd remember that."

"Maybe you did it unintentionally in your sleep."

"I'm sorry if I did, but I don't think so."

It felt like a blatant falsehood, but how she said it made me second-guess myself. The accusation came up twice more, always the next morning. If it

253

had happened, why hadn't she woken me up? I wondered if it was a recurring bad dream tied to the trauma of her sexual abuse.

Erin the Angel

July 2nd & July 3rd, 2024

I noted questions for Erin the Angel, preparing for what could be my last chance to communicate with Melanie directly.

As I typed into my phone, *"What was the energetic shift that happened in June of last year?"* two letters appeared after it: *"nb."*

My hand wasn't even on the screen. Brandie once said spirit communicates easiest through technology because it vibrates at a similar frequency. The only other time I'd seen something like this was when my phone randomly copied the beginning of the Quora article titled, *"If a loved one…"*

I searched, *"What does NB mean?"* The answer: *"Nota Bene."* Latin for *"note well."* This was a message telling me to pay attention to that question.

As I attempted to make sense of it, my thoughts returned to the idea that had been consuming me: bringing Melanie back as my daughter. Was that what I was supposed to note? I wrestled with it until I eventually fell asleep, only to wake up to Mel's voice, *"Let it be, Beau."*

My sister Kaylie texted a video. *"Have I ever shown you videos of Blue howling?"*

The video played. Her dog Blue, head tilted back, howling in sync with fire engine sirens.

"What a legend," I replied.

"Hahaha, any time there are sirens, he sounds off!" she wrote.

"Sounding the alarm like a good boy."

I scrolled through my emails, wading through my dad's usual flood of forwarded messages. One subject line caught my eye: *"FW: Jackson Hole 2021 Vacation VIDEO."* It was a TikTok my sister Morgan had made, set to "Sleep on the Floor" by The Lumineers. The video opened with the lyric about taking out your savings and leaving town.

That song had come through days prior before I realized Mel was using music to communicate with me. As I sat with its significance, my phone buzzed.

Eight AM. Erin was calling. After a brief introduction, we got into it.

"This will be an interactive reading. I'm not sure if anyone has explained how this works.

First and foremost, we're both human, communicating with spirit on the other side. Sometimes, they give us glimpses through words, pictures, or feelings, and I'll share everything I receive.

When I asked, 'How do you resonate with sunflowers?' it was because Melanie mentioned there are sunflowers around him, and then you showed me pictures of the sunflowers at the daycare center.

It doesn't matter if it's an actual sunflower, a picture, or the paintings on the side of the building. She knew you'd recognize it, and she conveyed it that way.

Does that make sense?" Erin began.

"Yeah," I acknowledged, my mind still lingering on the sunflowers. *Was there more to that message I wasn't picking up?*

"Are you writing a book?" she asked.

"I am, yeah," I replied, feeling a spark of excitement. I had not told anyone I was writing a book yet.

"Okay… so it will be a powerful book," she laughed. "I just want to tell you, I didn't know that, but I heard, '*Ask about the book.*' A lot will come through, not just from this experience but from others in your life as well.

Before we go further, I always tune in and connect our energies with a prayer. If anything in my prayer doesn't resonate with you, just fill in what does, and we'll go from there. Then we'll ask and invite your angels to come in because, first and foremost, I'm an angel intuitive, and I work with both your angels and mine.

I do see two people right behind you at this moment, one female and one male. Do you have a grandfather or uncle in heaven?" Erin asked.

"My Grandpa Marty, yeah." I could barely get it out as I choked up.

"Okay… so he actually is on your right side, and Melanie is on your left side. They have their hands on your shoulders and want you to know that your grandfather's been with you this whole walk…I don't know if you've felt him. Have you had other experiences with him in your life?"

"We didn't have a great relationship. He passed when I was pretty young. He was Grandpa Marty, but I called him Grumpy Marty," I said, laughing through some tears.

"Yeah. He looks like a Grumpy, but he's much softer… He shows me a squirrel tail. Is there something you know about a squirrel tail?" she asked.

"Nothing that I remember about a squirrel tail."

"Okay… Well, we'll just hold onto that. Before we go any further, I want you to drop into your heart center. Here's your high heart. Here's your heart center. We're just going to connect our energies," she said, exhaling.

"Good morning, good evening, God, Universe, Source, Spirit, Great Spirit, Goddess, angels.

We come to you today in gratitude for Beau and the beautiful light he shines into the world.

We thank you for the magic, the mysteries, and the miracles you bring forth for us. We also thank you for the lessons that keep us growing and moving along our path.

We ask and invite all of Beau's team to be here: his angels, archangels, guardian angels, spirit guides, and anyone on the other side who wants to be a part of our session. We ask you to step into the light.

We welcome your energy. We welcome your words. We welcome your wisdom.

We ask and invite my team to be here. We ask and invite Archangel Michael to surround both of our areas with his white light of protection and send any energies that are not here for our highest good into the light.

And Archangel, I ask that you work through me with clarity, honesty, compassion, wisdom, love, laughter, and joy so that I can give Beau the messages in the same manner.

We thank you in advance for your divine wisdom, divine guidance, and divine love.

And so it is. Amen."

As Erin finished her prayer, my thoughts returned to my grandfather.

"It could be my mom's dad, too, because after this happened, I was in his house, but he passed when I was one or two years old. His name was Johnny."

"No, I get that this other grandfather…it's really interesting…so I'm not political, but what he shows me in a political arena is him shuffling like Joe Biden. He's just showing me that that's how people related to him, that he didn't flow like water."

That comparison was spot on. Grandpa Marty had been a shuffler with jet-white hair and the same hairstyle as Biden.

Erin shifted. "How are you connected to water?"

"I've been ice bathing every day."

"Are you doing that Wim Hof breathing?"

"I'm doing breathwork, but not while I'm icing. Melanie was a breathwork therapist, and so I've been breathing, practicing pranayama every day."

"Okay, so what is with the number ten or the month of October?" Erin asked.

"Ten could be how long she would have considered us together, 10 moons, which came through in a song she sent me. Her birthday is also October 29th."

"So she was a very energetic person. She had really big energy. The other thing she showed me is that she went within. She felt like she had this big energy and went into her heart. There's something… did she have a heart issue?"

"She didn't have a heart issue, no. But this leads me to my first question for you. She kept saying there was a big energetic shift that happened with her in June of last year, and she wished she hadn't cleared that energy because she couldn't go back."

On our third date in May of last year, she put me through my first breathwork session. Afterward, she said, 'Feel this,' took my hand, and placed it on her breastplate. It was literally purring like a cat.

'What is that?' I asked.

She said, 'That's my heart chakra vibrating.'"

"So, was she connected to Tigers somehow?" Erin asked.

I thought back to when she placed my hand on her heart chakra, and our eyes locked just before I pounced on her like a tiger. Mel was letting me know she was really there.

Erin continued, "I'm not sure what she means by the energetic shift or not being able to go back, but I'll tune into that some more, and we'll try to figure it out.

I keep hearing the song 'Three Little Birds' by Bob Marley. '*I woke up this morning… don't worry, every little thing's gonna be alright. Three birds outside my door.*' There's something with Bob Marley or three birds."

"'*Don't worry about a thing…cause every little thing's gonna be alright,*'" I started singing.

"Do you sing?"

"No," I laughed.

"Well, you sing better than me," Erin replied. "Ever since you texted me that first time and I asked you about the sunflowers, I keep hearing that song. And I'm not a Bob Marley fan, so…"

"She'll send me songs, and when I play them on YouTube, more songs will come through. She sent me a twenty song communication the other day.

So if I put on 'Three Little Birds' after this, a bunch more songs will come through. She usually ends it with a commercial or a song that tells me, '*Okay I have to go back to resting now,*' or a sign that I should breathe and move on with my day...

So I'll play that later and see what comes from it."

"Wow, you know... I want you to know that because you've been communicating with her through music, you don't need me. You're obviously receiving what she's bringing forth.

Not that I don't want to help you; I absolutely do. But what I'm trying to tell you is that you are very gifted. Most people in your situation wouldn't be able to recognize the signs she's been sending you."

"There have been so many signs. It's been out of control," I replied emotionally.

"Have you been getting signs of butterflies?"

"Yeah... She was my butterfly." I choked on the words.

"She shows me butterflies in all colors, not just blue or yellow, all different colors. They're beautiful.

And what's really interesting is they come in pairs, like a dance. She's dancing with your energy through the butterflies. That's the picture she shows me.

And I know this is around the Fourth of July, but I'm smelling fireworks. Is there a reason I'm smelling fireworks? Do you have fireworks?"

"I've been burning a lot of... what's the little wood you burn before..." I paused, trying to think of the name.

"Palo Santo," Erin interjected.

"Yeah, I've been burning Palo Santo... I think it's Palo Santo. It's a little wood stick..."

"Yep," Erin confirmed.

I then explained how I was led to her through my dad, who contacted her client about the Chris Stapleton song dedication and how the number twenty-two kept coming up.

"So... what I want you to know, and I don't know if you've added this up, but May 18th, 2024, adds up to twenty-two. There's your twenty-two again, a Master Builder day." Erin said.

$$0+5+1+8+2+0+2+4 = 22$$

"The eighteenth was like the perfect storm. The night before was her ex-boyfriend's birthday, and we had broken up. She said she wanted to go back to him to see if anything was still there.

I told her, 'If that's what you need to do, do it... but I can't promise I'll be around, and you need to do it the right way. There shouldn't be any attachments.'

So, on May 9th, she asked for no attachments, and I told her I was going to sell the Chris Stapleton tickets. She always asked how my dad's heart surgery was going…"

"Oh, that's the other heart thing," Erin interjected. "That's the other heart thing."

"My dad was going through a cardiac ablation. She had asked about his last procedure on May 16th, and I told her it went really well.

The next day was her ex's birthday. The day after that, May 18th, she took her life. She used my shotgun in my bedroom, and it just so happened to be my busiest day of the week."

I told her about the floating caterpillar going against the wind, a metaphor for Melanie's struggles with abuse and addiction.

"Another message that keeps coming through is that '*out of tragedy comes great triumph.*'

I feel like we are still together, and I have been launched into something greater.

With her death, there was a rebirth in me," I continued.

"Absolutely," Erin interjected.

"And she has now become my guardian angel to help me carry out that process."

"What I will tell you is that actually, she is a spirit guide for you. She is a guide, not an angel.

You have three personal guardian angels who came with you from birth, two male and one female. The female is at the front, representing your softer side. Her name is Willow.

And Melanie comes as a guide, and she will always be with you as a spirit guide, continuing to bring you signs.

I'd be surprised if you don't see a tiger somewhere because she shows me the fierceness of a tiger yet the gentleness of a kitten. I really feel there's big cat energy around you.

And there's something about orchids and sandalwood. Those two things," Erin said.

I explained that there were purple orchids in the bathroom on the plane to Bali. I told her about the flower that fell on my bike seat before "Something in the Orange" played, and the moment our connection began when she raised my hand."The big question I wrote yesterday was: '*What was the energetic shift last June?*'

She told me she was sexually abused when she was four by a fifteen-year-old boy in the neighborhood. Her mom said she didn't know what to do and didn't tell anybody. I never got all the details, but it didn't feel like the whole truth.

Later, when I talked to her breathwork therapist, whose sister does colonics, he told me that during a colonic, Melanie had said all of her siblings had been abused.

And I'm thinking... that doesn't sound like a fifteen-year-old boy in the neighborhood.

Her mom wants to frame this as 'mental health awareness,' but I'm like, no. She was sexually abused, nothing was done, and at fifteen, she was depressed and put on Adderall.

Her dream was to facilitate breathwork to help young girls struggling with abuse and addiction, but she felt she couldn't share her story because it would upset her family. Her throat chakra was locked up.

Now, I'm getting that she wants me to tell her story.

That is crystal clear to me.

I'm supposed to share her story, and it's going to help a lot of people..." I continued.

"Yep... so I feel like she had a thyroid issue. And that comes from not being able to speak your truth.

And I have to tell you, I don't think it was a fifteen-year-old boy. The hair on my arms and the back of my neck stood up when you said it didn't sound like a fifteen-year-old boy. It gave me the creeps like you're on the right track.

And she'll show you... she'll give you a picture of a train track or something on a track to let you know you're on the right path. She knows you know how to communicate with her already.

What she wants you to know is this, '*it's really hard, and it's a bummer that they want to pass it off as a mental health issue.*' That's so sad for her, but it's part of the culture where they don't want to bring up anything that could be seen as bad or negative. Mental health is more acceptable to them, but she's like, '*That's not the way this happened.*'

She's also saying that the day she was born was already written in the Book of Life, as was the day she would go to her forever home. And if we believe her, that's great... if not, she'll prove it," Erin said.

"What do you mean by that... the day she was born and the day she died was written before she was born?" I asked.

"Yep... she says, '*I did everything I came here to do. I chose to depart this way from my earthly journey, and I will remain with you in spirit,*'" Erin continued.

"My question in regard to that is… I feel that, but I also feel like this was a soul contract she and I made before coming here. That is the message coming through to me.

I have always felt like she was my soulmate. It was a nine-year dance for one year together where we really got to know each other.

I prayed the other night, asking how to bring her back."

I explained all the signs that followed, suggesting she wanted to come back as my daughter.

"Then, this morning while I was sleeping, I heard Mel's voice in my head say, *'Let it Be, Beau.'* And I'm sure I will hear 'Let It Be' by The Beatles in the next day or two.

I think the message is not to force it, to let things happen as they are meant to. Mel would get attached to ideas. She could see things, entities, and energies.

When she got off Adderall and birth control, it became overwhelming for her."

"There was a lot swirling in her head... What she shows me is rainbow energy, cloud energy, just swirling around, and every now and then, she'd grab a color and walk with it for the day," Erin said.

"Yeah, she would get stuck in loops about things, but it got worse when she went back on the Adderall. Her nervous system was shot... there's just so much. Are you getting any signs about what might have happened to her on that last night?"

"What's really interesting is she says, *'I was tricked.'*

There's something about her being tricked or duped... something wasn't honest about that whole situation. I keep hearing, 'I didn't really want to, but it was easier to go along than to put up a fight.'

He said something that made her feel like everything was going to be... ah... like everything was going to be alright.

Remember the song '*Don't Worry About a Thing*?' She believed everything was going to be alright, but then she woke up. It was okay for him but not for her.

And she felt lost, unsure of what to do," Erin explained.

I revealed the "Suicide after sex" communication.

"I think he pitched her a drug-fueled fantasy about having a baby together that night. She woke up in a state of despair, convinced she had ruined everything with me. She could not see a way to repair what she had done.

Despite her struggles, she still had a strong moral compass."

"Yeah... so just know all the things, you've got it spot on, actually. Everything is exactly the way you said.

She was worried about being pregnant, but she now knows she wasn't... and remember, she said, '*I was tricked.*'

And I'll tell you, if it hadn't been that place at that moment, she would have found another way to leave this life on that day," Erin affirmed.

"She had ropes in the back of her car."

"So, this is the other thing she really wants me to tell you.

She's saying, '*I have learned since I've been in heaven... a lot of people think that when you take your own life, you don't get to go to heaven, but guess what... you do.*

You have your life review, and then you go to heaven. And if you've watched the movie The Shack, it's even better than how they depict it.'

She said, '*Earth is our school, and life is full of choices. Always choose love above everything else because that's your light. Your personal light is the light of love.*'"

As the idea of *Earth school* surfaced again, I thought back to what Erin had said earlier—she did everything she was supposed to do here. *Had she come back to help me graduate?*

"She always said she was happy about what we were building but couldn't get this other guy out of her mind," I said. "The fact that she went back to him right before his birthday, that she was potentially his mother in a previous life, and that she took her life the day after his birthday... it's like everything lined up so perfectly for this to happen the way it did.

And I just can't believe that this would be an agreement I made before coming here, to do this to myself, because it's just been really hard."

"It is really hard, and yet we make all kinds of soul agreements.

I'm just going to tell you all the people who passed away during COVID, that was their soul agreement. They agreed to come here, live through that, and depart through that.

People come into our lives for a season or a reason, and she came to teach you about love, about how to rise above, and about yourself. She says you have a purpose.

She shows me a white dove flying around you... some kind of white bird. I don't know if you've seen it yet, but she says, '*This is my spirit. The butterflies I show you, the white bird flying free, I am no longer a prisoner of my own mind.*

And I'm going to help you write your book, to tell my story,'" Erin shared.

"This is where it gets tough for me, figuring out what to share. I'm writing this book, and her parents are not going to like it," I replied.

"So let me tell you what she's saying," Erin said. "She's telling me, '*When you stand in your truth, the truth stands with you. Write that down: When you stand in your truth, the truth stands with you.*'

The other thing she's telling me is that you will find a new love, and she probably will come back to you as a daughter."

Maybe Melanie was the baby girl she always felt was circling. Maybe she would become baby Grace.

"You deserve to heal your heart first and finish this part of your journey.

What's really interesting is she's showing me the *Three Little Pigs*, the house built with bricks, and how the foundation is built brick by brick. That's what you two were building: a strong foundation of friendship.

And she literally... I just want to tell you what she says: '*I was out of my head, I was out of my right mind and didn't know how to get back to who I was,*'" Erin shared.

"Why did she stop practicing breathwork and start taking Adderall again?" I asked.

"She was in a place of fear.

The breathwork cleared her head so much that it was part of the shift and started to scare her.

She was becoming very clear and making sense of things, but people around her told her a false story about herself.

So she went back. Someone convinced her that she needed Adderall, that she needed that."

"Her parents are trying to protect their image right now. That's why her mom doesn't want to tell her story, and I think she wants to keep me close…"

"So you don't tell the story," Erin interjected.

"Yeah," I agreed.

"And so, this is the thing... oh, interesting... '*Don't be taken in by false prophets.*' I hear that for you," Erin said.

"Yeah," I acknowledged.

"And that's not me. That's her saying it. She makes me feel like some of her family was very Bible-oriented, and others were not."

"I know who she trusted."

"She shows me you doing a TED Talk or speaking on stage. What do you do for work?"

"I have been in the events business for a long time, and I'm also building an RSVP website, where I'll be gathering all this data in a low vibrational space, which will allow me to market high vibrational events. The book, the website, and *Butterfly Breathwork* all have the potential to come together.

The saddest part is that I envisioned us doing this together. And in some way, we still are... but it would be so much better if she were here in the flesh.

I think we could have gotten there if she was still here."

"Well, she's still going to be there, giving you all of her wisdom, knowledge, and energy through songs and other people.

I keep hearing the name, Michelle. I don't know what that means, but I hear she's a breathwork person. I don't know anything else, just that a Michelle will come into your energy field to help you build this as a friend.

I hear coast to coast, Florida to California. I also sense something in Texas or Mexico, like in the Gulf or somewhere in Mexico.

She's bringing Michelle through, and it's like it's in lights... neon lights flashing *Michelle, my belle, Michelle, my belle.*

So, again, with the songs," Erin said.

"'Michelle, my belle'... I know that song," I replied. "She's just someone that I'm supposed to work with because *my belle* means…"

"Right… she may be bigger than just someone you're going to work with, friend.

And this is the thing, though, honestly: The grief journey is your own time. It is nobody else's timing and will take as long as it takes.

I really see you doing some sort of talk, either on a podcast or on a stage. And it's not to promote the book, the book comes up, but it is to talk to people about your journey.

And this is important: 2025 is all about things coming to completion. It isn't that things are finished. Completion means that things are complete.

It's like a puzzle. You put the last piece in and the puzzle is complete. Then you put it in a box, so you can start over again.

I feel like 2025, in a year's time from now, you will learn how to navigate grief differently. She will always be a part of who you are and what you do.

Even in your new relationship, you will share that she is now a guide for you, and your new person will feel her energy too. She will be as involved as you need her to be.

If you don't need her, she won't feel bad if you say, 'Thank you for your help and guidance. I will call you when I need you.'

By the laws of the spirit world, she knows, even in this little bit of time that she's been there, that she needs to pull back and let you navigate your walk in your time.

Now remember, you have these three guardian angels who came with you from birth. They have never been with anyone else, only you.

They've never walked the earth. They were assigned to you the day you were born.

You have two male angels, and then there's Willow. Willow is your soft side. She leads you to your divine feminine within so that you can experience all the feels that you need to experience."

"Is one of them a Native American man?" I asked.

"That's a spirit guide. You have a Native American spirit guide. He's not an angel for you. He's a spirit guide, like Melanie and your grandfather Marty.

People who've walked the earth come back as guides for you. I feel like this Native American man has an eagle feather hanging down, just one feather.

When I see him behind you, he can touch the ceiling. He's that big. Big and protective. I feel like his name has something to do with an elk.

Have you met him?"

"No, my buddy Leo's mom is psychic. She once told me, 'You have a big Native American chief watching over you,'" I said, laughing.

"Yeah... interesting. You know, Native Americans are named for the first thing the father sees. Elk... Dancing Elk is what I get for you... He's super powerful. I feel like he came from the Lakota tribe somewhere around South Dakota. He's from that part of the country," Erin said.

"Maybe that's why I have this desire to raise my family in Flathead Lake, Montana," I responded. "I remember going there when I was younger, and I kept telling Melanie I wanted to take her there so she could see it."

"Yeah... go for it, friend," Erin encouraged. "Okay... a couple of things. How do you resonate with a rainbow? That Kacey Musgraves song, '*There's always a rainbow hanging over your head.*' I'm hearing that.

I don't know what it means, but I see rainbows around you. I also see what Melanie calls Angel hearts, a heart with angel wings. I see those fluttering around you."

"At her celebration of life, I said... 'When I arrive at the gates of heaven, I'll ask Saint Peter where I can find the angel with the butterfly wings.'" I barely managed to get the words out.

"Yep... So she's showing me angel hearts with wings. Just know, I didn't know that. You knew that. She knew that.

She feels like the tribute to her was very... how does she want me to say it? Very heartfelt... and she says, '*Wow, better than... I know I did not deserve that, and yet, thank you so much.*'

She says she's flying on the wings of an eagle. Something about an eagle... Oh, the eagle feather! She's saying she feels like this little fairy, holding onto the eagle as you soar.

She wants you to know... this is really important; she's sorry for the pain she caused everyone, but she needs you to know her head is clear.

She feels bad that her body is not physically there. And yet, you know she's there because you've realized every sign she's brought to you."

"So the title for my book is *One Year with My Soulmate*, and I want to make sure that the title is true.

Maybe our ideas of soulmates, how we see them in life through the lens of the human ego, isn't exactly how it works in the spirit world.

Maybe we're not supposed to know. But the very first time I ever saw her, it was like a tractor beam to her eyes.

I knew then she was going to be an important person in my life."

"Yep... the eyes are the seat of the soul, and that's how you know when you can look into someone's eyes and feel something special.

She says, '*The title is perfect unless you decide to change it. At this moment, it's absolutely perfect.*' I don't know why, but she's showing me a blue cover. Is there something with you and blue?"

"It's interesting because another medium I spoke to, who wouldn't do a reading, also mentioned something about blue to me. 'You should wear blue'... I don't know…" I trailed off, trying to figure it out.

"She's showing me a blue cover on the book.

I feel like there's a reason she keeps showing me two butterflies, the dance of the butterflies. There's something about that. It's either going to be a chapter, or it's going to be on the back of the book."

"There was a song that came through in the first reading, from Erykah Badu, called 'Next Lifetime,' and there's a line in that song about meeting in the next life as butterflies," I replied.

"Yeah," Erin said.

"And it was like I was taken in this lifetime.

So she had this soul contract, which I think was a twin flame thing, this idea that her ex was a broken reflection of everything she was not. He was all of the trauma, pain, and suffering she was dealing with. And she felt like she needed to take care of him; that's what gave her purpose.

She always said, 'I wish you needed me more.' I'd tell her, 'I do need you,' and I guess she understands how I needed her now."

"She does."

"But I was super independent," I continued.

"That's not bad."

"I wanted her to get her thing going, something she was passionate about outside of us so that when we came together, it could be magical for both of us."

"You are so much in the light... You have such a big light.

Don't let anyone dim that for you. And your intuition is spot on... I want to tell you that. And I think any psychic, medium, or angel person would tell you the same."

"Brandie is the other woman that Melanie led us to. Apparently, they're soul sisters," I replied. "She's been telling me, 'You have a lot of gifts. You need to decide whether it's breathwork or energy work that you want to lean into.'"

Erin continued, "There's a band called WookieFoot. A song called 'We're All Travelers' or something like that, something about traveling together. I don't know anything about them; I just hear that.

Another thing is public speaking, and it's on an energetic level. It isn't something common; it's something very deep.

Oh, my head's tingling so much. You will bring forth a lot because the paradigm is shifting in our world.

You will be touching people who want to bring forth their gifts, and I feel a lot of tonal healing around you. So again, the music thing, tonal healing is something that will be developed through you."

"I think I'm supposed to awaken and enlighten people, but I want to do it in way where they figure it out for themselves by heightening their own intuition, rather than saying, 'Hey, this is how things are happening.'"

"So what's happening is people planted their seeds and anchored something in. You're going to be the waterer, the wayshower. You'll help them unhook their anchors so they can bring it out to the world," Erin explained.

"I found something cool the other day.

'Remember that you are water: cry, cleanse, flow, let go.
Remember that you are fire: burn, tame, adapt, ignite.
Remember that you are air: observe, breathe, focus, decide.
Remember that you are earth: ground, build, produce, give.
Remember that you are spirit: connect, listen, know, and be still.'

I think it's super powerful to know that you are all those elements in one," Erin said.

This mirrored my daily routine in Bali: fitness as fire, ice baths as water, writing as earth, and breathwork as air, all while connecting to spirit.

Alcohol is often referred to as spirits, so perhaps avoiding it helps unlock spiritual gifts. I had been free from alcohol and coffee for months.

Maybe my healing routine could inspire others to discover their gifts, offering a path to unhook the anchors weighing them down and nurture their seeds to grow from within.

"I appreciate it, Erin. Is there anything else Mel wants to tell me before we end?"

"'*Love is never ending, love continues on.*' She absolutely wants you to watch for her signs. And another thing, sunflowers are a big deal, whether they're on a wall, in a field, or on a plate."

"What about 'Sunflower' by Post Malone?"

"There you go. Yes, absolutely. And the other thing is this:

'I wish I would have told you more often how much I love you... how much I love you.'

She said you'll hear that through different things, through different people, through different songs, through different readings you do.

And when you hear her voice as you remember it, strong, healthy, sincere, and gentle, that's her speaking. That is her talking to you. She doesn't want you to think you're making it up in your head. That's her whispering in your ear.

When you hear and remember her and her beauty, she wants you to know, *'Thank you for believing in me when I couldn't believe in myself.'*

You were a champion for her, and she knows that," Erin said.

After hanging up with Erin, I sat in silence, processing everything. The reading validated so many of my intuitive feelings about Melanie wanting her story told, our soul connection, and the divine timing of it all.

While the pain of losing her remained, I felt a renewed sense of purpose. She was helping me share her message so that others might find their way from darkness into the light.

Scar Tissue

February 25th - March 14, 2024

Mel tagged me in an Instagram post by @theangrytherapist. The first image said, "*Sun people.*" The second read:

"There are some people, very few, who have sun inside them. It's hard to explain. Their presence brightens up your world. It's not what they say. It's how they show up.

They don't want anything back. They have an internal being that leaks pure light and feels like the sun on your cold face. It's a calm energy. An inner peace. A heart-driven confidence in self. An acceptance of their story."

I replied with a sun and heart-kiss emoji. Her simple recognition of the light I tried to shine for her meant the world to me.

Being a sun person made me think about what Southern California does best. I knew Mel wanted out of LA, but maybe I could buy some time. She loved the outdoors, so I figured she might enjoy biking. My mom had given me a baby blue beach cruiser, which was barely used but in need of a tune-up. I fixed it up and gave it to Mel, hoping rides down the boardwalk and afternoons by the water might bring us closer.

The first time we rode together, we took the path around the marina to Playa Del Rey for happy hour. The ocean breeze energized us both. As we settled into our outdoor table, I tried steering the conversation towards future adventures along the coast, but Mel had something else on her mind.

"Do you think humans are meant to be monogamous?"

"I used to wonder about that, too," I replied. "They say some of the happiest couples are swingers. I think it depends on the person, though. Some animals mate for life, others have multiple partners."

"Forever with one person seems so long," she said. "I thought I'd be with my last boyfriend forever. Then, one day, it was just over. And now I'm here with you. Life is so impermanent, you know. Would you ever consider an open relationship?"

"Is that something you want?"

"No, just curious."

"Not with you, and not at this stage in my life. I'm looking for someone to have a family."

"What if I can't give you kids? Are you still going to want to marry me?" she asked, her voice tinged with recurring doubt.

"Why put that out there? It's not something we have to worry about right now," I replied.

Her question about monogamy lingered as we rode back to my house. I wasn't sure if she was testing my character or questioning her own desires. As the sun fell behind the Santa Monica Mountains and the air cooled, the ride felt good, washing away some of the tension from our conversation.

Back home, the quiet of the evening settled around us. Mel seemed pensive, her energy still unsettled.

"Want to do some breathwork before dinner?" I suggested, hoping it might center us both. "Maybe try something different tonight?"

She nodded, her eyes brightening slightly at the idea. Mel had been focused on entities for most of our relationship, so I suggested David's gratitude meditation instead.

Following his instructions, I let out a loud growl, which made Mel laugh.

"Please don't do that again."

She was notorious for making noises during solo sessions, so I didn't think it would bother her. We kept going with the two-step breathing. Afterward, I asked her if she was vibrating.

"Not really, no. Were you?"

"Big time," I said. "I still am."

She studied me. "How are you so clear?"

"You weren't vibrating, really?" I asked, remembering when I felt her heart purring like a kitten.

"I think I've cleared enough energy to start using Adderall again," she said. "I think I can control it."

"I really don't think that's a good idea for you."

"Would you break up with me if I did?"

"I can't answer that question because you're not on it."

"Becky is on it, and she's having a great time."

"Do you think that's true happiness?"

"She did try and make out with my ex one time."

"While you were still together?"

"She was drunk, but still, how fucked up is that?"

Then, just as quickly, she pivoted.

"Do you think I'm pretty?"

"I tell you all the time how pretty you are."

"I know you do, but sometimes I just need to hear it. I used to be so hot."

"You still are. You're a beautiful thirty-two-year-old woman."

"Maybe, but I used to be the hottest chick in the bar. Everybody used to check me out when I walked into a room."

"You still are the hottest chick in the room; you just cover yourself up. Look at what you're wearing: a big blue life preserver vest like Marty McFly that is two sizes too big for you and completely hides your figure.

Stand up.

I'm going to take a picture so you can see it for yourself."

I scrolled between the two photos. "Look at how hot you look without the vest."

Mel let out my favorite yelp. "I'm still wearing the vest to the movie tonight."

"Then don't complain about nobody checking you out," I said, smiling.

She slipped the vest back on, and we saw *Dune: Part Two*. It was enjoyable but the storyline lost us. We agreed that we needed to re-watch the original.

The following Sunday, perfect spring weather inspired a spontaneous bike ride to Manhattan Beach. We planned to watch Dune again afterward and make a day of it. Despite the brilliant sunshine, Mel's mood remained clouded and distant. She was barely engaging, only briefly perking up when she pointed out the hot rollerblader chicks on the strand.

The ten-mile ride along the boardwalk to the pier left us ready for lunch. When we sat down, Mel finally shared what was on her mind.

"Life is so boring without Adderall," she said. "Where is the excitement supposed to come from?"

"It won't look the same, but it'll last longer," I said. "It'll come from helping people through similar struggles. I promise the reward you get from that will be greater than any high from Adderall. That's real passion."

"I don't know, I feel like a fraud."

"Why? You've worked so hard to heal yourself."

"I just do."

"Well, you're not. I'm super proud of you, and you should be too."

"I don't know why, but I'm really struggling."

"Should we breathe when we get home?"

"I've cleared so much energy. I really wish I wouldn't have cleared that last bit."

"Maybe try the creativity meditation. You've spent a lot of time on entity release."

"That's not it, Beau.

You don't understand.

There was an energetic shift that happened in June, and now I can't go back."

"What energetic shift?" She was right. I didn't understand.

Before I could push any further to ease my confusion, she quickly changed the subject.

"I think I'm going to cancel my breathwork retreat next week."

"I thought you were looking forward to it?"

"I was, but we're going to Italy next month, and I don't want to use all my vacation time during tax season."

"Didn't you already request the time off?"

"I did, but I'm tired of spending so much money on healing. When does it end?"

"You're only a couple of years into this journey. You're recovering from a fifteen-year Adderall addiction."

"How long is it going to take?"

"I know it feels like you're lost deep in the forest, but there's a light shining through. All you need to do is take the next step toward it. Your next step is helping others heal. I promise the reward from that will change your life."

"Yeah, maybe."

Her slow decline was on my mind the entire bike ride home. The fact that she didn't want to go to her breathwork retreat was the most troubling.

That night, we snuggled on the couch for an escape into *Dune*. I noticed a slow, nervous twitch in her finger, a consistent rhythm as she tapped my hand. Mel broke from the movie early to take her nightly shower. Afterward, she stood in the hallway, naked.

"Do you think I'm fat?"

"What are you talking about?"

"My legs used to be ripped."

"Listen, you're not twenty-five any more. That picture you've got of me on your phone with a six-pack when I was twenty-six, I could get that again, but I'd have to be a psycho about working out and dieting. It's just harder after thirty. If you want your legs ripped again, you need to increase the intensity of your workouts."

"My workouts used to be fun on Adderall. Now they're so boring."

I was starting to worry about her cravings.

"What if I bought rollerblades and skated to the Manhattan Beach Pier and back every day?" she continued.

"You'd probably get pretty ripped."

"That would be fun, yeah?"

"You'd get a great tan, and vitamin D is really good for you."

That night, Mel ordered new rollerblades. When they arrived, she strapped them on, and we went outside to take them for a spin.

"This is harder than it looks," she admitted, realizing she'd need practice before the ten-mile skate.

"You'll get the hang of it."

I had no idea it would be the last time she'd ever wear them.

As I helped her unstrap, her growing insecurity took over once again. "Do you think I'm pretty?"

"I think you're beautiful, Melanie."

"Even though I'm breaking out?"

"So you've got a little acne. It's no big deal."

"It's so annoying. How am I breaking out at thirty-two?"

Between the acne, the mood swings, and her cravings, I had to ask.

"Are you back on Adderall?"

"No. I think it's my body regulating itself after being on birth control for so long."

"It's like you're going through puberty at thirty-two," I teased, trying to offer comfort in any way that I could.

"I know. It's annoying."

I looked at her, unsure what to say.

"But you still think I'm pretty?" she continued.

"Yes, I still think you're pretty."

"David talked me back into the retreat."

"I love that. Are you excited?"

"Yeah, I guess so."

She left for New Mexico a few days later. I was hopeful her community would help get her back on track.

Erin's Songs

July 3rd, 2024

The mysterious *"nb"* that appeared after my question regarding June's energetic shift continued to nag at me. Something significant had happened that I didn't yet understand. With a list of songs still to go through, I hoped the message would reveal itself in the music Erin had given me.

ALL TOGETHER BY WOOKIE FOOT

The message was clear: live with purpose, step outside your comfort zone, and make an impact, not just a living. It wasn't about gold or silver but something deeper: connection, meaning, and the kind of wealth you couldn't hold in your hands.

In a growing chaotic world, what passed for sanity wasn't always a sign of well-being. Real joy would come from letting go of fear, embracing imperfection, and finding my place in something bigger than myself. Life wasn't about having it all but about coming together to create something that mattered.

I was swirling with the idea of building a new community. As the video wrapped, a commercial cut in, ending that communication. I moved on to the next song, which kicked off another six-song message.

RAINBOW BY KACEY MUSGRAVES

The song was multidimensional, like a "Rain Beau." I arrived at the end of Melanie's storm. The lyrics spoke of a rainbow always hanging over her, reminding me of the rainbow energy Erin said clouded Melanie's mind. She would grab a color and walk with it for that day.

Bear saw it too, the way her mind got caught in loops, spinning the same questions: *Am I pretty enough? Am I fat? Do I love him? Why does he love me?*

Butterflies appeared throughout the music video, eventually taking flight from the interlocked hands of a couple. I waited for Melanie to take flight, always urging her to trust her wings. Now, from the other side, she carried me.

We were flying together.

SOUL MATE BY FLORA CASH

I had just asked Erin about the book title, and hearing "Soul Mate" answered my question.

Mel had mentioned that we were here in *Earth school* to learn to always choose love. The lyrics felt like proof of that, telling the story of two soulmates who had traveled through lifetimes together, always finding their way back to each other.

Through every hardship, they treated the world as a classroom, a place to grow together. No matter what came, they vowed to find each other again in each new life. Even when the world grew dark, their love remained the light. As long as they kept fighting for it, their journey would never end, transcending time, hardship, and even death.

At the end of the video, the main character loses his partner. As he grows old, she is still there, holding his hand from the other side. Erin told me Melanie would do the same, guiding me for the rest of my life.

WILD ONE BY ZACH BRYAN

Melanie once asked why I was still single. I told her I hadn't met the right person, though I knew it was her from the moment we met.

Erin had just shared that Mel wished she had told me more often how much she loved me. The song revealed why she loved me: I was a "wild one," independent, resilient, and shaped by hardship. She admired my free spirit and love of freedom over convention.

The night of our last kiss, when she came back to me, I made it clear that no matter how strongly I felt for her, I would choose myself over being treated like a "punk ass bitch." She confessed then that it was what she loved about me.

WHERE'S MY LOVE BY SYML

Cold bones. That was Mel. Distant from everything warm. She hid away, unable to let her walls down, incapable of receiving, unsure how to truly love herself.

She was still with me in spirit, but she had to rise into the heavens to cleanse her soul. Only then could she return, ready to bleed the same and love the way she longed to.

BODY BY SYML

Mel struggled with her sense of self, always yearning to change and grow, especially in love. She felt trapped in a broken body, battling inner demons that left her conflicted and inadequate. Desperately seeking healing, she longed to love with strength, devotion, and stability.

Yet, she fought between self-destruction and the steady love I offered, knowing she could not accept it. Her plea to "*give my new body a chance*" felt like a cry for patience. She often wished we had waited to begin our relationship, saying she was not ready and had not finished healing.

She needed to stop viewing herself as broken and embrace healing as an ongoing process, not an endpoint. She guided me to do the same. Together, we would bring her story out of the shadows, helping others on their own journeys of transformation.

My mind swirled, trying to decipher all the messages that came through. At breakfast, I opened Twitter, and the first post I saw reported a hurricane headed for Texas and Mexico. I remembered Erin saying Mel was showing her something about Texas and Mexico.

Then I thought about the Lumineers video my sister Morgan used to edit the family trip in Jackson Hole. My dad sent it to me at 6:57 a.m., and I was on the phone with 9-1-1 after Melanie's accident at 6:57 p.m. I had also sent the TikTok to Brandie at 6:53 a.m., the moment I dialed the call.

All my savings were in crypto. If something awful happened, and with how bad my work had been, I might never be able to leave L.A.

I felt uneasy and rushed back to the hotel to dive deeper into what all this could mean. I pulled up the song on YouTube.

SLEEP ON THE FLOOR BY THE LUMINEERS

As I began watching the video, "*If you don't leave now, you may never make it out*," was whispered into the ear of the lead actress. Just then, the phone rang.

It was the front desk. "Is Mr. Josh there?" they asked.

"No."

"Is Miss Tara there?"

"No."

Josh and Tara were permanent residents of a hotel suite, but they were both out of town, and I was staying in their place. I took it as a sign that I may have overstayed my welcome.

"You've got to be kidding me," I thought as I packed up my things and headed for the lobby.

"Are you checking out, sir?" the receptionist asked, curious.

"Yes," I replied.

This is nuts, I thought as I loaded two pieces of luggage onto the front of my bike and left in search of a new place to stay.

As I waited at reception in a new hotel, I asked myself, *Am I overthinking this*? My whole body lit up with vibrations. I took a deep breath and checked into my new room.

I raced through the rest of Erin's songs, in search of more answers.

SUNFLOWER BY POST MALONE

Mel's ever-changing emotions defined the push and pull of our relationship. She was always on the move, coming and going like a butterfly, while I stayed bright, vital, and constant in my love, like a sunflower she kept returning to.

Erin said sunflowers were significant for me. The message was that "*I was her sunflower*," and she was still my butterfly, not just passing through but shaping me with every return, pollinating me with insights from the other side.

"Last Dance" came on again. I had already listened to it a dozen times and took it as a sign to move on.

THREE LITTLE BIRDS BY BOB MARLEY

Erin clarified that this song was about Mel's ex on his birthday, the last night of her life when her family and I suspected some kind of "illicit drug" use. He assured her everything would be all right.

In the animated music video on YouTube, one of the three little pigs is smoking pot with the Big Bad Wolf. It felt too on the nose.

He told her not to worry. Things weren't all right.

I WANNA LOVE YOU BY BOB MARLEY

Mel needed to understand what she still felt for him—if it was love. The feeling created an uncertainty about us.

He promised that if she came back, he would love and treat her right.

She threw her cards on the table, risking everything we had built to see what that was about.

WAITING IN VAIN BY BOB MARLEY

It did not take long after returning to him for her to realize she did not love him anymore.

He did not want to wait around for her love. He was entitled, and he wanted her love on his birthday.

The three-song Bob Marley communication ended as another commercial played. I pulled up Erin's last song, feeling the messages shift back to me.

MICHELLE BY THE BEATLES

Erin said I was destined to meet a breathworker, Michelle, who would help with my vision.

The name *"Belle,"* which means *"beautiful"* in French, stood out to me, as did Beau, its masculine counterpart. The song's second line, *"These are words that go together well,"* connected Michelle and Beau.

I believed I was meant to look for a Michelle in the breathwork community, maybe even a new business partner.

AND I LOVE HER BY THE BEATLES

Upon recognizing that *"Belle"* meant *"beautiful woman,"* Erin suggested she might be more than just a friend. Maybe Michelle was the woman I was meant to love so I could bring Melanie back.

HERE COMES THE SUN BY THE BEATLES

Mel was communicating she was ready to go back to the light.

LET IT BE BY THE BEATLES

And there it was. *"Let it be, Beau,"* coming to me again as my mind continued to search for answers. She was suggesting it was time to give it a rest.

"Somewhere Only We Know" by Keane played again, signaling it was time for breathwork. Still, I wasn't ready and kept pushing forward, playing "Sleep on the Floor" by the Lumineers again.

With all of the emergency signals, there was one line I could not shake. The one telling me to take my savings out and leave town.

287

"When am I supposed to get out, and where am I supposed to get out of? Was I meant to leave Bali? Was I supposed to leave LA?"

I sold my crypto—it was all the savings I had. I needed financial stability to make a real change. When I got back to LA, my next step would be packing up my things and putting them in storage. I didn't have all the answers yet, but I had to start somewhere.

The next video was:

THE BALLAD OF CLEOPATRA
BY THE LUMINEERS

The five-song music video told Melanie's story. It opened with "Ophelia." The lyrics spoke for both of us. I was in a good place in life, but Melanie was always on my mind like a drug. I couldn't shake her, and she couldn't shake her ex. Mel was confessing that she should have known better, but something in her wouldn't let go. When she told him she had a new boyfriend taking her to Italy, he felt like he was losing her for good. It wasn't love—he wasn't capable of that, still trying to figure out how to love himself. For him, it was a game. His ego just wanted to win.

The next song was "Cleopatra." Mel was admitting she'd been late for the love of her life. If she could go back, she'd marry me in an instant. But she died on time, leaving bloodstains behind. As I heard the lyric, *"I've read the script and the costume fits, so I've played my part,"* a charge surged through my chakras. It echoed what Erin had said: while free will existed to a certain extent, Melanie's book of life—even the day she would leave this world— had already been written.

Then came "Sleep on the Floor," where a man convinces a young woman to leave her family behind. Melanie had once left her family for her ex, and that choice created a rift between them.

"Angela" came next, and again, my chakras lit up with the opening line. Melanie believed she was leaving *"with the wilderness inside."* Erin had revealed that Mel had been "duped." She had been on birth control during their relationship. Erin said, "It was easier to go along with it." Maybe it wasn't a drug-fueled fantasy. Maybe he persuaded her to have unprotected sex. Maybe he finished inside of her. When she woke up in the morning, she thought he had gotten her pregnant, which was okay for him, but not for her.

In the video, the woman who left her family for her boyfriend ends up walking away from him too, unwilling to raise a child with someone who built her up *"just to cut her down"*—not only did Melanie not love him, she didn't trust him.

The line *"but you held your course to some distant war, in the corners of your mind"* gave me goosebumps again. Mel couldn't stay still, always running from the pain of her past.

The video closed with "My Eyes," which spoke of the devil inside and asked, *"What did you do to my eyes?"* That was my question—the look I'd always known was gone in her final days. She told me the Concerta was making her crazy. I think she did Molly the night of his birthday and woke up in a state of guilt-ridden despair. Her ex said that by the time she left his house to go to mine, "She was all jacked up." She likely tried to beat her comedown that day by overloading on her stimulants. Dolores said that when one's karma becomes severely imbalanced, as hers would have been from multiple drugs, it creates a void in the energy field that acts like a magnet, pulling in disorganized elementals. I believed she was possessed by the entities she'd been running from throughout our entire relationship when she took her life.

This five-song ballad wasn't just hers—it was ours. A script neither of us could rewrite. She left her family for him, then left him for herself. She found a healing community. She taught me her ways. But then, she backpedaled. The Adderall opened the door for the entities to retake control of her mind, which led her back to him. She thought she was pregnant—by someone she no longer wanted to be with. That belief became the trigger that forced her to leave me for good, so she could guide me from the other side. I was still walking through the fire, but with every step, my desire to finish what she started burned brighter.

Last Dance

March 31st - April 21st, 2024

It was Easter morning, and Mel woke me in a panic. "Someone is trying to break into the house!"

I jumped out of bed and rushed to the front door. Through the window, I saw a homeless man trying the handle. As he moved toward the back gate, I pounded on the door.

"Get the fuck outta here!"

"I'm sorry," he called back, rushing away.

This was the second time a homeless person had tried to break into a place where we were staying and the third unsettling encounter, including the unstable guy with the broomstick in Malibu. I wanted Mel to know how to protect herself.

"If someone breaks into the house, the rule of thumb is to use the handgun to get to the shotgun," I instructed. "Do you know where my guns are?"

"No," she replied.

During COVID, amidst the BLM riots, I exercised my Second Amendment right and bought two handguns, a shotgun and a rifle. I showed her the Glock 40 mounted under my bedside table and the 9mm hidden under my desk.

"Where's the shotgun?" she asked.

"The shotgun is too big for you," I said. "I'll take you to the range and teach you how to use the handguns."

The morning adrenaline settled on our drive to Newport Beach, where we met her parents, Jimmy, Becky, and Ray for Easter lunch at an Italian restaurant.

Jim and Liz were eager to get us in the spirit for our trip to Italy, which was just nine days away. The chef, a boisterous man, discovered we were heading to his homeland and shared stories over a fantastic Italian wine.

In a spontaneous moment, Mel grabbed my face and kissed me. I loved it, but I wished I always felt this special to her. Part of me wondered if it was a spectacle for her parents.

I hated that I was questioning the sincerity of that kiss, but Mel kept showing inconsistencies that fed my doubts. A few days later, she returned from a breathwork session with David unsettled.

"I need to talk to you about something."

I prepared myself for the worst.

"David said I shouldn't keep any secrets from you." Her eyes ready for confession.

"I'm listening."

"My ex reached out to let me know he found my grandmother's ring, and we met up for coffee."

She had told me he was blocked on everything, and the story didn't add up.

"Did you tell him about us?"

"I did."

"Did you mention we were going to Italy?"

"No, it was just a quick catch-up."

"Well, I appreciate you telling me," I said, though I had grown weary of hearing about this guy.

I spent the next few days scrambling to get ahead on work to be fully present for our trip to Europe. Mel seemed to be doing the same, but she had another confession when she called me the Tuesday before our flight.

"Hi, Butterfly."

"I'm really struggling."

"What's wrong?"

"I wanted to finish my website before Italy, so I took some Adderall yesterday. I couldn't sleep last night and have been having really bad panic attacks all day."

"Where did you get it from?"

"I still had some from my last prescription," she said. "Are you upset?"

"I don't want to see you jeopardize your progress. Flush the rest of the pills."

"I will. I hate feeling like this."

"We have a few days before the flight. You'll be fine by Sunday."

Her last prescription had been over two years ago. Again, the story didn't add up. Had she really kept them this long? I didn't press. I wanted to believe her. I wanted to be supportive.

In the days before our trip, Mel wavered between excited and anxious. The morning of the flight, she woke up unsettled. I'd secured some anti-anxiety medication from a friend just in case we needed it, and by the time we got to the airport, she was still on edge.

"I don't know if I can get on this flight."

"What's wrong?"

"I'm afraid you're not going to like me anymore if you get a chance to see the real me."

"You practically live at my house and we spent two weeks in Colorado together."

"I don't know what's wrong with me."

"Do you want to try the Xanax?"

"I'm scared. I've never done it before. What's it going to do to me?"

"It'll calm your nerves. You'll likely sleep the entire flight and wake up in Amsterdam."

"I really don't want to take something new on a plane. I need to call John."

I didn't want to push it on her, as even the thought of taking it seemed to heighten her anxiety. After the call, she returned seemingly more settled. We lined up to board as panic took hold once again.

"I don't think I can do this."

Twice, as we approached check-in, she asked to move to the back of the line.

We eventually scanned our boarding passes, this time managing to get through the gate as the last two passengers onto the jetway.

"I can't do this," she said.

"Are you sure?"

"I'm freaking out."

"Come on." I walked her toward the ticketing counter.

"You can't go this way, sir," security said, stopping us.

"She's having a panic attack. She can't fly. Can I pick up her bags in Amsterdam?"

"She has to fly with her bags. Do you have her boarding pass?" he asked.

Mel handed him her boarding pass.

"I'll take care of it," he said.

"It's final boarding, sir. We're about to close the gates," the attendant added.

"I'm going, Mel. Everything's booked, and I've been looking forward to this."

"I'm sorry. I promise I'll come tomorrow." She kissed me deeply before I boarded.

I settled into my seat, defeated. With our relationship hanging in the balance, I took the Xanax I had gotten for her and passed out.

By the time the wheels hit the runway in Amsterdam, I still didn't know if she'd follow through.

Then I saw her text:

"The airline re-booked my flight. When do we leave for Italy?"

"Wednesday morning."

"Great, I'm on the same flight. I land at the same time tomorrow."

After a sleepless night, I woke to a text: she was in the air. I Ubered to the airport. We were thrilled to see each other, celebrating with a passionate kiss as she came through security. I grabbed her bags, and we headed to the hotel.

Desire took over the moment we walked through the door. We spent the day in bed, wrapped around each other, lost in bliss.

"I love you so much," she confessed.

"I love you too."

It was the best sex of our relationship, and the first time since Las Vegas— outside of our Valentine's session with David—that she told me she loved me. It felt like a reset, like Europe might be exactly what we needed.

By 5 AM, we were wide awake, hitting the hotel gym, indulging in a long breakfast, and strolling along the canals during the morning commute. Locals bustled past on bikes and on foot.

"Look at how happy everyone is," I said.

"I know, it's so refreshing. I could totally see myself living like this."

Back at the hotel, we packed up and hailed a car to the airport for our flight to Milan, officially beginning the Lake Como portion of our adventure.

"I'm glad you made it," I said, kissing her.

"Thanks for being so patient with me," she said. "John was really sweet. He talked me into coming."

"Did you tell your mom what happened?"

"She was screaming at me."

"Gotta love Liz for always having my back," I said, making Mel laugh.

"She loves you. My friend from Austin said, 'Wow, he flew to Amsterdam without you? I would have gotten off the plane.'"

"We never would have made it here if I got off the plane."

"I know," she said. "I don't know what's wrong with me."

"That guy clearly wants to be more than just friends. I don't like that he tried to cut me down the first chance he got."

"You're probably right. I won't talk to him anymore."

The whirlwind of the past 48 hours, from her almost backing out to flying solo to meet me, sparked a commitment in her I hadn't seen before. She finally surrendered to the relationship, letting carefree energy lead, and everything began to flow. It felt like a turning point.

We booked an Uber from Milan and stopped at a grocery store before heading to our Airbnb in Moltrasio. Maria, our host, met us at the market to pick us up. She was a petite, fit woman in her sixties with a deep tan. We barely fit our luggage and groceries into her Suzuki. She gave us a quick town tour, pointing out restaurants and sights to check out.

Approaching a steep, narrow stone pedestrian path, Maria said, "I go up here now."

Mel and I laughed, thinking she was joking, but she wasn't.

"You come with me, or you walk. Many guests prefer to walk."

"What do you think?" I asked Mel.

"I'm fine," she said, a hint of excitement in her voice.

"Okay, we go now," Maria said.

Though she had obviously done this drive many times, it felt like the car might tip at any moment as her Suzuki crawled up the increasingly steep and winding steps.

Once we settled into our top-floor condo, I made a move, which was met with mutual excitement. This was the most physical we had ever been in such a short period, and it felt effortless.

We capped off the day with dinner and wine overlooking Lake Como at magic hour. For the first time, I felt like Melanie was truly all in. It was refreshing.

I fell asleep easily that evening but woke at 3 AM, unable to drift off again. By 5 AM, I gave up and decided to start my day. The day before, Maria had shown us how to use a classic Italian Moka pot, so I fired up the stove to give it a shot.

As I waited for the coffee to brew, I rummaged through the kitchen, looking for utensils. The loose drawers rattled as I pulled them open.

Mel emerged from the bedroom, her voice laced with concern. "Is everything okay in here?"

"Yeah, sorry. Did I wake you?"

"I thought you were mad about something. It's really loud."

"My bad, the drawers are really loose." I softened my voice. "Want some eggs?"

"No, I'm going to try and sleep a little longer," she said before retreating back to bed.

I took advantage of the quiet morning to get some work done as the sun crept over the mountains on the far side of the lake.

A couple of hours later, Mel reemerged. "How was the Moka?" she asked.

"I'm not sure I did it right."

"Want me to make you one?"

"That would be great."

She wasn't satisfied with the result. Without the foam she expected, it wasn't what she wanted. "Let's go get a cap," she suggested.

We sat midway up the hill outside at Bar Al Centrale, sipping cappuccinos and sharing a croissant.

"It's so good!" Mel said, slurping hers down. "I should've gotten a double. I think I'm going to get another."

"Why not? You're on vacation."

Coffee had become such a normal part of our mornings by then that I didn't think anything of it. We spent mid-morning in the condo. Mel stretched out in the sun on the balcony while I crafted our Friday boat adventure.

Maria had recommended a waterfront restaurant for lunch. The town's historic charm, with stone steps winding to the lake, cast us as leads in what felt like a Renaissance play.

"Would it be bad if I had a glass of red wine right now?" I asked.

"Not at all. I'm going to get a Prosecco."

We shared prosciutto and melon, linguini with clams, and finished with a decadent chocolate cake. To my surprise, Mel picked up the check, which was another first.

Maria's was a good half mile uphill from the lake. Mel took her time on the steps as I waited at intervals.

"I can't believe I ate that much. I'm so full," Mel said.

We crawled into bed for an afternoon nap before our scheduled massage and Tibetan sound healing.

The Shiatsu massage wasn't for me, but the Tibetan bowl therapy was incredible. Emanuela had us lie on our backs, side by side, holding hands as she placed small bowls on us and played them. The vibrations pulsed through my body, pulling me into a lucid, meditative state. In that moment, I felt completely connected to Melanie.

After the session, she was glowing. "I want her life. Everything is so perfect. I'd love to own a house here, Airbnb the top floor like Maria does, and do sound healing. That would be the dream."

"There's no reason why that can't happen. It really is peaceful here. A simple life would be nice. LA is such a rat race."

"Such a rat race. Can we please move here?"

"As soon as EventReply hits," I said with a smile.

Jet lag took over early that evening, which worked to our advantage as we had an early start the next morning. We started our day with Cappuccinos at Bar El Centrale before catching the first ferry to Como, where we planned to take the fast boat to Bellagio. During our forty-five-minute wait, Mel glanced at me.

"Is it bad that I want another cappuccino?"

"I kind of do, too," I admitted.

By the time we got on the boat, she was feeling it.

"I'm so wired. That second cappuccino was a really bad idea. The coffee is so strong here."

"It'll wear off," I reassured her.

The cruise past timeless towns with rolling hills and green vineyards seemed to relax her. When we reached Bellagio, we quickly boarded another ferry to Lenno. We sat on the top deck, letting the crisp air and morning sun wash over us.

The ferry docked in Lenno, and we strolled along the waterfront marina toward Villa del Balbianello, the grand estate Maria had told us about. A winding path led us through the lush landscape, where exotic plants looked as if they had been taken from another world.

In the villa's garden, Mel became my muse against a dramatic backdrop of vibrant lakeside flowers. I snapped photos and videos as she explored the manicured estate while wedding photographers worked nearby, capturing couples draped in tuxedos and gowns.

"How amazing would it be to get married somewhere like this?" Mel asked.

The life that I had always envisioned with her seemed to be unfolding.

We retraced our steps to the Lenno ferry and crossed the water to Bellagio for lunch, where Mel insisted on picking up the check again. The walking didn't let up as we wound through narrow alleys, wandering in and out of shops while she picked out gifts for her family.

"I need a new pair of sunglasses," she said.

"I mean, we're at the Gucci store in Bellagio. If you're going to get a pair, this would be the place."

She turned the moment into a personal fashion show, playfully walking the catwalk before settling on a pair.

The coffee crash hit as we waited for the ferry back to Como. I could tell Mel was back in her head a little, but whatever she was spinning, she kept to herself.

Despite the exhaustion from two more boat rides and another walk up the hill to Maria's, things were peaceful. Our time in Europe had been the best our relationship had ever felt.

Travel anxiety crept in as we prepared to check out the next morning. Our flight wasn't until 5 PM, and I needed to figure out how to fill the day.

Maria dropped us off at the Grand Hotel Imperiale, where we left our bags at the bell desk. I went downstairs and booked us massages and a spa day, complete with a steam room, meditation space, and a place to shower before heading to the airport. It was exactly what we needed to decompress before the flight.

When we landed in Naples, Mel lit up.

"This is where they invented pizza, right?" she asked. "We have to get some!"

By the time we arrived at Hotel Romeo around 9 PM, that excitement had faded. Jet lag hit hard, and the idea of pizza became a distant memory as we crashed into bed.

By 6 AM, we were in the hotel gym for a quick workout before exploring the city. Naples reminded me of *Game of Thrones*, and I was eager to show Mel the castles. However, we had to settle for seeing them from the outside, as both were closed for renovations.

After a couple of miles of walking, we found almost nothing for breakfast. The city was practically devoid of morning cafés, so we settled for a quick bite at a small coffee shop near our hotel. The sun was relentless, and while I was glad Mel got to experience Naples, we decided to leave early for Amalfi.

After a windy drive along the coast, we arrived at our grand finale: Hotel Miramalfi, built into the cliff overlooking the Mediterranean. Our room wasn't quite ready, so we left our bags with the bell desk and had lunch by the pool.

"Front-row seats to the end of the world," I joked as we toasted.

Mel had been troubled by the Russia-Ukraine conflict and escalating tensions between Israel and Palestine, frequently asking if I thought we were heading toward *World War III*.

"Italy has the best Negronis," I said, taking a sip. "How's your drink?"

Mel rarely drank, but she had been indulging on this trip. She ordered a limoncello cocktail. "It's so good," she said, offering me a taste.

The hotel upgraded us to a suite with a yard and a deep bathtub, which Mel took full advantage of that evening. We ordered room service and called it a night. I had big plans for us the next day.

Breakfast at Hotel Miramalfi was one of the highlights of the trip. The dining hall opened onto a balcony overlooking the sea, and Mel was in a great mood.

We walked down the narrow street to the Amalfi Harbor for a private yacht tour along the coast. Snuggled up on the back of the boat, we listened as our captain pointed out Dolphin Island and the Dolce & Gabbana archway just off Capri. We circled the island before reaching Nerano, where we moored and waited for a water taxi to take us to Il Cantuccio.

Our waiter, a charismatic Italian man, greeted us with Limoncello shots.

"If you no like the meal, I pay!" he boasted.

The place filled quickly, and each table received the same warm welcome. Another staff member walked around with a boom box, playing hit songs from every era.

We danced along to "YMCA," me sipping my usual red wine while Mel had a glass of Prosecco.

"I'm drunk from one glass of Prosecco and that Limoncello shot," she laughed before jumping into "Dancing Queen."

The journey continued to Positano, where Mel shopped for her nieces. We wandered the town's steep stairs before stopping at a cliffside restaurant, where I ordered a Negroni, and we took in the unreal view.

Mel's cocktails wore off, and I could tell she was running on empty. I tried to entice her with an ocean dip to wake her up, but she wasn't into it. Still, she was a good sport as we made our way back to the harbor and tackled the quarter-mile walk up the hill to our hotel.

Mel unwound with a bath, and we fell asleep watching Equalizer 3, which had been filmed just down the road in Atrani.

After another incredible breakfast, we lounged on the cliffside deck. I sipped a Negroni, staring at the horizon before summoning the courage to jump into the sea.

As I climbed back up, Mel asked, "How was it?"

"Exhilarating. A little cold, but it feels good. You should try it."

"I think I'm going to get a workout in," she said, heading to the gym.

When she rejoined me on the ocean deck, she sat silently, staring at the horizon, lost in thought before asking the question that always seemed to return to her.

"What's your idea of fun?" she asked.

"What do you mean? Wasn't yesterday fun?"

"No, it was."

"Did you have fun in Como?"

"I had a lot of fun."

"So where is this coming from?"

"I don't know. I know it shouldn't be, but everything feels so boring."

Maybe she was hungover from the day before, or maybe it was something deeper. Either way, we'd taken a huge step backward.

"How about a massage?" I suggested.

"They have massages here?" she asked, her interest piqued. "That sounds amazing."

I had the waiter call the front desk to book one for her.

Her questions about us still lingered. We had just been on a boat trip along the Amalfi Coast, staying at a breathtaking hotel with every amenity imaginable. *How could she possibly be bored?*

After her massage, she wanted to explore the town. We wandered through a few stores, but as the rain started, we ducked into a waterfront restaurant for a bite.

As I settled the bill, Mel asked, "Can you call the shuttle?"

"The shuttle picks up at the other end of town," I said. "We're closer to the hotel."

"I bet if you called, they'd pick us up."

"I promise they won't. I've been in this predicament before. The designated pickup is back where the boat dropped us off, and we'd have to wait in the rain."

Mel was frustrated, but our options were limited.

"We can either run for it or wait for the rain to stop," I said.

"This is so annoying."

As we started up the stairs, the rain came down harder. Mel trailed behind.

"Wait for me!" she shouted.

I stopped under a tree at the landing.

"It would be nice if you waited so I don't get mugged," she snapped.

"What are you talking about? That was just a family of tourists."

The rain refused to let up all the way back to the hotel.

"I bet the shuttle would've picked us up."

"Ask Erica in the morning," I said, referring to our maître d' at breakfast.

When we finally got to the room, I asked if she wanted me to draw her a bath.

"I'm really not happy about that," she muttered, still stewing.

"You're in Amalfi. Get over it!"

I tried to shake it off, but it gnawed at me. *Was she even enjoying any of this?*

I hoped a warm bath would soften her mood, but her saltiness lingered into the next morning.

"I'm still not happy about last night."

As Erica walked by at breakfast, she asked how our night was.

"We got caught in the rain after dinner," I said. "I told her the shuttle has a designated pickup spot, but she didn't believe me."

"Yes, you must wait at the center for the shuttle," Erica confirmed. Noticing Mel's frustration, she tried to soften things. "What's wrong with a little rain? You're in Amalfi."

"That's what I said," I added.

Despite Erica's attempt to lighten the mood, Mel remained tense. As Erica walked away, Mel muttered, "What a bitch."

"What are you talking about?" I asked, surprised. "Erica is the sweetest person on the planet."

"I really don't appreciate you guys teaming up on me like that."

Shortly after, Erica returned with an umbrella. "For your hike today, in case it rains," she said. "We have umbrellas at the front desk for all our guests."

"Thanks, Erica," I replied.

I had planned a beautiful trek from Amalfi to Ravello, hoping it might reset the mood. Hiking was Melanie's favorite, and I had thought this would be the highlight of our trip. As we got ready, she slipped on her sneakers.

"I forgot to pack my hiking shoes."

"You asked me if we were going hiking?" I said, puzzled.

"I know. These will have to do."

Mel never hiked without her shoes and litter pouch. This wasn't like her.

Hand in hand, we navigated the morning foot traffic in town. But as we began our climb into the Lattari Mountains, the root of her uncertainty about us surfaced again.

"Would you be okay if my ex and I were friends?" Mel asked. "I miss his friendship."

My blood boiled. This was her favorite thing to do in the world, and she was thinking about him.

"No, I wouldn't be cool with that. You've repeatedly told me how toxic that relationship was and how this guy is a narcissist. Honestly, I'm not confident enough in your commitment to our relationship to say yes to that."

"He's really not that bad of a guy."

"Maybe I'm not what you're looking for."

"It's not that. I just miss his friendship."

"I'm done talking about this guy," I said, trying to keep the day from spiraling.

This was supposed to be magical. Instead, my head spun. *Was last night really about the rain, or was it just an excuse to push me away?* If that was the case, it was working. I needed space.

I continued ahead, pausing at a turn-of-the-century flour mill and then a majestic waterfall. I offered Mel a chance to take pictures, but she declined. I waited again as we passed through the quiet town of Pontone, then stopped once more to lead her up the staircase to Ravello.

The three-hour climb settled my thoughts. No matter my doubts, I wasn't going to let them ruin the trip.

I had told Mel the pasta at Cumpa' Cosimo was the best I'd ever had, and I was excited for her to try it. The restaurant was run by an elderly woman, everyone called Grandma. Her son said it had been in the family for over a hundred years. We ordered fettuccine Bolognese and gnocchi, followed by another round of fettuccine with a couple of glasses of red wine.

An older English couple smiled as our third plate of pasta landed.

"We're eating like we're going to the electric chair," I joked.

They laughed, and Mel seemed to enjoy our banter.

Grandma stopped by, impressed with the damage we'd done.

"Best pasta in the world," I told her.

She smiled and brought us complimentary gelato.

"She has really good energy," Mel said.

The hike, the meal, the restaurant's strong family atmosphere, and bonding with our neighbors helped put the stress of the last twenty-four hours behind us.

"That was so good, but I'm so full. I need to walk it off," Mel exclaimed.

We wandered the charming side streets, climbing again through alleys until we stumbled upon Villa Cimbrone. Perched on a cliff, its English gardens boasted beautiful trees with purple flower blossoms framing breathtaking ocean views.

"I can't believe someone actually lived here," I said.

"The flowers are so pretty."

My hip throbbed from all the walking we'd done in Europe. This wasn't normal pain; it felt different. We sat silently on the lawn outside the café, overlooking the sea. I could see Mel's wheels turning again. She always seemed to struggle in moments of stillness, something constantly going on in her head.

Afterward, we took a cab back to the hotel. Mel went straight for a bath. Despite the rough start, the day had turned romantic, so I asked if she wanted company. Again, she turned me down.

I realized her nightly breathwork had disappeared. Nine days in, other than the sound bowl healing, she hadn't practiced once.

The next morning, we noticed bloodstains on the sheets.

"Are you on your period?" I asked.

"That would make a lot of sense considering the last couple of days," she said, looking at the bed.

"Do you want me to run into town and grab you tampons?"

"That's okay. I don't think it's too heavy. I'll just use some tissue paper."

I found that odd, but I didn't question it.

After breakfast that morning, we took a little break from each other. I enjoyed the vastness of the ocean from the cliff deck while Mel explored the town. When she returned, she suggested we go into town together.

Before we left, I noticed a Ziploc bag full of pills in the bathroom.

"What are these?"

"Oh, just some anti-anxiety meds for flying that John gave me."

Eleven pills for a couple of flights? That didn't seem right. *Was she lying about being back on Adderall?*

We walked along the coast to Atrani for a quick lap of the square before heading back to Amalfi.

"My hip is screaming."

"What's it from?"

"I don't know, but Clark has had both hips replaced. I really don't want to end up needing surgery."

"You're getting old, man," she teased.

"I know. What the heck."

"You should get it checked out when we get home."

"I'd rather rehab it naturally first. They're so quick to cut these days."

"Why do I feel another conspiracy theory coming on?" she said.

"Western medicine. Always quick to make a buck," I said, and we both laughed.

We stopped at a wine shop in Amalfi, where I asked the owner for his best bottle and bought it as a gift for her parents.

"They're going to love it," she said. "Thanks for being so sweet."

Mel woke up excited for our last day in Italy. Breakfast was phenomenal, and after our cappuccino, we enjoyed a more intimate and fulfilling morning, gazing out at the Mediterranean from our suite. She seemed to be emerging from the funk she'd been in.

That afternoon, we lounged on the cliffside before heading across the street for an early dinner at a restaurant we'd been eyeing since our arrival in Amalfi. The food was just okay, but the views were breathtaking. We took some pictures before wandering back into town.

At a charming bookstore, Mel had a custom journal made for her sister Sarah's birthday.

"Is this your shop?" she asked the owner, a woman about her age.

"It's my father's, but it will be mine someday," she said.

"That's so cool. Do you have an online store in case I want to order more?" Mel asked.

"We do," the woman said, handing her a business card.

"I love it here. There's so much character," Mel said.

We watched as the bookstore owner pressed a wax Taurus emblem onto the front of Sarah's journal.

"She's going to love this," Mel said, thrilled.

I just smiled, savoring her happiness. The culture and the family-run businesses passed down through generations were refreshing. Melanie's rhythm in life aligned perfectly with the pace of the locals. That night, we packed our suitcases, now heavier with all the gifts she had picked up for her family.

"I can't believe it's our last night," she said.

"We've still got breakfast tomorrow," I reminded her.

She responded with her classic yelp and snuggled into me as we drifted off t sleep.

Our last breakfast together offered peaceful views of the sun reflecting off the morning blue sea, with Mel savoring every last drop of her coffee—one final slurp and a smile before saying goodbye to Amalfi.

"I really appreciate you," Mel said. "Thank you for planning such a great trip."

"You're welcome."

"Erica was really sweet," she added, her tone much warmer than a few days prior. "I'm going to miss our morning breakfast so much."

"Maybe we can make this a yearly thing," I suggested.

Her face lit up. "That would be amazing."

During the drive back to Naples, Mel nestled into my arm. Our driver, obviously energized from his morning espresso, excitedly practiced his English with and shared an engaging history lesson. He recounted the story of Mount Vesuvius and the eruption that claimed nearly twenty thousand lives.

"You have to visit Pompeii," he said. "So much history."

"I'd love to visit next time," Mel said.

"Let's do it," I replied with a smile.

That evening, in Amsterdam, Mel wanted to go out for one last dinner in Europe. We found Joseph's Bistro, a cozy wine bar in a neighborhood that reminded me of the trendier spots in Venice and Brooklyn. The food was excellent, and we both had a glass of wine.

When Mel ordered a second, I hesitated. "Are you sure?"

"What? I'm still on vacation," she snapped. "Don't be such a square."

I threw up my hands in surrender. When the bill came, she insisted on covering it.

"I did pretty good picking up some nice checks on this trip."

"You did. And thank you, it hasn't gone unnoticed."

After our early meal, we strolled the neighborhood, but a light drizzle cut our walk short. One thing I learned on that trip was that Mel did not like the rain.

The next morning, we squeezed in a quick workout, had breakfast, and hit the airport.

When we landed at LAX, our bags never appeared on the carousel. Just what we didn't need after a long flight, but the KLM baggage desk quickly arranged for delivery to the house.

When we got home, Mel went straight for her nightly shower. I watched her let out a satisfied sigh as her head hit the silk pillowcase. Maybe we hadn't outrun the chaos, but she seemed at home for now, and I was still holding on.

(Scan for Amsterdam - scroll down for Lake Como and Naples + Amalfi.)

Karmic Cycle

July 4th - July 7th, 2024

On my first night at the new hotel in Bali, I was startled awake by a single ring on my phone. I got out of bed to silence it. It was already on silent. Strange. The time was 12:12 a.m.

The next morning, I searched "*1212*" and found an article on *willowsoul.com* titled "*3 Reasons Why You Keep Seeing 1212.*" The featured image depicted an angel; I felt it was a message from my guardian angel, Willow, whom Erin had mentioned. The article urged me to release my worries, maintain a positive mindset, and pursue my dreams with a calm spirit. It spoke of becoming a change-maker, connecting with others, and trusting the Universe to guide me.

That morning, butterflies danced around me in pairs as I weaved through Bingin on my scooter. After settling into a bean bag at Santai, I answered a call from my dad, who was eager to hear about my session with Erin.

"Grandpa Marty was there. She said he had been with me since the accident. He showed her a squirrel's tail. Does that mean anything to you?"

"Squirrel's tail, huh? I'll have to think about that one."

"She also said I have a guardian angel named Dancing Elk from the Lakota tribe in South Dakota."

"Dancing Elk? Maybe that was William Peligrimia Williams, my grandfather. He died of tuberculosis at 32 when Marty was two."

"No, his name was Dancing Elk," I said, laughing, already sensing his skepticism. "The other thing that was pretty wild is that she knew I was writing a book."

"What's the book about?"

"It's called *One Year with My Soulmate*. It's about Mel and me. I'm hoping to release it on her birthday."

"When's her birthday?"

"October 29th."

"Wait. October 29th? That's Grandpa Marty's birthday."

"What are the chances of that?"

"Do you think you'll be done by then?"

"The 29th of this year probably isn't realistic. May 18th, the day I lost her, might be though."

After my ice bath, I returned to Alchemy. In my journal, I had written notes about the video of Kaylie's dog, Blue, howling along with the fire engine sirens. The color blue had surfaced repeatedly during my session with Erin and was also mentioned by David's psychic, Chris.

Three emergency messages had come through Morgan's "Sleep on the Floor" TikTok video. And then there was Kaylie's dog, Blue—sounding the alarm.

Erin had mentioned Texas and Mexico. Now, a hurricane threatened both.

I need to get out of LA.

That night, I was jolted awake again, this time by a flashing light on my phone. It felt as though I was being pushed out of bed. The time was 12:22, ten minutes later than the night before.

In the morning, I searched "*1222.*"

Willowsoul.com appeared again, this time with "*6 Reasons Why You're Seeing 12:22.*" The image showed a cartoon resembling Mel in a saddle, riding a white dove.

I recalled Erin mentioning a white dove circling me and how Mel felt like she was soaring on an eagle. Brandie had also seen a white dove.

"1222 encouraged embracing new perspectives, breaking free from old thought patterns, and taking meaningful steps forward. Letting go of the past was key."

Okay. I was being guided down a new path, possibly letting go of my weekly events. But if I gave up my venues, how could I make EventReply work?

The final meaning emphasized that a positive outlook would open a gateway for solutions to flow. The first step was clear: finish the book. To do that, I needed to free up my time.

After my morning routine I returned to Alchemy to write. The place had great energy. As I organized my notes from the July 3rd call with Erin, I kept thinking about Grandpa Marty and my dad's grandfather, William Pelligrimia Williams, who had died at 32. Each time my dad had mentioned him, I felt an undeniable connection.

My mind drifted back to when I wrote my first screenplay, fresh out of college, in my dad's office. I would lose myself in moments of writer's block, staring at William's Mameluke sword from the Marines, which hung above Dad's desk.

I remembered riding across the Dumbarton Bridge as a child, my dad telling me about William, and an odd certainty settling in back then. I had believed I might have been him in a past life.

Then it struck me. Mel had also died at 32.

Erin mentioned Marty had been with me as a spirit guide since the accident. Melanie had the same birthday as him. I recalled asking Mel, after my first breathwork session in our room following her passing, if anyone was with her. Her response was a clear, resounding yes.

I wrote in my journal:

"Was I William?"

Immediately energy coursed through my body.

"Mel was my wife.

Marty was our son."

With each new realization, the euphoric surge intensified, butterflies dancing through my chakras.

"Grandpa Marty had been there since the accident to help his mother transition, and now both were spirit guides for me."

The realization hit like a jackpot.

She was the subject of my *Dear Soulmate* poem, the one I wrote when I was eighteen. I sensed she was out there. I knew she would come into my life when the time was right.

I had been searching for her since my past life had ended at 32, only to find her in this one and lose her at the same age. A karmic soul contract written across two lives, now fulfilled.

I texted my dad, asking for his grandmother's name.

"Lucille McKee," he replied.

My mind was blown. *Lucille* and *William, the marine, her* "*knight in shining armor.*"

Time froze around that look Mel had always given me, the one I had been trying to understand since the moment our eyes first met.

How was this happening?

Some things defy logic. Some things stretch probability so far they demand to be noticed.

I kept turning the numbers over in my head, trying to make sense of them.

Melanie and Grandpa Marty shared a birthday. William and Melanie both died at 32. *So what are the odds?*

I searched for an answer. According to CDC actuarial life tables, the probability of any person dying at exactly 32 years old was *one in 667.* The chance of two unrelated people dying at that age was *one in 444,444. The angel number that kept surfacing.*

Then there was the birthday. The odds of two people sharing a birthday were one in 365.

When these probabilities combined, the likelihood of all of this aligning was staggering. *One in 162 million.*

I was 135 times more likely to be struck by lightning in my lifetime than to have this exact sequence of events occur by chance.

If this was just coincidence, then coincidence was telling a whale of a story.

I knew she was my soulmate the moment I laid eyes on her.

I texted Erin to share the news. She responded:

"Well, hello, friend. I also get that you guys were married in a past life.

I love music and do not usually get messages for myself through songs. This morning, I woke up at 4:12, and Melanie was on my mind. She brought the song 'California Dreamin'' loud and clear. Message for you? Big hugs."

I pulled up "California Dreamin'" by The Mamas and the Papas. Maybe the message was Mel wanted me to come back to California. Then I clicked on another version of the song by Sia, accompanied by an image of a cruise ship getting rolled over by a tidal wave.

CALIFORNIA DREAMIN' BY SIA

The video was for the *San Andreas* movie trailer. It showed Los Angeles and San Francisco being destroyed, buildings collapsing, and tsunamis swallowing entire cities. As it played, a harrowing surge of electricity shot through my chakras, like a live wire snapping loose in a storm, charged with fear.

Oh my God. The emergency messages Mel had been sending me. They were about the San Andreas Fault. The Big One. The disaster they had warned about my entire life.

The rush of realizing she was my soulmate had been electrifying, but this hit like a ton of bricks. My perception of reality was collapsing.

What is happening to me?

I struggled to process it all. I needed to breathe, to slow down long enough to make sense of it. Breathwork rocked me to sleep that night, but I was pushed out of bed again—this time at 12:32, ten minutes later than the night before. The number 10 kept following me.

When I woke up, I researched "*1232*." It symbolized spiritual awakening and enlightenment, a reminder that angels and spirit guides were leading me.

During my morning relax at Santai, I searched for answers about the San Andreas Fault message. Brandie offered an interesting insight.

"*It sounds like you've tapped into the Akashic records*," she wrote.

I recalled reading about them in Dolores Cannon's *Between Death and Life*, which described the Akashic records as a vast archive of every event in the universe.

Mel had been convinced something catastrophic would happen in LA before the election. She also had a strong feeling about Maui before the fires hit. *Was this the energetic shift that she had been burdened with in June?*

I replied to Brandie, "*I think Mel was tapped into them, and she has even greater access now that she is on the other side.*"

"*It's possible to pull information from the Akashic records across different timelines of parallel universes. Probably best not to make any rash decisions*," she wrote back.

Why was this information given to me, and what am I supposed to do with it?

If I had known Mel would take her life, I would have done everything to stop it. *But this? An earthquake?*

Was this what Erin had envisioned as the topic for a podcast or TED Talk, was I supposed to warn people about a potential disaster? *How would this come across? People are going to think I'm crazy.*

I iced my body and let the thought settle before heading to Alchemy to write.

As I organized songs and lyrics from the past few days, I came across the final words in Wookiefoot's "All Together": "*A revolution without dancing is a revolution not worth having.*"

I thought about the dancing butterflies Erin had mentioned. Somehow, dance needed to be part of the *Butterfly Breathwork* experience, with music and movement serving as a bridge to something entirely new. As I journaled, my chakras lit up again. I was on the right track.

What if Mel was sending me this music to inspire an experience centered on dance? What if I incorporated my entire Bali routine into a multi-day festival? Not just musicians and dancing but headlining energy workers, breathwork facilitators, yoga teachers, fitness instructors, Reiki healers, mediums, and sound healers. Ice baths. A coworking space where people could journal their experiences. Maybe it was more than just *Butterfly Breathwork.* Maybe it was the *Butterfly Effect,* a festival or retreat giving people the tools to tap into their higher selves.

I slipped into David's 28-minute meditation and dropped into a deep psychedelic state. "A thousand different women." "Darling." "Birth." The message remained the same: *She is going to reincarnate as my daughter.* Melanie's loving energy filled the room. I reached up, clenched my fist three times, our silent *I love you,* and went to sleep.

I woke up struggling with the San Andreas Fault message. I couldn't shake the feeling that this was part of our divine plan, that Melanie's loss was tied to it. Her proof that there was nothing she could have done to prevent her loss. Erin had called us "wayshowers."

Was I supposed to show people out of harm's way?

While stretching at BTC, a new song played.

TALK 2 ME BY MONETL FISH

The refrain in the song's title played in my head for the rest of the day. I thought back to the breathwork session the night before, when I had felt Mel's presence but asked nothing, only telling her I loved her before bed. Tonight, I planned to go deeper to find out what I was supposed to do with this knowledge.

Brandie had advised me not to make any rash decisions, but I gave my landlord one month's notice on my place in Venice, where I had made a home for nine years. I also gave my two weeks' notice at The Buffalo Club and The Victorian.

That night, I slipped into a breathwork meditation. As I lay in a state of relaxation, I intuitively remembered Erin mentioning someone's heart.

"Is there something wrong with my dad's heart?"

My chakras lit up slightly.

"Is there anything I can do to help him? To buy him more time?"

The second set of questions did not receive a yes, but I realized I had run them together, which likely muddled their clarity for a response.

My sister Morgan entered my mind. Her middle name was Mary Ann, after my dad's mother, who struggled with alcoholism and died of cirrhosis at forty-eight. Mel had said Morgan's struggles were likely energetic, and Dolores Cannon believed that negative entities can remain attached to a soul even after death. I wondered if Morgan carried attachments from her past life that she needed to clear.

"Was Morgan… Mary Ann Moots in her last life?" My chakras lit up—Yes. She was my dad's mother, Marty's wife."

I recalled Erin mentioning 10 and October.

"Is the San Andreas Fault going to go on October 10th?" A slight buzz, confirmation I was on the right track.

"Was the energetic shift last June you tapping into the Akashic records?" Another electrical confirmation.

"Was I William Pelligrimia Williams?" Bingo.

"Were you Lucille McKee in your last life?" Another strong surge.

A wave of loving sadness poured over me.

"It took me so long to find you; I'd just love for it to be easier next time, to find you at a young age, and for it to last a really long time."

My tears dried as I drifted from meditation into a deep sleep, only to be pushed out of bed again at 10:23. *Was Mel using 1 2 3 to reply to my I love you from the other night, or was it something else?*

Could October 23rd be the earthquake date?

Slipping Away

April 22nd - May 7th, 2024

Upon returning to LA from Europe, Mel spent two days at my place. After two weeks together, I thought some space might be good, but we were still waiting for our lost bags. In the mornings, she fired up the espresso machine while we caught up on work; in the afternoons, we did HIIT workouts and sauna sessions in the garage to sweat out our vacation.

At night, we snuggled on the couch to watch movies. Her nervous tic had intensified, now showing up as finger tapping or a slow, repetitive curl of her toes. I wasn't sure if she even noticed. I thought about asking what was going on, but I didn't want to hurt her feelings.

We watched *The Way,* about a man walking the Camino de Santiago with his son's ashes.

"I would love to do that," Mel said.

"I'm down, but I need to get my hip squared away first."

Having her there felt natural, and any lingering doubts about our relationship faded over those two days. When our bags finally arrived, she thanked me for the trip and offered to make dinner later in the week.

Mel spent the next week in Malibu with John and Katie, in Carlsbad to see Sarah, and at a bachelorette party in San Diego. We had planned to go to the shooting range that Sunday, something she was eager to try.

On Saturday, she said she was coming back early for a pool party in Topanga and asked to stay at my place. She had given up her Airbnb when we went to Italy and still had a couple of days before she could move back in.

"Is the Austin guy from Aviator Nation throwing it?" I asked.

"Yeah, it would be nice to make some new friends."

I bristled. She knew how I felt about him.

"It's disrespectful and unattractive that you're still talking to him. He clearly doesn't respect our relationship. That's not what I'm looking for in a partner."

"I really appreciate you setting boundaries," she replied. *"I know I need to get better at making more girlfriends. I'm not going to go. I'm excited for the range with you tomorrow."*

Sunday morning, she texted:

"Hey, I'm gonna spend some time with Britt and the kids this morning. Can we postpone the range?"

"No sweat."

"Maybe we can go hiking instead?"

"That sounds great."

I made the most of my day off, catching up on laundry, watching the NBA playoffs, and scrolling Instagram when a post caught my eye. I forwarded it to Mel:

"Kissing for at least six seconds triggers the release of oxytocin, helping couples bond and trust each other."

"Six seconds, baby!" she replied.

Mel was running late, and I was growing restless. I checked my phone.

"Looking like closer to 5 p.m."

"Do you want to go for a bike ride instead?" I suggested.

"Sure."

When she finally arrived, I greeted her with a six-second kiss, which she eagerly returned.

"Sorry I'm late. I was really looking forward to the range."

"We'll go another time."

"Can you show me how to use the guns?"

Drawing from my COVID-era handgun training, I walked her through the basics.

"Rule number one: never point a gun at anything you're not ready to kill."

I made sure my 9mm was empty and demonstrated grip, racking the slide, and ready stance.

"Your voice, combined with the firearm, is your most powerful tool," I explained. "If there's an intruder and you have enough space, use it: 'Get the fuck out of my house or I'll shoot you!'"

She followed my instructions carefully, checking the chamber and toggling the safety with focused precision.

"Can we go to the range next weekend?" she asked enthusiastically.

We seemed to find something she was excited about.

With the sun starting to dip, we took off on our bikes toward Venice Beach Bar, weaving through side streets until we reached the boardwalk. Upstairs, we grabbed a spot just in time for sunset. Over skinny margaritas, she asked, "Do you think we're compatible?"

The question was all too familiar and one I was tired of answering.

"Where is this coming from?"

"I mean, I wanted to go hiking today."

"You were supposed to be here early for the range, then said you'd be here by three for a hike, which I was down for. But you didn't get here until five, and the last thing I wanted was to sit in the car for thirty minutes after waiting around all day."

That seemed to settle her, and she shifted the conversation.

"So, I just got some new acne medication. I think it should help."

"Are you worried about the side effects?"

"I've tried everything naturally. I'm so over it." Her tone was sharper than usual.

She ordered a second margarita, rare for her. I had only seen this side of her once before, but I kept quiet, remembering her second glass of wine in Amsterdam.

The bike hop continued to a sushi spot for Toro and a glass of red wine. The alcohol loosened me up enough to ask a question that had been on my mind.

"How come I don't ever see you breathing anymore?"

"I'm still breathing in Topanga and Malibu."

"It used to be part of your nightly routine."

"I've cleared enough energy. I don't need to do it all the time."

She was drinking more and had abandoned breathwork. This wasn't the woman I had started dating, and my attraction to her was fading.

Mel spent the next few days in Topanga, until she unexpectedly showed up at my house later in the week.

"Hi-eee," she said, coming through the door.

I got up to greet her with open arms.

"What is this?" she mocked. "I'm not your kid! Come hug me like you're excited to see me."

"I am excited to see you."

"But do you miss me?"

"Of course I do. But I also enjoy my alone time. That doesn't mean you're not on my mind. Everything I do, I do with you in mind."

"You're so independent. I need passion and romance. We need to work on building our love."

"I don't understand how I'm not giving you that. We spend so much time in your head, Mel, and it can be exhausting."

She flinched. I softened.

"You come and go as you please. Would you really respect me if I was always chasing you?"

"Probably not," she admitted.

"The inconsistency makes it hard to gauge, and the only thing that works is giving you space. You take what you need, and I do my best to cater to that."

"I know. I'm sorry. Thanks for being patient with me."

Mel bubbled with excitement that evening. A friend had offered her an outdoor space in Topanga for private breathwork sessions.

"Do you think any of your friends might want to try breathing with me?"

"It's tough to get people to pay for a private session on their first go, but I promise I can help fill your classes."

"Would you be okay if my friend from AV did a session with me?"

"You're still talking to that guy?" I sighed. "No, I wouldn't be okay with that. You know how I feel."

"I know, but I really want to get my business going."

"This guy wants to fuck you, Mel. You don't build a business like that."

"But you did," she shot back.

I gave her a weary look. Not only was that untrue, but nightlife and breathwork were completely different industries.

"Hey," she said softly, "I want you to know I would never cheat on you. If I wanted to hook up with someone else, I'd break up with you first."

"I trust you."

"I'm going to stop talking to him."

"I appreciate you asking me."

The disrespect kept coming. A couple of days later, I saw her scrolling through her ex's Instagram in the mirror behind her.

"Whatcha doing?"

"Just scrolling."

"You sure you're not looking at your ex's Instagram?"

Her jaw dropped.

"Someone tagged him, and I just clicked real quick," she said, floundering.

I didn't have the energy to argue. I began to withdraw, hoping that space would help her appreciate what we had.

She wanted to hang out for Cinco de Mayo, then canceled that morning.

"*Hey, I think I need some space to figure things out,*" she texted.

"*Okay, are we still going to your mom's parade next Saturday?*"

"*I don't think so.*"

That afternoon, she texted, wanting to see me again, but I had already made other plans.

"*I'm at a Lo Siento event, but I'll be home later if you want to stop by,*" I replied.

"*I'll probably just stay up in Topanga then.*"

"*Okay.*"

Mel seemed unsure how to handle the distance. I buried myself in work to avoid the weight of it.

Two days later, Mel texted: "*How's the day?*"

"We're almost sold out at Buffalo Club on EventReply. It's working!"

"That's amazing, I'm so proud of you."

"Thanks, but there's still a long way to go… lots of bugs, which sucks because you only get one chance to make a first impression. Super frustrating and a little stressful."

Then she surprised me:

"I can come over, and you can use my body to take out your frustration if you like."

I stared at my phone. This wasn't like her. But it was arousing.

"Yes Please !" I sent, with the drool-face emoji.

"Lol. Okay, I'll be over soon."

The encounter felt different. She seemed dissociated from her body, a sinister smile on her face, as if I were with someone else entirely.

The Mel I knew seemed to resurface as we lay in bed afterward.

"I really wish you needed me more."

"I do need you. You're my motivation. Every day, I wake up excited to build a foundation for us, so we can have a family someday."

"Would you even miss me if we broke up?"

"Of course, I'd miss you, but I'd be okay."

"What would you do?"

"Honestly, I'd probably move to Bali and live a simple life."

"Would you be sad?"

"Yeah, I'd be sad, but I'm emotionally stronger than I've ever been, and I've already grieved this relationship once."

"How could you grieve the relationship when we were never together?"

"Because I've always known this was meant to be."

"How can you be so sure?"

"Something about my intuition must have been right. You're here in my bed right now."

She studied my eyes, looking for the answer.

"How come I don't feel it like you do?"

My girl was still in there, but she couldn't see it.

"I don't know."

She broke eye contact changing the subject.

"I think I'm going to get an apartment in Topanga. There's a really cute one opening up in my friend's building. Then I can get a dog."

She showed me pictures on her phone.

"A dog would be great for you." Mel always said she was happiest with Lady.

She kept scrolling through images of the apartment, her expression unreadable.

"Do you think we're meant to be monogamous?"

"We've already had this conversation."

It was the second time she had brought it up, another crack in her certainty. I wanted desperately to save what we were building, but letting her figure things out on her own was the only thing that had ever worked for us.

Still, I kept the door open.

Featured Photos

July 8th - July 10th, 2024

Since the "California Dreamin'" video had come through Erin, I sought her advice, and she suggested we set up a call.

After a quick hello, I got straight to the point.

"What am I supposed to do with this information?"

Erin pulled a tarot card.

"The card that came out is about being a Sacred Activist, letting love lead, and protecting what's right. There's a lion on her chest. Haven't you been seeing big cats?"

"I can be fiercely abrasive at times. I thought there might be a way to activate people's intuition through breathwork. But with this new information, if it's correct…"

Erin pulled a second card.

"Archangel Michael comes out. You are receiving upgrades, which we already know. The card is telling you to move forward in a way that feels right.

It comes with the sacred activist. There is a reason you are receiving this information. I don't usually hear music… you and I are different. But for three days, I kept hearing that song. I told my husband, 'Oh my God, I'm still hearing that song. I wonder what it means.' Then there you were with that video, and as soon as I watched it, I stopped hearing the song, which meant the message was received.

You are on an accelerated spiritual path, so much so that you recognized the first couple of versions of the song you heard were not doing it for you. Then you got to that one. When you sent it to me, I said to my husband, 'Oh my God, watch this. This is about an earthquake in California.' And he said, 'Whoa, that is nuts.'"

"People are going to think I'm crazy if I put out a video saying that this is going to happen."

"To be the activist, standing in your wisdom, knowledge, and truth, is simply saying, 'I've been told there will be an energetic shift. It could be the San Andreas Fault, clear across the country, or within you.' At this point, better to play it safe than have people think you're crazy. I absolutely believe you. Anyone I know in California, I'm telling to get out because I feel like something big is shifting, especially with the election year, people are all over the map... there's so much ugliness."

"Erin, I'm buzzing right now, and I start to buzz whenever I get a *'yes'* to my thoughts. I think it's going to be even bigger than 9/11."

"Remember, Beau, when you stand in your truth, the truth stands with you. You have a message for people, and a podcast could be the place to share it. Those who understand will believe you, and they'll tell others, and the message will spread.

I know there are places where you can share that message. You can say whatever you want, but in the beginning, it might be better to stand in your truth about the energetic shifting and not label it as the earthquake we suspect it might be. Let people come to their own conclusions," Erin explained.

"Okay…That's heavy," I said.

"It is," Erin confirmed. "But remember, the free will of one can change the outcome for many. And you're not the only one receiving messages about this. Others will come forward eventually."

"I think right now, for me... I'll probably just share it with people I'm close to, and they can do what they want with it... I mean, they're still gonna think I'm nuts, but at least it's people who love me, you know…"

"And you know what? I don't think they're going to think you're nuts. Look at all the proof you have. There are no coincidences. Everything has lined up, and you got something through somebody else from her, to give to you.

Not saying that I'm great because I'm not, but what I'm saying is she came through somebody else to bring you a message that you've now connected, and it's a thing. Dates, times, numbers."

I then explained how I had woken up four nights in a row at 12:12, 12:22, 12:32, and 10:23.

"When you wake up at 12:12, you have the power to bring healing and light to the world. That's significant. And notice how you're already doing that, just by being who you are."

"*1 2 3* is also how we communicate 'I love you,'" I added.

"Right," Erin agreed. "Sequences like *1 2 3*, *3 4 5*, or *7 8 9* show you're climbing the spiritual ladder. Most people spiral up gradually, but you're doing it at an unusual rate. When you see those numbers, it means you're on a rocket ship. So, yay for you being psychic," Erin said, laughing. "That's incredible. And everything you're saying to me makes perfect sense. I'm like, 'Yep... yeah... uh-huh... I believe it.'

Things are orchestrated by divine beings for divine timing. For us to be connected at this time, at this place, it's like when you mentioned twenty-two days. You and I were meant to connect," Erin confirmed.

I then told her about my realization that Melanie and I were soulmates and that her death completed some kind of karmic cycle.

"Yep, absolutely. You two wrote this life together, and you will have another. Everything is now complete, and you go out together in your next life."

"You mean we die together?"

"Yep... but not until you're old. It's like you're in your 90s, from what I'm being told. And it's a beautiful life. You have three children, oh, there's that 3 again. And the two of you live your life in such harmony and balance, and you go out together in your nineties."

"It's refreshing to hear that from you today," I replied.

"Yeah... interesting... you guys will meet at a circus. You're not circus performers, but you somehow connect at a circus."

"In the next life?"

"Uh-huh... yep... and it's not like in a real old-time setting. It's in the 2000s, in this kind of era. It's going to be really interesting how you two come back to be with each other."

"I appreciate it, Erin. Thank you so much."

"You're so welcome, honey... I hope you're doing well."

"Did you want me to take care of you for this session?"

"Just a big hug," Erin said with a smile.

I needed to clear my mind and hit BTC for a training session. The sweat was good, but the relief didn't last. Afterward, I sat down at Cashew Tree for breakfast. Erin's words about my spiritual acceleration plan stared me in the face. A *Featured Photos* sequence in my iPhone's *For You* page, starting with an image of Melanie, jumped out at me. *Was this a new form of communication?*

(Please scan QR codes in this chapter for clarity.)

The ten images felt like a message had been arranged for me, carefully chosen from the eleven thousand pictures on my phone. The first shot of Me in front of Atrani, taken the day after we watched *Equalizer 3*, where Denzel uncovered a terrorist plot. I had just told Erin that I felt the energetic shift would be bigger than 9/11.

The second image was also of Melanie. It seemed to point to two messages.

The third was a flyer selected from the hundreds of event flyers I had saved on my phone. The clock tower in the fourth photo seemed to signal the timing I had been searching for, pointing directly to the date on the flyer.

The fifth photo showed me with friends at a day club called Ushuaïa in Ibiza. When I Googled the name, I found that Ushuaïa is also known as the "*End of the World*," the southernmost city in South America. This took me back to the "end of the world" joke I made with Melanie in Amalfi.

The first message had me thinking of a terrorist attack on the San Andreas Fault or a world-altering energetic shift, and it seemed to suggest October 22nd as the date.

The second message appeared to be about my family, related to what Erin had said about somebody's heart. I was concerned by the look on my dad's face in the sixth photo at the end of the Rose Bowl and hoped that wasn't a game-over sign for him, but my sister Brittany sitting in front of the fireplace seemed to hint at an emergency.

The next photo of my family and me in New York had me thinking family emergency, and again, I was worried about my dad.

The last two photos, one of my ex walking a path on Christmas and another of Melanie in deep thought, suggested that there may have been another message. I needed to follow the path of Christ to meet a woman in order to bring Mel back as my daughter.

I also wondered if the final photo of Melanie was an indicator of the weight of her visions, the access to the Akashic records, or the energetic shift, as she referred to it, that she could not return from.

There was a quote by Dick Gregory that kept appearing on my Instagram feed: *"When the Universe picks you, and you put on the magic glasses, there are rules that go with them: You can never take them off, you never see things as they're supposed to be, you see things as they are, and you can never force anyone else to wear them."*

Mel tried, but there was no going back. I was getting first-hand experience with that, and my worldview would never be the same.

As I tried to make sense of everything, the next sign came through my body. I began experiencing involuntary twitches in my left arm. I thought it might have been from all the workouts I had been doing, but I had never felt anything like this before. Erin said Mel would show me when I was on the right track. Maybe that's what the twitches were about.

Then a pattern emerged: three twitches, then two, followed by one final long twitch. The message hit me immediately. Mel was saying, *"I love you."*

I woke up on my last day in Bali to a new series of *Featured Photos* on my phone.

Again, the message began with two pictures of Melanie. The first was at Christmas Tree Cove in Palos Verdes, where her dad grew up, followed by an image of her walking through a path of sunflowers, holding up two fingers.

The next photo was of us on her birthday at Hozier. The timing of my screenshot in that photo captured a text that read, "Don't forget about me," which felt like no coincidence.

Next, she pointed to sunflower seeds in my mouth, reinforcing the idea that her path to a second life with me—indicated by her two fingers in the second photo—was a new birthday, as my daughter through my sunflower seed.

The fifth photo showed Mel in her sun and moon necklace, pulling me back to the lyric from Tanner Usrey's "Beautiful Lies": "I'd steal the moon from the stars, just to get to where you are." It felt like a sign—proof she was doing everything she could, from the other side, to make that happen.

The next picture began the second message. It showed my dad putting a life jacket on my sister Kaylie, followed by my buddy's son wearing a number 85 George Kittle jersey. The 49ers won the Super Bowl in 1985. I wondered if Mel was giving me gambling plays to protect my family from the earthquake.

The last three photos showed my dad and me at the lake, then Mel with a smirk, followed by the Rose Bowl shot.

I was excited by the idea of Melanie giving me football futures to help me buy my dream house on the lake.

Even in the air, signs kept coming. On my flight from Bali to Taipei, I met Mike Mercer, a pastor from Oregon who runs a charity that helps girls who have survived sex trafficking in Indonesia. Given Melanie's abuse, I took this as another sign.

The twitches in my arm intensified during the long flight from Taipei to Los Angeles. It felt like Morse code.

When I landed at LAX, my phone revealed a third set of *Featured Photos.*

The series began with an orange sunset, symbolizing "Something in the Orange" and a message from the light—a sign that Melanie and I were not done yet.

A photo of the rock bar at Ulu Cliffhouse in Bali, with a single tree rising above, resembled the Tree of Life.

A family picture of my dad, my sister Kaylie, her boyfriend Josh, my ex, and me made me wonder if my dad might return one day as Kaylie's child or mine.

Then came a sequence: a photo of my dad and me on the day we both got COVID, an image of the Green River in Chicago from when I contracted COVID at Lollapalooza (the time I got it really bad), and a picture of a Philly cheesesteak hinting at a heart attack.

I saw the message as foreshadowing my dad's potential sickness and a heart attack.

The sequence closed with an image of me walking away, Mel's service flyer, a female DJ I once booked, and finally, a photo of me in a Buffs Helping Buffs shirt.

The shot of the DJ and me walking away had me thinking of the "Something in the Orange" lyric, *"Please turn those headlights around."* I felt I might be able to prevent his funeral—as long as I was there for him, unlike the Saturday I lost Melanie.

The thought of losing him brought tears to my eyes as I exited the plane.

When I arrived home, I collapsed into bed, drained from my travels. I was unsure if I was about to fall into a dream state or if I had been in one this entire time.

The Wolves Won

May 9th - May 18th, 2024

After a HIIT workout in the garage, I received a call from Mel. My endorphins were high when I answered.

"Hi, Butterfly," I said. "How's your day?"

"I just finished a Zoom session with David."

"Nice, how'd it go?"

"I think we need some space."

"Is this you wanting to break up?"

"I feel like I need to see if there's anything still there with my ex, and David said that if I'm going to do that, I need to cut off all attachments."

"If that's what you feel you need to do, then you should come get your stuff and drop off your key."

"Are you upset?"

"I'm tired of hearing about this guy. If you need to go see if there's something there, then do it. I'm going to sell the Chris Stapleton tickets."

"Well, don't sell them yet. There might not be anything with him, and then we could still go."

"You said no attachments, Mel."

"What am I supposed to tell my family?"

"Tell them you broke up with me, and I sold the tickets."

"But you gave those to me as a birthday present," she protested.

"I just took you to Italy for two weeks. I'm not paying for you and your family to go to that show without me," I said. "People give back engagement rings all the time."

"Can you at least save two for me?"

"Why, so you can take your ex?"

"I wouldn't do that. It would be nice if you held on to two so we could potentially still go."

"Honestly, Mel, I'm not sure I'm going to want to go with you after this."

"Wow, you're really hankering to sell those tickets, aren't you?"

"I'm getting off the phone now."

The next night was the USC graduation event. Buffalo Club was sold out, and everyone had pre-paid. I had just finished my shower and was getting dressed when I heard a rattle at the front door, which swung open.

Melanie burst through with a guilt-driven, apologetic look on her face.

"I'm so sorry for being a brat."

"You come over now? It's my busiest night of the year."

"I know, but I really wanted to see you."

"I have to go."

"I'm so sorry. I really need to talk to you," she pleaded.

"I'm not a punk ass bitch, Mel. I've been super patient with you and put a lot of work into this relationship, but I'm not going to let you walk all over me."

"And that's what I love about you. I manifested you. I don't want to lose you."

She then planted a ten-second kiss on my lips. I can still close my eyes and feel the electricity from that moment. It would be our last kiss ever.

"Have a great night at work. I'm going to come back over on Sunday so we can talk."

"That sounds great."

I wanted to stay, but there were too many people celebrating one of their proudest accomplishments, and I needed to make sure everything ran smoothly.

Mel attended her mom's parade in Newport the next day. On Sunday, May 12th, she said she was going to come over and talk but canceled and rescheduled for Monday.

Then I got a text:

"Hi there! Can I come by this afternoon? Want to grab some things and would love to chat with you. Let me know."

"What time are you thinking? Tonight would be better for me."

"What time?" she asked.

"7:30 would be great."

"Tomorrow night might be better, but I'll let you know in a few hours."

"Tomorrow night would be better for me as well," I added.

"OK."

Later that night, I received a text from an unknown number. It was Mel's mom Liz:

"Hi Beau, we missed you on Saturday. Thank you so much for the exquisite bottle of FURORE. We will enjoy it in good health and think of you. Hope to see you soon. Liz and Jim."

I considered my reply carefully, knowing Melanie would likely see it. If things were going to improve between us, she would need to put real effort into maintaining the relationship. If she wasn't willing to do that, I was ready to part ways.

"You are welcome. I hope it hits all the right notes. I wanted to be there."

On Tuesday, the 14th, we continued to discuss meeting up before finally settling on dinner at my house.

I was making salmon and rice and asked Mel if she wanted to help with the salad, but she declined. When she finally came over, she seemed like a completely lost version of herself. She didn't hesitate to unload her thoughts as she burst through the door.

"Alesandra said the world isn't ending anytime soon. Just great!"

I was caught off guard, thinking we were going to have a civil talk, but her energy was like nothing I had ever seen.

"I'm really not happy about you manipulating me into this relationship," she said.

"What are you talking about?"

"You were always pushing so hard."

"That's not true, Mel. We didn't talk for almost four years. I've always been honest about my feelings for you. I've been patient with this relationship and have always given you as much space as needed."

Mel opened a bottle of red wine and poured herself a glass, shifting the blame onto herself.

"I'm mad at myself for giving us a chance. I wasn't ready, and now I can't go back."

"Go back to what?"

"There was an energetic shift in this relationship, and now I can't go back. It's like you have this weird power over me."

"You said you wanted to see if there was anything still there with your ex."

"It's not that. I don't love him anymore."

"Then why can't we move forward?"

"Because… you're just my friend."

I froze. I wanted to tell her, *You're my best friend*, but the words wouldn't come. I was crushed. She knew it.

"We don't have any fun together," she said, twisting the knife.

"I've never heard that from anybody in my life. You're always so excited about our next adventure, but then, when we actually do it, you spend half the time in your head and don't fully enjoy it."

She seemed unsure how to respond to that.

"Did you have any fun in Italy?" I asked.

"I did, but why does it always have to be some big vacation? Why can't we just have fun doing nothing, just being at the house together?"

"Did you enjoy biking to Venice for sunset the other day?"

"Yeah, that was fun."

"What about doing HIIT classes in the garage, or ice bathing, or cooking dinner together? What does your idea of fun look like?"

"Laying in bed, doing nothing, and having sex all day."

"I'd be open to that every once in a while."

"I don't want that with you."

"We haven't had good sex?" I asked.

"No, we have."

"I don't understand, Mel."

"I don't know... I'm really struggling. At the parade on Saturday, my mom said, 'You gotta do something.' I wish I had never started this healing journey. Now, there's no going back, and everything just feels so boring."

I was mentally exhausted. She had completely given up on breathwork, and I didn't know what to say.

"Today, I was searching online for ways to commit suicide so that I don't mess up and end up brain-dead or in a wheelchair," she continued with a sinister, excited look on her face.

I was confused. The entire conversation had felt manipulative.

"When I was twenty-six and still heartbroken over my ex, I was struggling to figure out what I was doing with my life. I remember driving home from work one night, thinking about how easy it would be to crash my car and end things. But I didn't do it. There were too many people in my life who loved me. And eventually, I worked through that."

"I literally don't care about anything anymore."

"What about your nieces' and nephew?"

"They're sweet, but even my love for them isn't the same."

"Are you back on the Adderall?" I asked again.

"No."

"I think you should try some NAD therapy."

"What's that?"

"It's like stem cells for the brain. I've tried it, and I've had a bunch of teammates who were struggling with depression who said it changed their lives," I replied. "I'll look into setting up an appointment for you."

"It won't help," she said. "You don't understand, this is energetic."

I watched her pour another glass of wine. We had been dating for almost a year, and I didn't recognize this version of her at all. I was speechless.

"Let's watch a comedy!" she said, changing the subject.

We pulled up a Nikki Glaser special on Netflix. I tried to hold Mel's hand, searching for a sign of comfort, but she pushed mine away. As the comedy went on, she seemed to lighten up, laughing hardest at the darker, more morbid jokes. This was unlike her. She left midway through the show with a suitcase full of her things in what felt like a quick, cold goodbye.

"Can I take the rest of this bottle with me?" she asked on her way out the door.

All I could think about was how out of character this was for her.

The next morning, worried about her, I sent her a text message with a link to Tupac's "Keep Ya Head Up," adding, "W*ait for the chorus.*"

"*You just don't get it... But thank you. I'm only 32. That's so long to live like this. That's why I'm so depressed.*"

"*It will pass. NAD will help.*"

"*It won't pass. It's not even the depression... It's just this boring life. I didn't want to clear that last energy. I wasn't ready. If I knew, I wouldn't have.*"

"*NAD will help.*"

"*You literally don't know. It won't. Because I can't go back. That's the only thing that will fix this... and that isn't possible.*"

"*Sounds like forward is the only way.*"

"*Well, maybe. And as grateful as I am for you, I also know this relationship shifted things for me... that's why I'm struggling with it. I just wasn't ready. I needed more time. Now my head is spinning.*"

"*What are the three things you love most in this world?*"

"*Nothing, really.*"

"*Person, place, or thing... three things.*"

"*Nothing, reallyyy.*"

"*Lies.*"

"*Actually no... I don't think I can really love anything. It's not in my tool belt. It's weird. That's why I'm feeling like this... What's the point, you know? That's sorta the point of life. It's not just depression. It's like seeing all the hopelessness in life. I wouldn't wish this on anyone.*"

"*You're evolving past the third level of enlightenment in this life. You still have so much more to experience to get there. Then your soul reaches the fourth level of enlightenment,*" I said, referencing *Many Lives, Many Masters*.

"*I don't really want to.*"

"*Then the fifth.*"

"*I just want to have fun.*"

"*And then you become a master soul.*"

"*And I can't anymore. I'm just numb.*"

"*There's still a lot of fun to be had.*" I encouraged.

"*For you... The things that you find fun don't do anything for me. We don't have the same versions of fun. I try, I really do. What's the point if there's no fun?*"

"*For you too!!*" I said, trying to stay confident.

"*It's just not there for me...it's just fake for me. I appreciate you so much, but this relationship changed a lot for me, and I'm really struggling with it.*"

"*Have you had your period since Italy?*"

"*It's not my period.*"

"*Have you though?*"

"*Yeah... it's the shift that's happened in the past year. And I'm not doing well with it. I wasn't ready for this energy to be cleared. I just wasn't. I didn't want it to be cleared.*"

"*What was the energy that was cleared?*"

"Whatever it was in the past year. I don't know... I just don't see the point in anything. The turning point was when you and I started spending time together."

I texted her a picture of my dream house on Flathead Lake and wrote, *"The Dream."*

"That's your dream... I don't really know if I have any right now, which makes me a little sad."

At this point, I didn't know what else to say. She was breaking up with me, yet I still loved her and wanted her to be happy. Hoping someone else's words might help, I sent her two of my favorite poems: *Invictus* by William Ernest Henley and *Footprints in the Sand* by Margaret Fishback Powers. I wanted to remind her that her soul was unconquerable and that God was there to support her through her struggles.

The next morning, I reached out by text again.

"I've got the NAD person," I wrote. *"They can come to the house. My buddy has gotten three tune-ups since he did it five years ago."*

"It's not the NAD..." Mel shot back. *"This past year is what fucked me up, and I can't go back now."*

"Yes, but NAD stimulates cellular production and DNA repair in your brain from all the damage that's been done. You'll start feeling a lot better about life. Let me know if you want me to set up an appointment. I think you should try it. I know multiple people who have said it changed their lives."

"That's not it, Beau."

"It'll help knock out the depression and the feeling of being lethargic and unmotivated, everything you said you're struggling with."

"You don't get it," she insisted. *"It's not my brain chemistry. It's what happened in the past year."*

"It's what's happened the last 18 years," I countered.

Mel's frustration grew. *"No... you don't get it."*

"You said you wanted to try something to help with the depression. This will knock it out."

"It started last June. It won't help. It's not chemistry, it's energetic."

"You don't know that."

"I know exactly..." Her tone turned bitter. *"And I'm sick of spending money on shit at this point. None of it helps. And I wish I was still on Adderall."*

"This is a form of stem cell treatment... it's different," I urged.

"This whole thing I've done is so dumb and has made life really pointless," Mel texted.

"I'll pay for the first one. 'You've gotta try something,'" I replied, quoting her mom's statement from the parade.

"This is bad..." she texted. *"You should have just left me alone. You kept telling me you saw a vision. Why did you do that? How come you kept saying that to me?"*

"Because it's true... my vision has remained the same. I never strayed from you, and I'm still here."

"This fucked everything up. You got inside my head. It was so manipulative. And I literally can't go back. And I don't have the heart to go forward... so I literally don't want to be here."

"It was honest," I wrote back. *"If you want my help, I'm here. But I'm not going to be gaslit into thinking what you're going through is because of me. That's bullshit."*

"It sounds dramatic, but it's not. You gaslit me a lot, and that's why I'm frustrated."

"That's garbage. I was honest about my feelings for you and always have been. And I'm still here, so I don't want to hear it."

"Yeah, you were always pushing so hard... you don't know what this has caused. Truly."

I was done defending myself. Thirty minutes later, she wrote back.

"Wow. I'm sorry for blaming you. You're just trying to help. It won't happen again. I'm going through it... Thanks for the NAD rec. I'll reach out today. I'm just pushing you away because I'm suffering, and it's not cool or right. I'm really sorry. Thank you for being here for me."

I liked her last text and went about my workday.

Three hours later, she texted me, *"Can you send me info for the NAD person?"*

I sent it over. *"Sorry... thought I sent that earlier,"* I added. *"Ask for a referral if she's not in LA?"*

Another couple of hours passed:

"Were you able to get an appointment set?"

She texted back before bed that night, saying she was *"working on it."*

On the morning of Thursday, May 16th, I wrote her another message:

"How are you doing today?" She responded with a thumbs-up emoji, which was a bit of a relief.

Late that night, she showed up at my house unannounced, bursting through the door while I was on a conference call with my website team in India.

"I'm going to grab some of my things," she announced and started making trips between my office and her car.

"I'd like to talk to you when you're done," she added.

I had made ground turkey with marinara sauce, rice, and corn for stuffed bell peppers, and it was sitting on the stove. When I finished the call, I walked into the living room and found Mel leaning over the sink, shoveling food into her mouth like she hadn't eaten in days.

"What would you say in my eulogy?" she asked suddenly.

"I don't want to talk about that."

"Oh, come on, you're no fun," she teased, her tone unsettling.

"That doesn't sound like fun to me, Mel."

"Do you think I'm fat?" she asked again, changing subjects abruptly.

"No."

"Getting old sucks," she muttered.

"You're not old," I scoffed.

"I'm fat and ugly, and there's literally nothing to look forward to."

"The seventy-two-year-old version of you is going to laugh at that statement."

"I don't even want to think about seventy-two," she replied, brushing off the thought.

"There's so much life left to live," I said. "What about the lake house? The kids? The dogs?"

"That's not my dream, that's your dream."

"What about the apartment in Topanga and a new dog?"

"Yeah, that's exciting, I guess," she settled. "All you want from me is to have your babies. I don't even know if I can have kids! What about me?" Her voice rose to a shout.

"What's your dream then, Mel?"

"To be madly in love. I could've had that six months ago, but I gave you a chance, and you ruined it!"

"How did I ruin it? You're going back to him, which is what you said you wanted," I said, trying to stay calm.

"I don't love him anymore," she said flatly.

"Love takes time to build."

"I could've gone back in June, but now I can't, and I'm really mad about it. Everything is so boring now. I'll take the chaos with the lows because the highs were so good," she snapped.

I searched helplessly for something—for the look I'd always known. Mel was barely in there, and I had nothing to say. She packed another suitcase and took it with her.

On Friday, May 17th, I woke up to a text from her:

"I'm sorry about last night. I'm really, really struggling. I'm sorry to put anything on you. It won't happen again."

"It's okay. I'm here for you if you need me."

"I just don't know what to do at this point."

"Try the NAD."

"It's not even that, though."

"I think you'll feel better about life."

"I don't think I ever will."

"You've gotta try it... I'll pay for the first one. The excitement will come back... just set it up at my house."

"It's okay... No, it won't."

"You won't know unless you try. Everyone I know who's tried it says it works like magic, including me."

My phone died, and two hours passed. When I turned it back on, I read her next message.

"I just want you to know that last night was the meds talking, not me. I'm trying to see if I can get some support from my family. Thank you for everything."

"What kind of medications are you on?" I asked. *"I'm sorry, but my phone was dead. I was just getting those messages."*

Another two hours passed without any response from her.

"I can book you an appointment for NAD therapy on Monday, May 20th, at 10 AM at Infuse Wellness in Santa Monica," I texted. *"I've gotten a bunch of IVs from them. They're great. Let me know, and I'll book it. Here's their calendar. They have appointments available on Monday for 12:15 and 2:15."*

"I can book it. Thanks. I'm going to come grab my stuff this evening."

"Ok," I texted back, encouraged that I might be getting through to her.

"Not because I need to do anything... but because I should. Because I should pick it up."

"If you want no attachments so you can go see if there's anything with your ex, then it's what you need to do."

I felt our only chance at moving forward was her going back to him, realizing it wasn't what she wanted and then working to get our relationship back.

"It's not about him. But you say, 'Do what you need to do,' and then put this weird pressure on me. So, I'm just going to get my stuff, so I don't have to deal with that... just for myself. I don't want my stuff being a thing held over me or something weird. That doesn't feel good. And it makes sense for me to just get it anyway."

"It's not about him? You said you wanted to reach out to your ex. I said if you need to see if there's anything still there with him, then you need to drop the key and pick up your stuff. It's not holding anything over your head... it's just fair."

She liked my text and responded with a wall of messages:

"Be there soon."

"40 mins."

"I've felt a lot of pressure to move forward with you in ways I was never ready for, and then it was held over my head when I felt like I needed to explore something but felt like I couldn't... I'm not happy about that.

I should have done things differently, but I was in an in-between place and felt beholden. That wasn't fair for me and changed the whole trajectory for me.

I know it was out of generosity, but also a weird power imbalance. I should have noticed and made a different choice. So I'm getting my stuff because I'm done feeling beholden. I'm angry at myself for going along with everything."

This was an endless back-and-forth. She was stuck in a repetitive cycle. Not long after, she burst through the door, heated and ready for another round.

"Thursdays and Sundays!" she shouted, referring to the days I told her I would be most present for date night.

"That was when we first started dating, Mel. It hasn't been that way for months," I reminded her, trying to ground the conversation.

She sat across from me on the couch, and we gazed into each other's eyes for an extended period. For the first time ever, I couldn't see my soulmate in there. Her eyes were demonic, as if she were possessed.

"I guess you were wrong about that look you always felt."

I recalled the vision from the Valentine's breathwork session with David.

"Maybe you were just supposed to lead me to breathwork," I said.

"That's so fucked up!" she screamed at me.

"I'm still here, Mel! I'm still here. What am I supposed to do?"

"I'm really not happy about being manipulated into this relationship," she accused, looking to load up again.

"David told you to lean into the relationship, and your family was rooting for me. But I never manipulated you into anything."

Then she shifted, abruptly changing the subject.

"How's your dad doing?"

Amid her chaos, she seemed genuinely concerned, knowing he'd just undergone another heart procedure.

"He said it went really well and that he's finally catching a full breath," I replied, briefly taken aback trying to make sense of her demeanor. "What meds are you on?" "What meds are you on?" I asked.

"My doctor put me on Concerta to help with my depression."

I had never heard of Concerta and wasn't sure how to respond. The inconsistencies in her personality were unlike anything I had ever seen, and I didn't know what to do.

Mel grabbed the last of her things and took them to the car. She then set her house key on the coffee table.

"That's everything," she said, her tone final.

"Do you want to take the coffee machine?"

"I'll pick it up some other time."

"Ok," I replied, feeling the sting of tears forming.

"What's wrong?" she asked, almost mockingly.

"I'm sad," I admitted, only to be met with her unsettling, almost evil grin.

She gave me the coldest goodbye hug, barely grazing my shoulder. I stood frozen in the entryway as she walked out of my life.

On Saturday, May 18th, I woke up to a text from Mel:

"Hi! Can you leave a key somewhere this evening so I can come by and grab the coffee machine and any last things, please?"

I made one last double cappuccino and savored it on the couch, wondering how we had gotten here. I had never worked so hard in any relationship.

"I'll put everything on the picnic table in the backyard." I texted.

I then unplugged the espresso machine and moved her things onto the picnic table. The pile included mementos from some of our amazing times together, like the thank you note from Hotel Miramalfi and the sideline pass with her name on it from the UCLA game. I wanted her to remember all the fun we had, the moments she somehow couldn't see. I was holding onto hope that things would work out.

"There are some other things I'd like to grab. If you could leave a key, that would be great... there's some other stuff I'm forgetting, I think... I'd like to do a sweep if that's okay with you. I'll be quick."

"Already swept the medicine cabinet and closet, everything is on the picnic table, but I'll leave a key under the ashtray so you can double check. Maybe check the front closet by the door."

"Thank you."

I placed her key under the ashtray next to her things.

"If there's anything you don't want to take, please just throw it away."

"Appreciate you," she responded.

I then dove into logging EventReply notes, trying to distract myself from the breakup.

Fifteen minutes later, she texted again: *"If you wanted me to come by while you're there, I can try, but evening is just better for me."*

Every time she came over, it felt like another breakup, and I didn't want to deal with that in the middle of my work weekend. My coffee buzz was working, and I was focused, trying to get everything done before my double shift at The Victorian in Santa Monica during the day and Baja Venice at night.

My phone died while I was testing the website, and by the time it had charged and I checked it again, I had another message from her: *"I probably don't need to go inside, actually... if you already did the sweep."*

"Front closet and garage may be the only places you have stuff. Got your supplements, the medicine cabinet, office closet, bedside table... coffee maker

stuff... earrings are in the candle... key is under the ashtray if you need to sweep.”

Everything she needed was there for her.

Later, she sent:

“What's up? Can't chat right now.”

“Buried right now.” I was.

“You called me,” she said.

Confused, I checked my call history and sent her a screenshot showing the last time I called her was the night before.

“Yesterday at 8:01 pm,” I replied.

“Oh lol,” she responded.

Around 4 p.m., I left for work. I had been grieving the relationship since the night before but still felt like she might show up at my house on Sunday. If she did, I wanted to have my wits about me, and if she didn't, a hangover would only make it worse. I decided not to drink and stopped at Erewhon for two CBD sodas and an iced coffee to get me through the events.

When I arrived at The Victorian, I tuned all the TVs to the Mavs vs. Thunder playoff game and settled in to watch it after greeting some of the staff.

My phone was about to die, so I checked the ADT security clips. Mel had come through the front gate at 5:09 p.m. I checked the back alley camera, but there were no clips. Her stuff was still on the picnic table. I assumed the camera had glitched, my drained phone failing to update the live feed.

I took my phone upstairs to charge in the storage closet, grabbed a burger and fries, watched some of the game, and then went back up to retrieve it.

I checked the ADT security camera again. Her stuff was still on the back table. I looked closer at the side gate, which was wide open. So was the back door. Then I noticed a palm frond rustle from the wind, something new on my screen suggesting the feed was live.

That didn't feel right. My phone was still low on battery, and I figured the camera was probably glitching, but I decided I had better go check, just in case. On my way out of The Victorian, I told the manager:

"I'll be back in thirty minutes."

That was the start of the worst day of my life.

Dear Grace

Your soul has loved me across many lives.
And now your unseen tongue sparks a beautiful rise.
I feel your electricity in the whispering wind,
A flutter of wings where the veil has thinned.

I've walked the dark forest and bathed in flames,
Surrendering gratefully to my karmic claims.
Yet I plant seeds with weathered hands,
Tending the soil, reshaping the land.

I'll meet you halfway under the new moon
Until it's time to grow in your belly cocoon.
Please wait for your garden, my butterfly soul,
I'm piecing together what will make this life whole.

I search for your mother as I journey within,
So your path through this sunflower to life can begin.
When I rest at night, I dream of your face,
My patient, my perfect, sweet baby Grace.

@SUNFLOWERSIGNALS

(Scan to continue following my journey)

Special Thanks

I would like to express my heartfelt gratitude to those who have supported me through this.

To my Mom and Dad, thank you for always believing in me, no matter what path I have taken. I know how difficult this has been for both of you.

To Melanie's family, thank you for your love during the toughest moments.

To my sisters, Jenny and Auntie Shawn—thank you for your continued support.

To Aunt Sue—thank you for the open-door policy.

To David, Chris, Brandie, Erin, Melani, and Ama'zjhi, you all have incredible gifts and have forever changed my life.

To my friends—Neil, Donna, Justin, Jynelle, Roger, Troy, Stevi, Lincoln, Brian, Landon, Caroline, Adam, Cass, Ryan, Serene, Bobby, GiGi, Asabi, Lucas, Josh, Tara, Bella, Jake, Made, Nicole, Chris, Bear, Kia, Emily, Mr. & Mrs. Z, Buddy Dave, Susan, Adir, Kyle, and Tony—thank you for your unwavering support.

And to everyone else who reached out to check in on me—thank you.

Without all of you, this book would not have been possible. I love you all.